JOE CELKO'S
TREES AND HIERARCHIES
IN SQL FOR SMARTIES

JOE CELKO'S
TREES AND
HIERARCHIES
IN SQL FOR SMARTIES

Joe Celko

ELSEVIER

AMSTERDAM • BOSTON • HEIDELBERG • LONDON
NEW YORK • OXFORD • PARIS • SAN DIEGO
SAN FRANCISCO • SINGAPORE • SYDNEY • TOKYO

Morgan Kaufmann is an imprint of Elsevier

Acquiring Editor: Rick Adams
Development Editor: Dave Bevans
Project Manager: André Cuello
Designer: Joanne Blank

Morgan Kaufmann is an imprint of Elsevier
225 Wyman Street, Waltham, MA 02451, USA

Notices
Knowledge and best practice in this field are constantly changing. As new research and experience broaden our understanding, changes in research methods or professional practices, may become necessary. Practitioners and researchers must always rely on their own experience and knowledge in evaluating and using any information or methods described herein. In using such information or methods they should be mindful of their own safety and the safety of others, including parties for whom they have a professional responsibility.

To the fullest extent of the law, neither the Publisher nor the authors, contributors, or editors, assume any liability for any injury and/or damage to persons or property as a matter of products liability, negligence or otherwise, or from any use or operation of any methods, products, instructions, or ideas contained in the material herein.

Library of Congress Cataloging-in-Publication Data
Application submitted

British Library Cataloguing-in-Publication Data
A catalogue record for this book is available from the British Library.

ISBN: 978-0-12-387733-8

Printed and bound by CPI Group (UK) Ltd, Croydon, CR0 4YY

Transferred to digital print 2012

Working together to grow libraries in developing countries

www.elsevier.com | www.bookaid.org | www.sabre.org

ELSEVIER BOOK AID International Sabre Foundation

For information on all MK publications visit our website at www.mkp.com

For Hilary and Kara
I love and believe in you both

C O N T E N T S

INTRODUCTION

An introduction should give a noble purpose for writing a book. I should say that the purpose of this book is to help real programmers who have real problems in the real world. But the "real" reason this short book is being published is to save me the trouble of writing any more emails and pasting more code on Internet forums, newsgroups, and blogs. This topic has been hot on all SQL-related Websites, and the solutions actually being used by most working programmers have been pretty bad. So I thought, why not collect everything I can find and put it in one place for the world to see.

In my book *SQL for Smarties* (Morgan-Kaufmann, 4th edition, 2010, ISBN 978-0123820228, Chapter 36), I wrote a chapter on a programming technique for representing trees and hierarchies in SQL as nested sets. This technique has become popular enough that I have spent almost every month since *SQL for Smarties* was released explaining the technique in Newsgroups and personal emails. Also, people who have used it have been sending me emails with their own programming tricks. Oh, I will still have a short chapter or two on trees in any future edition of *SQL for Smarties*, but this topic is worth this short book.

The first section of the book is a bit like an intro college textbook on graph theory so you might want to skip over it if you are current on the subject. If you are not, then the theory there will explain some of the constraints that appear in the SQL code later. The middle sections deal with programming techniques, and the end sections deal with related topics in computer programming.

The code in this book was checked using a SQL syntax validator program at the Mimer Website (http://developer.mimer.com/validator/index.htm). I have used as much standard SQL code as possible. When I needed procedural code in an example, I used SQL/PSM but tried to stay within a subset that can be translated easily into a vendor dialect (for details of this language, see Jim Melton's book *Understanding SQL's Stored Procedures*, ISBN 0-55860-461-8).

There are two major examples (and some minor ones) in this book. One is an organizational chart for an unnamed organization and the other is a parts explosion for a Frammis. Before anyone asks what a Frammis is, let me tell you that it is what holds all those widgets that MBA students were manufacturing in the fictional companies in their textbooks.

These choices were made because a parts explosion will have the same part in many places (i.e., a #5 machine screw gets used a lot) and an employee usually holds only one position within the organization.

I invite corrections, additions, general thoughts, and new coding tricks at my email address or my publisher's snail mail address.

Joe Celko

Graphs, Trees, and Hierarchies

LET'S START WITH a little mathematical background. Graph theory is a branch of mathematics that deals with abstract structures known as graphs. These are not the presentation charts that you get out of a spreadsheet package.

Very loosely speaking, a graph is a diagram of "dots" (called nodes or vertices) and "lines" (edges or arcs) that model some kind of "flow" or relationship. The edges can be undirected or directed. The edges might have values (the distance of a road on a map), as can the nodes (the weight of packages in the city of the map). Graphs are *very* general models. In circuit diagrams, edges are the wires and nodes are the components. On a road map, nodes are the towns and edges are the roads. Flowcharts, organizational charts, and a hundred other common abstract models you see every day are all shown as graphs.

A directed graph allows a "flow" along the edges in one direction only as shown by the arrowheads, while an undirected graph allows the flow to travel in both directions. Exactly what is flowing depends on what you are modeling with the graph.

The convention is that an edge must join two and only two nodes. This lets us show an edge as an ordered pair of nodes, such as ("Atlanta," "Boston") if we are dealing with a map or (a, b) in a more abstract notation. There is an implication in a directed graph that the direction is shown by the ordering. In an undirected graph, we know that (a, b) = (b, a), however.

A node can sit alone or have any number of edges associated with it. A node can also be self-referencing, as in (a, a).

The terminology used in graph theory will vary, depending on which book you had in your finite math class. Here, in informal language, are the terms used in this book.

Order of a graph: number of nodes in the graph.

Degree: number of edges at a node, without regard to whether the graph is directed or undirected.

Indegree: number of edges coming into a node in a directed graph.

Outdegree: number of edges leaving a node in a directed graph.

Subgraph: a graph that is a subset of another graph's edges and nodes.

Walk: a subgraph of alternating edges and nodes connected to each other in such a way that you can trace around it without lifting your finger.

Path: a subgraph that does not cross over itself—there is a starting node with degree one, an ending node with degree one, and all other nodes have degree two. It is a special case of a walk. It is a "connect the dots" puzzle.

Cycle: a subgraph that "makes a loop" so that all nodes have degree two. In a directed graph, all nodes of a cycle have outdegree one and indegree one. See Figure 1.1.

Connected graph: a graph in which all pairs of nodes are connected by a path. Informally, the graph is all in one piece.

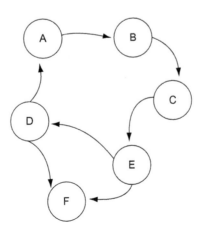

Figure 1.1

Forest: a collection of separate trees. Yes, I am defining this term before we finally get to discussing trees. There are many equivalent ways to define a tree, and I want to spend some time with them. For now, let's say that it is a graph without any cycles.

There are many more terms to describe special kinds of graphs, but frankly, we will not use them in this book. We are supposed to be doing SQL programming, not learning graph theory.

The strength of graphs as problem-solving tools is that nodes and edges can be given extra attributes that adapt this general model to a particular problem. Edges can be assigned "weights," such as expected travel time for roads on a highway map. Nodes can be assigned "colors" that put them into groups, such as men and women. Look around and you will see how they are used.

1.1 Defining Tree and Hierarchies

There is an important difference between a tree and a hierarchy, which has to do with inheritance and subordination. Trees are a special case of graphs; hierarchies are a special case of trees. Let's start by defining trees.

1.1.1 Trees

Trees are graphs that have the following properties:

1. A tree is a connected graph that has no cycles. A connected graph is one in which there is a path between any two nodes. No node sits by itself, disconnected from the rest of the graph.

2. Every node is the root of a subtree. The most trivial case is a subtree of only one node.

3. Every two nodes in the tree are connected by one and only one path.

4. A tree is a connected graph that has one less edge than it has nodes.

In a tree, when an edge (a, b) is deleted, the result is a forest of two disjoint trees. One tree contains node (a) and the other contains node (b).

There are other properties, but this list gives us enough information for writing constraints in SQL. Remember, this is a book about programming, not graph theory, so you will get just enough to help you write code, but not enough to be a mathematician.

1.1.2 Properties of Hierarchies

A hierarchy is a directed tree with extra properties: subordination and inheritance.

A hierarchy is a common way to organize a great many things, but the examples in this book will be organizational charts and parts explosions. These are two common business applications and can be understood easily by anyone without any special subject area knowledge. And they demonstrate that the relationship represented by the edges of the graph can run from the root or up to the root.

In an organizational chart, authority starts at the root, with the president of the enterprise, head of the Army, or whatever the organization is and it flows downward. Look at a military chain of command. If you are a private and your sergeant is killed, you still have to take orders from your captain; subordination is inherited from the root downward.

In a parts explosion, the relationship we are modeling runs "up the tree" to the root, or final assembly. If you are missing any subassembly, you cannot get a final assembly.

Inheritance, either to or from the root, is the most important property of a hierarchy. This property does not exist in an ordinary tree. If I delete an edge in a tree, I now have two separate trees, not one.

Another property of a hierarchy is that the same node can play many different roles. In an organizational chart, one person might hold several different jobs; in a parts explosion, the same kind of screw, nut, or washer will appear in many different subassemblies. And the same subassembly can appear in many places. To make this more concrete, imagine a restaurant with a menu. The menu disassembles into dishes, and each dish disassembles into ingredients, and each ingredient is either simple (salt, pepper, flour, etc.) or it is a recipe itself, such as Béarnaise sauce and Hollandaise sauce. These recipes might include further recipes. For example, Béarnaise sauce is Hollandaise with vinegar for the water and adds shallots, tarragon, chervil, and (sometimes) parsley, thyme, bay leaf, and cayenne pepper.

Hierarchies have roles that are filled by entities. This role property does not exist in a tree; each node appears once in a tree and it is unique.

1.1.3 Types of Hierarchies

Getting away from looking at the world from the viewpoint of a casual mathematician, let's look at it from the viewpoint of a casual database systems designer. What kinds of data situations will I want to model? Looking at the world from a very high level, I can see four kinds of modeling problems.

1. Static nodes and static edges. For example, a chart of accounts in an accounting system will probably not change much over time. This is probably best done with a hierarchical encoding scheme rather than a table. We will talk about such encoding schemes later.

2. Static nodes and dynamic edges, for example, an Internet Newsgroup message board. Obviously, you cannot add a node to a tree without adding an edge, but the content of the messages (nodes) never changes once they are posted, but new replies can be posted as subordinates to any existing message (edge).

3. Dynamic nodes and static edges. This is the classic organizational chart in which organization stays the same, but the people holding the offices rotate frequently. This is assuming that your company does not reorganize more often than its personnel turnover.

4. Dynamic nodes and dynamic edges. Imagine that you have a graph model of a communications or transportation network. The traffic on the network is changing constantly. You want to find a minimal spanning tree based on the current traffic and update that tree as the nodes and edges come on and off the network. To make this a little less abstract, the fastest path from the fire station to a particular home address will not necessarily be the same route at 05:00 hours as it will be at 17:00 hours. Once the fire is put out, the node that represented the burning house node can disappear from the tree and the next fire location becomes a node to which we must find a path.

Looking at the world from another viewpoint, we might classify hierarchies by usage—as either searching or reporting. An example of a searching hierarchy is the Dewey Decimal system in a library. You move from the general classifications to a particular book—down the hierarchy. An example of a reporting hierarchy is an accounting system. You move from particular transactions to summaries by general categories (assets, liabilities, equity)—up the hierarchy.

You might pick a different tree model for a table in each of these situations to get better performance. It can be a very hard call to make and it is hard to give even general advice. But it is hoped that I can show you the trade-offs and you can make an informed decision.

1.2 Network Databases

Conference on Data Systems Languages (CODASYL) was a consortium formed in 1959 to develop portable programming languages for commercial use. Their best effort was COBOL, which still dominates commercial programming today, but they also had a database standard. This project was assigned to the Data Base Task Group, and its first report in January 1968 was entitled *COBOL Extensions to Handle Data Bases*.

In 1969 the DBTG published a language specification for the network database model, which became generally known as the CODASYL Data Model. It is based on directed graphs that were traversed by an imaginary cursor.

Like SQL, there were sublanguages. It had a data definition language (DDL) that defined a schema, much like the DDL in SQL. Then there was a data manipulation language (DML), which defined new verbs for COBOL. Back in those days, nobody thought about other languages.

ANSI and ISO adopted CODASYL database specifications under the name Network Database Language (NDL), with work taking place within the same working group (X3H2) as SQL standardization. An ISO standard for NDL was ratified as ISO 8907:1987. It never went anywhere and finally expired in 1998.

Several commercial products were based on the network model. Some of the implementations were:

1.   Integrated Data Store (IDS/2) from Honeywell

2.   Integrated Database Management System IDMS from Cullinet (nee Cullinane Database Systems)

3.   IDS (Integrated Database System). This was the very first DBMS. It was designed by Charles Bachman in 1960.

4.   DMS-1100 from Univac

5.   DBMS32 from DEC (Digital Equipment Corporation)

6.   IMAGE/3000 from Hewlett-Packard (a port of TOTAL from the mainframes to HP3000 computers)

7.   IMS from IBM. This hierarchic DBMS is still a dominate database product that uses a tree data model. It may well have as much or more data in its files than SQL. I have given it Chapter 15 by itself.

1.3 Modeling a Graph in a Program

Long before there was SQL, programmers represented graphs in the programming language that they had. People used pointer chains in assembly language or system development languages such as 'C' to build very direct representations of graphs. However, the later, higher level languages, such as Pascal, LISP, and PL/I, did not expose the hardware to the programmer like the system development languages. Pointers in these languages were abstracted to hide references to physical storage and often required that the pointers point to variables or structures of a particular type (see PL/I's ADDR() function, pointers' data types, and based variables as an example of this kind of language construct).

Traditional application development languages do not have pointers, but often have arrays. In particular, because FORTRAN only had arrays for a data structure, a good FORTRAN programmer could use them for just about anything. Early versions of FORTRAN did not have character string data types—everything was either an integer or a floating point number.

This meant that the model of a graph had to start by numbering the nodes and using the node numbers as subscripts to index into the arrays.

Once the array techniques for graphs were developed, they became part of the "programmer's folklore" and were implemented in other languages.

1.4 The Great Debate

The Great Debate was a debate between proponents of the relational and network approaches. It was held at the ACM SIGMOD Workshop on Data Description, Access, and Control in 1974. Dr. E. F. Codd spoke for the relational approach and Charles W. Bachman for the network, or CODASYL, approach.

Part of the debate was a moderately complicated business problem. Dr. Codd solved it correctly in a small number of steps. Mr. Bachman gave an elaborate solution that was wrong. This was the point at which RDBMS began to replace CODASYL models. ANSI X3H2 was formed, SQL became the standard, and you know the rest.

However, one of the objections to RDBMS was that it could not represent hierarchies easily. Because almost all commercial programming and Western thought is based on hierarchies, set-oriented RDBMS tools would only be good for ad hoc queries and never for serious, large databases. Well, that was wrong.

Ironically, object-oriented (OO) programming picked up hierarchies for classes.

1.5 Note on Recursion

I am going to take a little time to explain it because trees are a recursive data structure and can be accessed by recursive algorithms. Many commercial programmers are not familiar with the concept of recursion. Recursion does not appear in early programming languages. Even when it did or was added later, as was the case in IBM's MVS COBOL product in 1999, most programmers do not use it.

There is an old geek joke that gives the dictionary definition: Recursion = (REE-kur-shun) self-referencing procedure or data structure; also see recursion.

This is really pretty accurate, if not all that funny. A recursive structure is made up of smaller structures of the same kind. Thus, a tree is made up of subtrees. You finally arrive at the smallest possible subtrees, the leaf nodes—a subtree of size one.

A recursive function is also like that. Part of its work is done by invoking itself until it arrives at the smallest unit of work for which it can return an answer. Once it gets the lowest level answer, it passes it back to the copy of the function that called it so that copy can finish its computations. And so forth until we have gotten back up the chain to the first invocation that started it all. It is very important to have a halting condition in a recursive function for obvious reasons.

Perhaps the idea will be easier to see with a simple example. Let's Reverse a string with this SQL/PSM function:

```
CREATE FUNCTION Reverse (IN instring VARCHAR(20))
RETURNS VARCHAR(20)
LANGUAGE SQL
```

```
DETERMINISTIC
BEGIN -- recursive function
IF CHAR_LENGTH(instring) IN (0, 1) -- halt condition
THEN RETURN (instring);
ELSE RETURN -- flip the two halves around, recursively
  (Reverse(SUBSTRING (instring FROM (CHAR_LENGTH(instring)/2+1))
  || Reverse(SUBSTRING (instring FROM 1 FOR CHAR_LENGTH(instring)/2))));
END IF;
END;
```

Given the string 'abcde', the first call becomes:

```
 Reverse('de') || Reverse('abc')
```

this becomes

```
 (Reverse(Reverse('e') || Reverse('d'))
 || (Reverse((Reverse('c') || Reverse('ab')))
```

this becomes:

```
 (('e'||'d')
 || (('c') || Reverse((Reverse('b') || Reverse('a')))))
```

this becomes:

```
 (('e'||'d') || ('c' || ('b' || 'a')))
```

this finally becomes:

```
 'edcba'
```

In the case of trees, we will test to see if a node is either the root or a leaf node as our halting conditions. The rest of the time, we are dealing with a subtree, which is just another tree. This is why a tree is called a recursive structure.

Graph Theory References

If you do not have graph theory in your mathematical background. Here is a short list of good introductory books.

Balakrishna, V., 1997. Schaum's Outline of Graph Theory. McGraw-Hill. ISBN 978-0070054899.

Berge, C., 2001. The Theory of Graphs. ISBN 978-0486419756.

Chartrand, G., Introductory Graph Theory. ISBN 978-0486247755. Fun and easy Dover reprint.

Cormen, T.H., Leiserson, C.E., Rivest, R.L., 1990. Introduction to Algorithms. McGraw-Hill Companies. ISBN 978-0262033848.

Even, S., 1979. Graph Algorithms. Computer Science Press, Rockville, MD. ISBN 978-0914894216.

Harary, F., 1994. Graph Theory. Addison-Wesley, Boston. ISBN 978-0201410334. Look for this author as he is a big name in the field.

Hartsfield, N., Ringel, G., 2003. Pearls in Graph Theory: A Comprehensive Introduction. ISBN 0-486432328.

McHugh, J.A., 1990. Algorithmic Graph Theory. Prentice-Hall, Englewood Cliffs, NJ. ISBN 978-013236159.

Ore, O. (revised by Robin J. Wilson), 1990. Graphs and Their Uses. American Mathematical Association. ISBN 978-0883586352. This is a classic book written at the high school level.

Trudeau, R.J., 1994. Introduction to Graph Theory. ISBN 978-0486678702.

Adjacency List Model

IN THE EARLY days of System "R" at IBM, one of the arguments against a relational database was that SQL could not handle hierarchies like IMS could and would therefore not be practical for large databases. It might have a future as an ad hoc query language, but that was the best that could be expected of it.

In a short paper, Dr. E. F. Codd described a method for showing hierarchies in SQL that consisted of a column for the boss_emp_name and another column for the employee in the relationship. It was a direct implementation in a table of the adjacency list model of a graph. Oracle was the first commercial database to use SQL, and the sample database that comes with their product, nicknamed the "Scott/Tiger" database in the trade because of its default user and password codes, uses an adjacency list model in a combination Personnel/Organizational chart table. The organizational structure and personnel data are mixed together in the same row.

This model stuck for several reasons other than just Dr. Codd and Oracle's seeming endorsements. It is probably the most natural way to convert from an IMS database or from a procedural language with pointer chains to SQL if you have been a procedural programmer all of your life.

2.1 The Simple Adjacency List Model

In Oracle's "Scott/Tiger" Personnel table, the "linking column" is the employee identification number of the immediate boss_emp_name of each employee. The president of the company has a NULL for his boss_emp_name. Here is an abbreviated version of such a Personnel/Organizational chart table (Figure 2.1).

```
CREATE TABLE Personnel_OrgChart
(emp_name VARCHAR(10) NOT NULL PRIMARY KEY,
 boss_emp_name VARCHAR(10), -- null means root
 salary_amt DECIMAL(6,2) NOT NULL,
 ...);
```

Personnel_OrgChart

emp_name	boss_emp_name	salary_amt
'Albert'	NULL	1000.00
'Bert'	'Albert'	900.00
'Chuck'	'Albert'	900.00
'Donna'	'Chuck'	800.00
'Eddie'	'Chuck'	700.00
'Fred '	'Chuck'	600.00

Use of a person's name for a key is not a good programming practice, but we will ignore that for now; it will make the discussion easier. The table also needs a UNIQUE constraint to enforce the hierarchical relationships

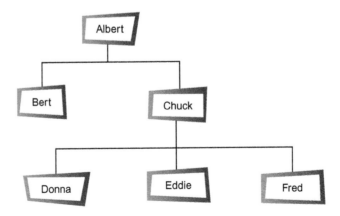

Figure 2.1

among nodes. This is not a flaw in the adjacency list model per se, but this is how most programmers I have seen actually program the adjacency list model. In fairness, one reason for not having all of the needed constraints is that most SQL products did not have such features until their later releases. The constraints that should be used are complicated and we will get to them after this history lesson.

I am first going to attack a "straw man," which shows up more than it should in actual SQL programming, and then make corrections to that initial adjacency list model schema. Finally, I want to show some actual flaws in the adjacency list model after it has been corrected.

2.2 The Simple Adjacency List Model Is Not Normalized

There is a horrible truth about the simple adjacency list model that nobody noticed. It is not a normalized schema. A boss is not an attribute of an employee any more than a book is an attribute of an author; subordination and authorship are relationships.

The classic normal forms are only part of normalization. The short definition of normalization is that all data redundancy has been removed and it is safe from data anomalies. Tom Johnston coined the phrase "non-normal form redundancies" for this particular kind of thing. I coined the phrase that a normalized database has "one simple fact, in one place, one time" as a mnemonic for three characteristics we want in a data model.

We will go into details shortly, but for now consider that the typical adjacency list model table includes information about the node (the salary_amt of the employee in this example), as well as who its superior (boss_emp_name) is in each row. This means that you have a mixed table of entities (Personnel) and relationships (organization) and thus its rows are not properly formed facts. So much for the characteristic one.

The second characteristic of a normalized table is that each fact appears "in one place" in the schema, that is, it belongs in one row of one table, but the subtree of each node can be in more than one row. The third characteristic of a normalized table is that each fact appears "one time" in the schema, that is, you want to avoid data redundancy. Both of these conditions are violated and we can have anomalies.

2.2.1 UPDATE Anomalies

Let's say that "Chuck" decides to change his name to "Charles," so we have to update the Personnel_OrgChart table:

```
UPDATE Personnel_OrgChart
   SET emp_name = 'Charles'
 WHERE emp_name = 'Chuck';
```

But that does not work. We want the table to look like this:

Personnel_OrgChart

emp_name	boss_emp_name	salary_amt
'Albert'	NULL	1000.00
'Bert'	'Albert'	900.00
'Charles'	'Albert'	900.00 ◄ change as employee
'Donna'	'Charles'	800.00 ◄ change as boss_emp_name #1
'Eddie'	'Charles'	700.00 ◄ change as boss_emp_name #2
'Fred '	'Charles'	600.00 ◄ change as boss_emp_name #3

Four rows are affected by this UPDATE statement. If a Declarative Referential Integrity REFERENCES clause was used, then an ON UPDATE CASCADE clause with a self-reference could make the three "boss_emp_name" role changes automatically. Otherwise, the programmer has to write two UPDATE statements.

```
BEGIN ATOMIC
UPDATE Personnel_OrgChart
   SET emp_name = 'Charles'
 WHERE emp_name = 'Chuck';
UPDATE Personnel_OrgChart
   SET boss_emp_name = 'Charles'
 WHERE boss_emp_name = 'Chuck';
END;
```

or, if you prefer, one UPDATE statement, which hides the logic in a faster, but convoluted, CASE expression.

```
UPDATE Personnel_OrgChart
   SET emp_name
       = CASE WHEN emp_name = 'Chuck'
          THEN 'Charles',
          ELSE emp_name END,
       boss_emp_name
       = CASE WHEN boss_emp_name = 'Chuck'
          THEN 'Charles',
          ELSE boss_emp_name END
WHERE 'Chuck' IN (boss_emp_name, emp_name);
```

However, as you can see, this is not a simple change of just one fact.

2.2.2 INSERT Anomalies

The simple adjacency list model has no constraints to preserve subordination. Therefore, you can easily corrupt the Personnel_OrgChart with a few simple insertions, thus

```
-- make a cycle in the graph
INSERT INTO Personnel_OrgChart VALUES ('Albert', 'Fred', 100.00);
```

Obviously, you can create cycles by inserting an edge between any two existing nodes.

2.2.3 DELETE Anomalies

The simple adjacency list model does not support inheritance of subordination. Deleting a row will split the tree into several smaller trees, as for example

```
DELETE FROM Personnel_OrgChart WHERE emp_name = 'Chuck';
```

Suddenly, 'Donna', 'Eddie', and 'Fred' find themselves disconnected from the organization and no longer reporting indirectly to 'Albert' anymore. In fact, they are still reporting to 'Chuck', who does not exist anymore! Using an ON DELETE CASCADE referential action or a TRIGGER could cause the entire subtree to disappear—probably a bad surprise for Chuck's former subordinates.

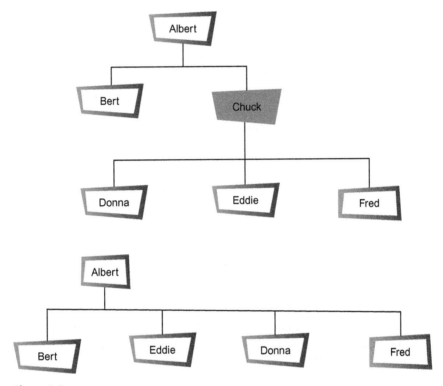

Figure 2.2

2.2.4 Structural Anomalies

Finally, we need to preserve the tree structure in the table. We need to be sure that there is only one NULL in the structure, but the simple adjacency list model does not protect against multiple NULLs or from cycles.

```
-- self-reference
INSERT INTO Personnel_OrgChart (boss_emp_name, emp_name) VALUES (a, a);

-- simple cycle
INSERT INTO Personnel_OrgChart (boss_emp_name, emp_name) VALUES (c, b);
INSERT INTO Personnel_OrgChart (boss_emp_name, emp_name) VALUES (b, c);
```

The problem is that the adjacency list model is actually a general model for *any* graph. Because a tree is a special case of a graph, you need to restrict the adjacency list model a bit to be sure that you do have only a tree.

2.3 Fixing the Adjacency List Model

In fairness, I have been kicking a straw man. These flaws in the simple adjacency list model can be overcome with a redesign of the schema.

First, the Personnel list and the Organizational chart could and should be modeled as separate tables. The Personnel table contains facts about the people (entities) who we have as our Personnel, and the Organizational chart tells us how the job positions within the company are organized (relationships), regardless of who—if anyone—holds what position. It is the difference between the office and the person who holds that office.

```
CREATE TABLE Personnel
(emp_nbr INTEGER DEFAULT 0 NOT NULL PRIMARY KEY,
 emp_name VARCHAR(10) DEFAULT '{{vacant}}' NOT NULL,
 emp_address VARCHAR(35) NOT NULL,
 birth_date DATE NOT NULL,
 ...);
```

I am assuming that we have a dummy employee named '{{vacant}}' with a dummy employee number of zero. It makes reports look nicer, but you have to add more constraints to handle this missing value marker.

Information about the positions within the company goes into a second table, thus

```
CREATE TABLE OrgChart
(job_title VARCHAR(30) NOT NULL PRIMARY KEY,
 emp_nbr INTEGER DEFAULT 0 -- zero is vacant position
     NOT NULL
     REFERENCES Personnel(emp_nbr)
     ON DELETE SET DEFAULT
     ON UPDATE CASCADE,
 boss_emp_nbr INTEGER -- null means root node
   REFERENCES Personnel(emp_nbr),
 salary_amt DECIMAL (12,4) NOT NULL CHECK (salary_amt >= 0.00),
 ...);
```

Note that you still need constraints between and within the tables to enforce the tree properties and to make sure that a position is not held by someone who is not an employee of the company.

The most obvious constraint is to prohibit a single node cycle in the graph.

```
CHECK (boss_emp_nbr <> emp_nbr) -- cannot be your own boss!
```

But that does not work because of the dummy employee number of zero for all vacant positions.

```
CHECK ((boss_emp_nbr <> emp_nbr) OR (boss_emp_nbr = 0 AND emp_nbr = 0))
```

If we want to prevent longer cycles, we cannot use the UNIQUE(emp_name, boss_emp_name) constraint, which limits an employee to one and only one boss. Again, multiple vacancies will mess up this model.

We know that the number of edges in a tree is the number of nodes minus one so this is a connected graph. That constraint looks like this in the original simple adjacency list table.

```
CHECK ((SELECT COUNT(*) FROM Personnel_OrgChart) −1 -- count of edges
    = (SELECT COUNT(boss_emp_name) FROM Personnel_OrgChart)) -- count of
nodes
```

The COUNT(boss_emp_nbr) will drop the NULL in the root row, which gives us the effect of having a constraint to check for one NULL:

```
CHECK((SELECT COUNT(*) FROM Personnel_OrgChart WHERE boss_emp_name IS
NULL) = 1)
```

This is a necessary condition, but it is not a sufficient condition. Consider these data, in which 'Donna' and 'Eddie' are in a cycle and that cycle is not in the tree structure.

emp_name	boss_emp_name
'Albert'	NULL
'Bert'	'Albert'
'Chuck'	'Albert'
'Donna'	'Eddie'
'Eddie'	'Donna'

One approach would be to remove all the leaf nodes and repeat this procedure until the tree is reduced to an empty set. If the tree does not reduce to an empty set, then there is a disconnected cycle.

```
CREATE FUNCTION TreeTest() RETURNS CHAR(6)
LANGUAGE SQL
DETERMINISTIC
BEGIN ATOMIC
-- put a copy in a temporary table
INSERT INTO TempTree
SELECT emp_nbr, boss_emp_nbr
  FROM Personnel_OrgChart;
--prune the leaves
WHILE (SELECT COUNT(*) FROM TempTree) -1
       = (SELECT COUNT(boss_emp_nbr) FROM TempTree)
  DO DELETE FROM TempTree
     WHERE TempTree.emp_name
            NOT IN (SELECT T2.boss_emp_nbr
                       FROM TempTree AS T2
                      WHERE T2.boss_emp_nbr IS NOT NULL);
  IF NOT EXISTS (SELECT * FROM TempTree)
  THEN RETURN ('Tree ');
  ELSE RETURN ('Cycles');
  END IF;
END WHILE;
END;
```

Checking for errors once they are in the tree with a function gives the result that there are errors, but to find the place is very hard in a large tree then. An alternative is to add a CREATE ASSERTION statement to the schema that will catch and prevent cycles when someone attempts to insert them. The general skeleton looks like this:

```
CREATE ASSERTION Valid_Tree
CHECK ((SELECT COUNT(*) FROM Tree)
      = (SELECT COUNT(*)
          FROM (SELECT parent_node FROM Tree)
         UNION
         (SELECT child_node FROM Tree)));
```

This solution is better because it prevents errors from the beginning. SQL Server and other SQL products do not have ASSERTIONs; however, this was ported easily to a VIEW, an INSERT trigger, and an UPDATE trigger.

These constraints will need to be deferred in some situations; in particular, if we reorganize a position out of existence, we need to remove it from the Organization Chart table and make a decision about its subordinates. We will deal with that problem in another section. The original Personnel_OrgChart is easy to reconstruct with a VIEW like this for reporting purposes.

```
CREATE VIEW Personnel_OrgChart (emp_nbr, emp_name, boss_emp_nbr,
boss_emp_name)
AS
SELECT E1.emp_nbr, E1.emp_name, E1.boss_emp_nbr, B1.emp_name
  FROM Personnel AS E1, Personnel AS B1, OrgChart AS O1
 WHERE B1.emp_nbr = P1.boss_emp_nbr
   AND E1.emp_nbr = P1.emp_nbr;
```

2.3.1 Concerning the Use of NULLs

I have shown a NULL-able boss_emp_name column in my examples in which NULL means that this row is the root of the tree; that is, that it has no boss_emp_name above it in the hierarchy. While this is the most common representation, it is not the only way to model a tree.

Alternatives are:

1. Use NULLs for the subordinates of leaf nodes. This leads to slightly different logic in many of the queries, reversing the "flow" of NULL checking.

2. Disallow NULLs altogether. This will record only the edges of the graph in the table. Again the logic would change. The root would have to be detected by looking for the one node, which is only a boss who reports to a dummy value of some kind and is never an employee, thus:

```
SELECT DISTINCT boss_emp_nbr
  FROM OrgChart
 WHERE boss_emp_nbr NOT IN (SELECT emp_nbr FROM OrgChart);
```

In many ways I would prefer the second option, but using the (NULL, <root>) convention guarantees that all employees show up in the emp_nbr column, which makes many queries much easier to write.

This convention was not done for that reason; historically, the boss_emp_name was considered an attribute of the employee in the data model. This is a violation of the second normal form (2nf).

2.4 Navigation in Adjacency List Model

The fundamental problem with the adjacency list model is that it requires navigation. There is no general way to extract a complete subtree.

2.4.1 Cursors and Procedural Code

The practical problem is that despite existing SQL standards, every SQL product has a slightly different proprietary cursor syntax. The general format is to follow the chain of (emp_nbr, boss_emp_nbr) values in a loop. This makes going down the tree fairly simple, but aggregation of subtrees for reporting is very slow for large trees.

This approach is fairly simple if you start at leaf nodes and travel to the root node of the tree structure.

```
CREATE PROCEDURE UpTreeTraversal (IN current_emp_nbr INTEGER)
LANGUAGE SQL
DETERMINISTIC
WHILE EXISTS
    (SELECT *
       FROM OrgChart AS T1
      WHERE current_emp_nbr = T1.emp_nbr)
DO BEGIN
  -- take some action on the current node of the traversal
  CALL SomeProc (current_emp_nbr);
  -- go up the tree toward the root
  SET current_emp_nbr
      = (SELECT T1.boss_emp_nbr
           FROM OrgChart AS T1
          WHERE current_emp_nbr = T1.emp_nbr);
  END;
END WHILE;
```

2.4.2 Self-joins

The other method of doing a tree traversal is to do multiple self-joins, with each copy of the tree representing a level in the Personnel_OrgChart.

```
SELECT O1.emp_name AS e1, O2.emp_name AS e2, O3.emp_name AS e3
  FROM Personnel_OrgChart AS O1, Personnel_OrgChart AS O2,
       Personnel_OrgChart AS O3
```

```
WHERE O1.emp_name = O2.boss_emp_name
  AND O2.emp_name = O3.boss_emp_name
  AND O1.emp_name = 'Albert';
```

This code is limited to a known depth of traversal, which is not always possible. This sample query produces this result table. The paths shown are those that are exactly three levels deep.

e1	e2	e3
'Albert'	'Chuck'	'Donna'
'Albert'	'Chuck'	'Eddie'
'Albert'	'Chuck'	'Fred'

You can improve this query with the use of LEFT OUTER JOINs.

```
SELECT O1.emp_name AS e1, O2.emp_name AS e2, O3.emp_name AS e3,
O4.emp_name AS e4
FROM Personnel_OrgChart AS O1
  LEFT OUTER JOIN
  Personnel_OrgChart AS O2
  ON O1.emp_name = O2.boss_emp_name
  LEFT OUTER JOIN
  Personnel_OrgChart AS O3
  ON O2.emp_name = O3.boss_emp_name
  LEFT OUTER JOIN
  Personnel_OrgChart AS O4
  ON O3.emp_name = O4.boss_emp_name
WHERE O1.emp_name = 'Albert';
```

Because any paths at a particular level not in the table will be displayed as NULLs, this query can be put into a VIEW and invoked.

Note that it produces:

e1	e2	e3	e4
'Albert'	'Bert'	NULL	NULL
'Albert'	'Chuck'	'Donna'	NULL
'Albert'	'Chuck'	'Eddie'	NULL
'Albert'	'Chuck'	'Fred'	NULL

This actually gives you all the subtree paths under 'Albert' to a fixed depth of three. The pattern can be extended, but performance will also go down. Most SQL products have a point at which the optimizer chokes either on the number of tables in a FROM clause or on the levels of self-reference in a query.

Aggregation based on self-joins is a nightmare. You have to build a table with one column that has the unique keys of the subtree and use it to find the rows to be used in aggregate calculations. One way to "flatten" the table is to use an auxiliary table called Series, which contains the single column seq of integers from 1 to (n), where (n) is a sufficiently large number.

```
SELECT MAX(CASE
      WHEN seq = 1 THEN e1
      WHEN seq = 2 THEN e2
      WHEN seq = 3 THEN e3
      WHEN seq = 4 THEN e4
      ELSE NULL END)
FROM (Series AS S1
      CROSS JOIN
      << Personnel_OrgChart query as above>>
      ) AS X(e1, e2, e3, e4)
WHERE seq BETWEEN 1 AND 4;
```

As you can see, this approach becomes insanely convoluted very fast and you do not gain generality.

2.4.3 Finding a Subtree with Recursive CTE

Standard SQL supports recursive CTEs, which can be used with the adjacency list model. You start the anchor or fixed point at the root and then attach each level. It is a good idea to track the depth of the recursion.

```
WITH RECURSIVE Traversal (emp_name, boss_emp_name, recurse_depth)
AS
(-- recursion starts at the anchor or fixed point query
SELECT P0.emp_name, P0.boss_emp_name, 0 AS recurse_depth,
FROM Personnel_OrgChart AS P0
WHERE boss_emp_name IS NULL
UNION ALL
```

```
SELECT P1.emp_name, P1.boss_emp_name, (T.recurse_depth +1) AS recurse_
depth
FROM Personnel_OrgChart AS P1, Traversal AS T
WHERE T.emp_name = P1.boss_emp_name
)
SELECT emp_name, boss_emp_name, recurse_depth
FROM Traversal;
```

This is actually implemented as a loop and cursors inside most SQL products. However, this declarative from has some chance of being optimized in the future, whereas loops and cursors do not.

2.4.4 Finding a Subtree with Iterations

This procedure will find the subtree rooted at the manager emp_nbr of your PersonnelOrg table. The idea is simple. Create a local working table and load it with the immediate subordinate emp_nbrs. Using the leaf nodes in a loop, find their subordinates. When you can add no more levels to the working tree, you have the whole subtree in the working table.

```
CREATE PROCEDURE GetSubtree(IN in_boss_emp_nbr INTEGER)
LANGUAGE SQL
DETERMINISTIC
CREATE LOCAL TEMPORARY TABLE WorkingTree
(LIKE PersonnelOrg)
ON COMMIT DELETE ROWS;

BEGIN ATOMIC
DECLARE local_prior_size INTEGER;
DECLARE local_curr_size INTEGER;

DELETE FROM WorkingTree; -- redundant unless table is external
INSERT INTO WorkingTree
SELECT *
  FROM Personnel_OrgChart
 WHERE in_boss_emp_nbr = boss_emp_nbr;

SET local_curr_size = (SELECT COUNT(*) FROM WorkingTree);
SET local_prior_size = 0;

WHILE local_prior_size < local_curr_size
   DO SET local_prior_size = (SELECT COUNT(*) FROM WorkingTree);
      INSERT INTO WorkingTree
```

```
SELECT *
  FROM PersonnelOrg
 WHERE boss_emp_nbr
       IN (SELECT W1.emp_nbr
             FROM WorkingTree AS W1
            WHERE W1.emp_nbr
            NOT IN (SELECT W2.boss_emp_nbr
                      FROM WorkingTree AS W2));
     SET local_curr_size = (SELECT COUNT(*) FROM WorkingTree);
END WHILE;
-- SELECT * FROM WorkingTree;
END;
```

I chose to use COUNT(*) for the loop control because it is usually fast and can be obtained from schema information tables. You can rewrite this as a recursive function, but it is probably not as effective.

This procedure involves some features you might not have in your SQL product.

Creating a temporary table inside the procedure is part of SQL:2003, but is not in the core standard. You can create a working table outside of the procedure body and insert into it.

The LIKE clause in the table definition copies table declarations and has some other options in SQL:2003. This can be done with a cut and paste instead.

2.4.5 Finding Ancestors

If you want to go up the tree for a known number of levels from a known employee, you can use this procedure:

```
CREATE FUNCTION GetAncestor_1
(IN in_emp_nbr INTEGER,
 IN in_lvl INTEGER) -- levels above employee
RETURNS INTEGER
LANGUAGE SQL
DETERMINISTIC

BEGIN ATOMIC
 DECLARE local_boss_emp_nbr INTEGER;
 SET local_boss_emp_nbr = in_emp_nbr;

IF in_lvl IS NULL
   OR in_emp_nbr IS NULL
```

```
      OR in_lvl < 0
THEN RETURN CAST (NULL AS INTEGER);
END IF;

WHILE in_lvl > 0
      AND local_boss_emp_nbr IS NOT NULL
   DO SET (local_boss_emp_nbr, in_lvl)
      = (SELECT boss_emp_nbr, in_lvl − 1
           FROM Personnel_OrgChart
          WHERE emp_nbr = local_boss_emp_nbr);
END WHILE;
```

If you prefer recursion over iteration, then you can use this version:

```
CREATE FUNCTION GetAncestor_2
(IN in_emp_nbr INTEGER,
 IN in_lvl INTEGER) -- levels above employee
RETURNS INTEGER
LANGUAGE SQL
DETERMINISTIC

RETURN
(CASE
 WHEN in_lvl IS NULL
     OR in_emp_nbr IS NULL
     OR in_lvl < 0
 THEN CAST (NULL AS INTEGER)
 WHEN in_lvl = 0
 THEN in_emp_nbr
ELSE GetAncestor
     ((SELECT boss_emp_nbr
         FROM Personnel_OrgChart
        WHERE emp_nbr = in_emp_nbr),
       in_lvl −1)
END);
```

The CASE expression first looks to see if the parameters make sense. If the level is zero, then you wanted this node. For greater levels, we traverse the tree recursively. The scalar subquery parameter might have to be written as (SELECT MAX(boss_emp_nbr) FROM Personnel_OrgChart WHERE emp_nbr = in_emp_nbr) to assure the compiler that it is a scalar value.

2.5 Inserting Nodes in the Adjacency List Model

This is the strong point of the adjacency list model. You just insert the (emp_nbr, boss_emp_nbr) pairs into the table and you are done. Assuming that they are valid, you are finished.

2.6 Deleting Nodes in the Adjacency List Model

Removing a leaf node is easy; just remove the row from the tree structure table. All of the tree properties are preserved and no constraints will be violated.

The code for deleting nodes inside the tree is much more complex. First you must make a decision about how to handle the surviving subordinates. There are three basic approaches.

1.   The ancient Egyptian school of management: when a node is removed, all of his subordinates are removed. When Pharaoh dies, you bury all his slaves with him.

2.   Send the orphans to grandmother: subordinates of the deleted node became immediate subordinates of their boss_emp_name's boss_emp_name.

3.   The oldest son takes over the shop: one of the subordinates assumes the position held previously by the deleted node. This promotion can cause a cascade of other promotions down the tree until a root node is left vacant and removed, or be stopped with other rules.

Because the adjacency list model cannot return a subtree in a single query, the constraints will have to be deferred while a traversal of some kind is performed.

2.6.1 Deleting an Entire Subtree

The simplest approach is to do a tree traversal down from the deleted node in which you mark all of the subordinates and then go back and delete the subset of marked nodes. Let's use −99999 as the marker for a deleted node and defer the constraint that forbids (boss_emp_nbr = emp_nbr).

```
CREATE LOCAL TEMPORARY TABLE Workingtable
(boss_emp_nbr INTEGER,
 emp_nbr INTEGER NOT NULL)
ON COMMIT DELETE ROWS;
CREATE PROCEDURE DeleteSubtree (IN dead_guy INTEGER)
LANGUAGE SQL
```

```
DETERMINISTIC
BEGIN ATOMIC
SET CONSTRAINTS <<constraint list>> DEFERRED;
-- mark root of subtree and immediate subordinates
UPDATE OrgChart
 SET emp_nbr
    = CASE WHEN emp_nbr = dead_guy
       THEN -99999 ELSE emp_nbr END,
    boss_emp_nbr
    = CASE WHEN boss_emp_nbr = dead_guy
       THEN -99999 ELSE boss_emp_nbr END
WHERE dead_guy IN (emp_nbr, boss_emp_nbr);

WHILE EXISTS -- mark leaf nodes
  (SELECT *
    FROM OrgChart
   WHERE boss_emp_nbr = -99999
    AND emp_nbr > -99999)
DO -- get list of next level subordinates DELETE FROM WorkingTable;

INSERT INTO WorkingTable
SELECT emp_nbr FROM OrgChart WHERE boss_emp_nbr = -99999;

-- mark next level of subordinates
UPDATE OrgChart
 SET emp_nbr = -99999
 WHERE boss_emp_nbr IN (SELECT emp_nbr FROM WorkingTable);
END WHILE;

-- delete all marked nodes
DELETE FROM OrgChart
 WHERE emp_nbr = -99999;

SET CONSTRAINTS ALL IMMEDIATE;
END;
```

2.6.2 Promoting a Subordinate after Deletion

This is tricky and depends on the particular business rules. One of the more common rules is that the senior subordinate moves the position of her deleted superior. This creates a vacancy in her old position, which might be filled by a sibling or by a subordinate.

I am leaving the node to the reader, but the general idea is to rearrange the tree structure so that the dummy employee number used earlier is finally moved to a leaf node where it is a degenerate case of removing a subtree. For example, we could remove "Chuck" and then promote "Donna" to his position. Her position is left vacant and can be removed, leaving "Eddie" as the senior subordinate.

2.6.3 Promoting an Entire Subtree after Deletion

You cannot delete the root or the tree unravels into a forest of disjoint subtrees. The constraints will prevent this from happening, but you can also test for the root in the insertion statement. Let's use the WorkingTable to hold intermediate traversal results again (Figure 2.2).

```
CREATE PROCEDURE DeleteAndPromoteSubtree (IN dead_guy INTEGER)
LANGUAGE SQL
DETERMINISTIC
SET CONSTRAINTS <<list of constraints>> DEFERRED;
BEGIN ATOMIC
DECLARE my_emp_nbr INTEGER;
DECLARE my_boss_emp_nbr INTEGER;

INSERT INTO Workingtable (emp_nbr, boss_emp_nbr)
SELECT T1.emp_nbr, T2.boss_emp_nbr
 FROM OrgChart AS O1, OrgChart AS O2
 WHERE dead_guy IN (O1.boss_emp_nbr, O2.emp_nbr)
   AND dead_guy
* (SELECT emp_name FROM OrgChart WHERE boss_emp_nbr IS
NULL);

UPDATE Personnel_OrgChart
 SET boss_emp_name = CASE WHEN OrgChart.boss_emp_nbr = dead_guy
     THEN WorkingTable.emp_nbr
     ELSE OrgChart.boss_emp_nbr END,
   emp_name = CASE WHEN OrgChart.emp_nbr = dead_guy
     THEN WorkingTable.boss_emp_nbr
     ELSE OrgChart.emp_nbr END
 WHERE dead_guy IN (emp_nbr, boss_emp_nbr)
 AND dead_guy <> (SELECT emp_nbr
     FROM OrgChart
```

```
    WHERE boss_emp_nbr IS NULL);

DELETE FROM OrgChart
 WHERE boss_emp_nbr = emp_nbr;
END;

SET CONSTRAINTS ALL IMMEDIATE;
```

2.7 Leveled Adjacency List Model

This next approach is credited to Dr. David Rozenshtein in an article he wrote in the now defunct Sybase user's *SQL FORUM* magazine (Vol. 3, No. 4, 1995). The approach he took was to do a breadth-first search instead of a depth-first search of the tree.

His objection was that processing a single node at a time leads to algorithms of complexity $O(n)$, whereas processing nodes by levels leads to algorithms of complexity $O(\log 2(n))$ instead.

His model is a modified adjacency list mode, with an extra column for the level of the node in the tree. Here is a sample tree, with levels filled in. Note that LEVEL is a reserved word in Standard SQL as well as some SQL products.

```
CREATE TABLE Tree
(boss_emp_name CHAR(1), -- null means root
 emp_name CHAR(1) NOT NULL,
 lvl INTEGER DEFAULT 0 NOT NULL);
```

Tree

boss_emp_name	emp_name	lvl
NULL	'a'	1
'a'	'b'	2
'a'	'c'	2
'b'	'd'	3
'b'	'e'	3
'b'	'f'	3
'e'	'g'	4
'e'	'h'	4
'f'	'i'	4
'g'	'j'	5
'i'	'k'	5
'i'	'l'	5

2.7.1 Numbering Levels

Assigning level numbers is a simple loop, done one level at a time. Let's assume that all level numbers start as zeros.

```sql
CREATE PROCEDURE RenumberLevels()
LANGUAGE SQL
DETERMINISTIC
BEGIN ATOMIC

DECLARE lvl_counter INTEGER;
SET lvl_counter = 1;

-- set root to 1, others to zero
UPDATE Tree
 SET lvl
   = CASE WHEN boss_emp_name IS NULL THEN 1 ELSE 0 END;

-- loop thru lvls of the tree
WHILE EXISTS (SELECT * FROM Tree WHERE lvl = 0)
DO
UPDATE Tree
 SET lvl = lvl_counter + 1
 WHERE (SELECT T2.lvl
          FROM Tree AS T2
         WHERE T2.emp_name = Tree.boss_emp_name) > 0
   AND lvl = 0;

SET lvl = lvl_counter + 1;
END WHILE;
END;
```

The level number can be used for displaying the tree as an indented list in a host language via a cursor, but it also lets us traverse the tree by levels instead of one node at a time.

2.7.2 Aggregation in the Hierarchy

Aggregation up a hierarchy is a common form of report. Imagine that the tree is a simple parts explosion and the weight of each assembly (root node of a subtree) is the sum of its subassemblies (all the subordinates in the subtree). The table now has an extra column for the weight and we have information on only the leaf nodes when we start.

```
CREATE TABLE PartsExplosion
(assembly CHAR(1), -- null means root
 subassembly CHAR(1) NOT NULL,
 weight INTEGER DEFAULT 0 NOT NULL,
 lvl INTEGER DEFAULT 0 NOT NULL);
```

I am going to create a temporary table to hold the results and then use this table in the SET clause of an UPDATE statement to change the original table. You can actually combine these statements into a more compact form, but the code would be a bit harder to understand.

```
CREATE LOCAL TEMPORARY TABLE Summary
(node CHAR(1) NOT NULL PRIMARY KEY,
 weight INTEGER DEFAULT 0 NOT NULL
) ON COMMIT DELETE ROWS;

CREATE PROCEDURE SummarizeWeights()
LANGUAGE SQL
DETERMINISTIC
BEGIN ATOMIC
DECLARE max_lvl INTEGER;
SET max_lvl = (SELECT MAX(lvl) FROM PartsExplosion);

--start with leaf nodes
INSERT INTO Summary (node, total)
SELECT emp_name, weight
  FROM PartsExplosion
 WHERE emp_name NOT IN (SELECT assembly FROM PartsExplosion);

-- loop up the tree, accumulating totals
WHILE max_lvl > 1
DO INSERT INTO Summary (node, total)
   SELECT T1.assembly, SUM(S1.weight)
     FROM PartsExplosion AS T1, Summary AS S1
  WHERE T1.assembly = S1.node
    AND T1.lvl = max_lvl
  GROUP BY T1.assembly;
 SET max_lvl = max_lvl - 1;
END WHILE;
```

```
--transfer calculations to PartsExplosion table
UPDATE PartsExplosion
   SET weight
       = (SELECT weight
             FROM Summary AS S1
             WHERE S1.node = PartsExplosion.emp_name)
 WHERE subassembly IN (SELECT assembly FROM PartsExplosion);
END;
```

The adjacency model leaves little choice about using procedural code, as the edges of the graph are shown in single rows without any relationship to the tree as a whole.

CHAPTER 3

Path Enumeration Models

O NE OF THE properties of trees is that there is one and only path from the root to every node in the tree. The path enumeration model stores that path as a string by concatenating either the edges or the keys of the nodes in the path. Searches are done with string functions and predicates on those path strings. For other references, you should consult *Advanced Transact-SQL for SQL Server 2000* (Chapter 16) by Itzak Be-Gan and Tom Moreau (ISBN 978-1893115828). They made the path enumeration model popular with this book. The code in this book is product specific, but easily generalized.

There are two methods for enumerating the paths: edge enumeration and node enumeration. Node enumeration is the most commonly used of the two, and there is little difference in the basic string operations on either model. However, the edge enumeration model has some numeric properties that can be useful.

It is probably a good idea to give the nodes a CHAR(n) identifier of a known size and format to make the path concatenations easier to handle. The other alternative is to use VARCHAR(n) strings, but put a separator character between each node identifier in the concatenation—a character that does not appear in the identifier itself.

To keep the examples as simple as possible, let's use my five-person Personnel_OrgChart table and a CHAR(1) identifier column to build a path enumeration model.

```
-- path is a reserved word in SQL-99
-- CHECK() constraint prevents separator in the column.

CREATE TABLE Personnel_OrgChart
(emp_name CHAR(10) NOT NULL,
 emp_id CHAR(1) NOT NULL PRIMARY KEY
   CHECK(REPLACE (emp_id, '/', '') = emp_id),
 path_string VARCHAR(500) NOT NULL);
```

Personnel_OrgChart

emp_name	emp_id	path_string
'Albert'	'A'	'A'
'Bert'	'B'	'AB'
'Chuck'	'C'	'AC'
'Donna'	'D'	'ACD'
'Eddie'	'E'	'ACE'
'Fred'	'F'	'ACF'

Note that I have not broken the sample table into Personnel (emp_id, path_string) and OrgChart (emp_id, emp_name) tables. This would be a better design, but allow me this bit of sloppiness to make the code simpler to read. REPLACE (<str_exp_1>, <str_exp_2>, <str_exp_3>) is a common vendor string function. The first string expression is searched for all occurrences of the second string expression; if it is found, the second string expression is replaced by the third string expression. The third string expression can be the empty string as in the CHECK () constraint just given.

Another problem is how to prevent cycles in the graph. A cycle would be represented as a path string in which at least one emp_id string appears twice, such as 'ABCA' in my sample table. This can be done with a constraint that uses a subquery, thus.

```
CHECK (NOT EXISTS
   (SELECT *
     FROM Personnel_OrgChart AS D1,
       Personnel_OrgChart AS P1
     WHERE CHAR_LENGTH (REPLACE (D1.emp_id, P1.path_string, ''))
       < (CHAR_LENGTH(P1.path_string)
         - 1) -- size of one emp_id string
   ))
```

Another fact about such a tree is that no path can be longer than the number of nodes in the tree.

```
CHECK ((SELECT MAX(CHAR_LENGTH(path_string))
    FROM Personnel_OrgChart AS P1)
  <= (SELECT COUNT(emp_id) * CHAR_LENGTH(emp_id)
    FROM Personnel_OrgChart AS P2))
```

This assumes that the emp_id is of fixed length and that no separators were used between them in the path_string. Unfortunately, the SQL-92 feature of a subquery in a constraint is not widely implemented yet.

3.1 Finding the Depth of the Tree

If you have used the fixed length emp_id string, then the depth is the length of the path divided by the length of the emp_id string, CHAR_LENGTH(emp_id).

```
CHAR_LENGTH(path_string)/ CHAR_LENGTH(emp_id)
```

I have made it easy to compute by using a single character emp_id code. This is not usually possible in a real tree, with several hundred nodes.

If you used a varying length emp_id, then the depth is

```
CHAR_LENGTH(path_string) − CHAR_LENGTH (REPLACE (path_string, '/', '')) +1
```

As explained earlier, the REPLACE() function is not a Standard SQL string function, but is quite common in actual SQL products. This approach counts the separators.

3.2 Searching for Subordinates

Given a parent, find all of the subtrees under it. The immediate solution is this.

```
SELECT *
 FROM Personnel_OrgChart
WHERE path_string LIKE '%' || :parent_emp_id || '%';
```

The problem is that searches with LIKE predicates whose pattern begin with a '%' wildcard are slow. This is because they usually generate a table scan. Also, note that using '_%' in front of the LIKE predicate pattern will exclude the root of the subtree from the answer. Another approach is this query.

```
SELECT *
 FROM Personnel_OrgChart
WHERE path_string LIKE (SELECT path_string FROM Personnel_OrgChart
          WHERE emp_id = :parent_emp_id) || '%';
```

The subquery will use the indexing on the emp_id column to find the "front part" of the path string from the root to the parent with whom we are concerned.

Traveling down the tree is easy. Instead of a '%' wildcard, use a string of underscore ('_') wildcards of the right length. For example, this will find the immediate children of a given parent emp_id.

```
SELECT *
 FROM Personnel_OrgChart
WHERE path_string LIKE (SELECT path_string FROM Personnel_OrgChart
          WHERE emp_id = :parent_emp_id) ||'_';
```

Many SQL products have a function that will pad a string with repeated copies of an input string or return a string of repeated copies of an input string. For example, SQL Server has a REPLICATE (<character exp>, <integer exp>), Oracle has LPAD() and RPAD(), and DB2 uses REPEAT(). This can be useful for generating a search pattern of underscores on the fly.

```
SELECT *
 FROM Personnel_OrgChart
WHERE path_string LIKE (SELECT path_string FROM Personnel_OrgChart
          WHERE emp_id = :parent_emp_id)
         || REPLICATE ('_', :n);
```

To find the immediate subordinates, assuming a numeric path string using periods, like the structure of this book:

```
SELECT *
 FROM Personnel_OrgChart
 WHERE path_string LIKE '01.02.01.%'
  AND path_string NOT LIKE '01.02.01.%.%';
```

The second search condition is there to prevent a table scan and to restrict the results to the immediate subordinates.

3.3 Searching for Superiors

Given a node, find all of its superiors. This requires disassembling the path back into the identifiers that constructed it. We can use a table of sequential integers to find the required substrings:

```
SELECT SUBSTRING (P1.path_string
      FROM (seq * CHAR_LENGTH(P1.emp_id))
      FOR CHAR_LENGTH(P1.emp_id)) AS emp_id
  FROM Personnel_OrgChart AS P1,
    Series AS S1
 WHERE P1.emp_id = :search_emp_id
   AND S1.seq <= CHAR_LENGTH(path_string)/CHAR_LENGTH(emp_id);
```

The problem is that this does not tell you the relationships among the superiors, only who they are. Those relationships are actually easier to report.

```
SELECT P2.*
  FROM Personnel_OrgChart AS P1,
    Personnel_OrgChart AS P2
 WHERE P1.emp_id = :search_emp_id
   AND POSITION (P2.path_string IN P1.path_string) = 1;
```

3.4 Deleting a Subtree

Given a node, delete the subtree rooted at that node. This can be done with the same predicate as finding the subordinates:

```
DELETE FROM Personnel_OrgChart
 WHERE path_string LIKE (SELECT path_string FROM Personnel_OrgChart
            WHERE emp_id = :dead_guy) || '%';
```

3.5 Deleting a Single Node

Once more we have to face the problem that when a nonleaf node is removed from a tree, it is no longer a tree and we need to have rules for changing the structure.

Assuming that we simply move everyone up a level in the tree, we can first remove that node emp_id from the Personnel_OrgChart table and then remove that emp_id from the paths of the other nodes.

```
BEGIN ATOMIC
DELETE FROM Personnel_OrgChart
 WHERE emp_id = :dead_guy;
UPDATE Personnel_OrgChart
   SET path_string = REPLACE (path_string, :dead_guy, '');
END;
```

There are other methods of rebuilding the tree structure after a node is deleted, as discussed earlier. Promoting a subordinate based on some criteria to the newly vacant position, leaving a vacancy in the organizational chart, and so forth are all options. They are usually implemented with some combination of node deletions and insertions.

3.6 Inserting a New Node

The enumeration model has the same insertion properties as the adjacency list model. The new emp_id is simply concatenated to the end of the path of the parent node to which it is subordinated.

```
INSERT INTO Personnel_OrgChart
VALUES (:new_guy, :new_emp_id,
     (SELECT path_string FROM Personnel_OrgChart WHERE emp_id = :new_guy_boss)
      || :new_emp_id);
```

This basic statement design can be modified to work for insertion of a subtree, thus.

```
INSERT INTO Personnel_OrgChart
SELECT N1.emp, N1.emp_id,
     (SELECT path_string FROM Personnel_OrgChart WHERE emp_id = :new_tree_boss)
       || N1.emp_id
   FROM NewTree AS N1;
```

3.7 Splitting up a Path String

Because the path string contains information about the nodes in the path it represents, you will often want to split it back into the nodes that created. This is easier to do if the path string was built with a separator character such as a comma or slash; I use a slash so this will look like a directory path in UNIX. You will also need a table called Series, which is a set of integers from 1 to (n).

CharIndex(<search string>, <target string>, <starting position>) is a vendor version of the Standard SQL function POSITION(<search string> IN <target string>). It begins the search at a position in the target string, thus when the <starting position> = 1, the two are equivalent. It can be defined as

```
CREATE FUNCTION CharIndex (IN search_str VARCHAR(1000), IN target
VARCHAR(1000), IN start_point INTEGER) RETURNS INTEGER
RETURN
  (POSITION (search_str
       IN SUBSTRING (target FROM start_point)) + start_point -1);
```

Version 1:

```
SELECT CASE WHEN SUBSTRING('/' || P1.path_string || '/' FROM S1.seq FOR 1) =
'/'
       THEN SUBSTRING('/' || P1.path_string || '/' FROM (S1.seq +1)
              FOR CharIndex('/', '/' || P1.path_string || '/', S1.seq +1)
                 - S1.seq - 1)
       ELSE NULL END AS emp_id
  FROM Series AS S1, Personnel_OrgChart AS P1
 WHERE S1.seq BETWEEN 1 AND CHAR_LENGTH('/' | | P1.path_string | | '/') - 1
   AND SUBSTRING('/' || P1.path_string || '/' FROM S1.seq FOR 1) = '/'
```

Version 2: This uses the same idea, but with two sequence numbers to bracket the emp_id embedded in the path string. It also returns the position of the subordinate emp_id in the path.

```
CREATE VIEW Breakdown (emp_id, step_nbr, subordinate_emp_id)
AS
SELECT emp_id,
    COUNT(S2.seq),
    SUBSTRING ('/' || P1.path_string || '/', MAX(S1.seq || 1)
          FROM (S2.seq - MAX(S1.seq || 1))
  FROM Personnel_OrgChart AS P1, Series AS S1, Series AS S2
 WHERE SUBSTRING ('/' || P1.path_string || '/', S1.seq, 1) = '/'
   AND SUBSTRING ('/' || P1.path_string || '/', S2.seq, 1) = '/'
   AND S1.seq < S2.seq
   AND S2.seq <= CHAR_LENGTH(P1.path_string) +1
 GROUP BY P1.emp_id, P1.path_string, S2.seq;
```

The S1 and S2 copies of Series are used to locate bracketing pairs of separators, and the entire set of substrings located between them is extracted in one step. The trick is to be sure that the left-hand separator of the bracketing pair is the closest one to the second separator. The step_nbr column tells you the relative position of the subordinate employee to the employee in the path.

Version 3: This version is the same as version 2, but is more concise and easy to comprehend.

```
SELECT SUBSTRING('/' || P1.path_string || '/'
        FROM S1.seq +1
        FOR CharIndex('/',
                '/' || P1.path_string || '/',
                S1.seq +1)- S1.seq - 1) AS node
   FROM Series AS S1, Personnel_OrgChart AS P1
  WHERE SUBSTRING('/' || P1.path_string || '/'
        FROM S1.seq FOR 1) = '/'
    AND seq < CHAR_LENGTH('/' || P1.path_string || '/');
```

Version 4: another way using the LIKE predicate:

```
SELECT SUBSTRING(P1.path_string
        FROM seq +1
        FOR CharIndex('/', P1.path_string, S1.seq +1) - (S1.seq +1))
   FROM Series AS S1
     INNER JOIN
     (SELECT '/' || path_string || '/'
        FROM Personnel_OrgChart) AS P1.(path_string)
     ON S1.seq <= CHAR_LENGTH(P1.path_string)
        AND SUBSTRING(P1.path_string
              FROM S1.seq
              FOR CHAR_LENGTH(P1.path_string))
          LIKE '/_%';
```

3.8 Microsoft SQL Server's HIERARCHYID

Microsoft added a HIERARCHYID data type to their MS SQL Server 2008 product. It is a path enumeration put into a VARBINARY(892) column. It is manipulated by methods in an OO format instead of with SQL statements.

This allows other languages to also invoke these methods and leave you with mixed system maintenance problems.

The representation uses a slash to separate the levels of the tree; the root is represented by a single slash. Nodes can be inserted anywhere using decimal numberings. Nodes inserted after /1/2/ but before /1/3/ can be represented as /1/2.5/. Nodes inserted before 0 have the logical representation as a negative number. For example, a node that comes before /1/1/ can be represented as /1/−1/. Nodes cannot have leading zeros. For example, /1/1.1/ is valid, but /1/1.01/ is not valid.

So, you're probably wondering how we know how to order nodes in the same level. This is accomplished by comparing node labels, like versioning in software. 0.5.1 comes after 0.5 and before 0.6. If we wished to insert a new node between 0.5 and 0.5.1, we could use 0.5.0.1 or 0.5.0.2, and so forth. Here is a list of the basic methods available to you.

GetAncestor(n): Returns a HIERARCHYID representing the nth ancestor of the affected node.

GetLevel: Returns an integer that represents the depth of the affected node in the tree.

GetRoot: Static method. Returns the root of the hierarchy tree.

IsDescendantOf(parent_node): Returns TRUE if the affected node is a descendant of the parent.

GetDescendant(child_node_1, child_node_2): Returns a child of the affected node, depending on child 1 and 2.

1. If affected node IS NULL, return NULL.
2. If affected node IS NOT NULL and both child_node_1 and child_node_2 are NULL, return a child of the affected node.
3. If affected node IS NOT NULL, child_node_1 IS NOT NULL, and child_node_2 IS NULL, return a child of the affected node greater than child_node_1.
4. If affected node IS NOT NULL, child_node_2 IS NOT NULL, and child_node_1 IS NULL, return a child of the affected node less than child_node_2.
5. If affected node, child_node_1, and child_node_2 are not NULL, return a child of the affected node greater than child_node_1 and less than child_node_2.

6. If child_node_1 IS NOT NULL and not a child of the affected node, an exception is raised.
7. If child_node_2 IS NOT NULL and not a child of the affected node, an exception is raised.
8. If child_node_1 >= child_node_2, an exception is raised.

Parse(input_string): Static method. Converts the canonical string representation of a HIERARCHYID to a HIERARCHYID value. Parse is called implicitly when a conversion from a string type to HIERARCHYID occurs. Acts as the opposite of ToString.

ToString: Returns a string with the logical representation of the affected node. ToString is called implicitly when a conversion from HIERARCHYID to a string type occurs. Acts as the inverse of Parse.

GetReparentedValue(old_root_node, new_root_node): Returns a node whose path from the root is the path to new_root_node, followed by the path from old_root_node to the affected node.

Here is how to modify the usual Personnel_OrgChart with an extra column.

```
CREATE TABLE Personnel_OrgChart
(emp_id INTEGER NOT NULL PRIMARY KEY,
 emp_name VARCHAR(25) NOT NULL),
 h_id HIERARCHYID NOT NULL UNIQUE,
 lvl AS h_id.GetLevel() PERSISTED,
 UNIQUE (lvl, h_id));
```

3.9 Edge Enumeration Model

So far, we have seen the node enumeration version of the path enumeration model. In the edge enumeration model, the "driving directions" for following the path from the root to each node are given as integers. You will also recognize it as the way that the book you are reading is organized. The path column contains a string of the edges that make up a path from the root ('King') to each node, numbering them from left to right at each level in the tree.

Personnel_OrgChart

emp_name	edge_path
'Albert'	'1.'
'Bert'	'1.1.'

emp_name	edge_path
'Chuck'	'1.2.'
'Donna'	'1.2.1.'
'Eddie'	'1.2.2.'
'Fred'	'1.2.3.'

For example, 'Donna' is the second child of the first child ('Chuck') of the root ('Albert'). This assigns a partial ordering to the nodes of the trees. The main advantage of this notation is that you do not have to worry about long strings, but there is no real difference in the manipulations. The numbering does give an implied ordering to siblings that might have meaning.

3.10 XPath and XML

I have avoided mentioning XML, as this is a book on SQL, but I cannot avoid it forever because the two are becoming more and more linked. XML is a mark-up language that shows a data element hierarchy by inserting tags into the text file that holds the data elements.

XML is becoming the "Esperanto" for moving data from one source to another, and there are many tools that are de jure or de facto standards for doing queries on data while they are in XML. One of these tools is XPath, which is based on a fairly simple notation to describe paths to nodes in an XML document in a notation that resembles a path enumeration but with wildcards and other higher level features.

The nodes on the path can then be sent as input to functions. Older programmers can think of XPath as a nonprocedural version of IMS or other hierarchical database query languages.

There are tutorials on XPath available on the Internet. At the time of this writing (2011), there is http://www.w3schools.com/xpath/.

XPath includes over 100 built-in functions. There are functions for string values, numeric values, date and time comparison, node and QName manipulation, sequence manipulation, Booleans, and temporal comparisons as you have programming languages. However, there are navigational functions for finding and manipulating nodes and sequences.

The XML document is a combination of schema and data. Here is an example taken from http://www.w3schools.com/xpath/xpath_examples.asp. The <> and </> pairs indicate the nesting of the hierarchical structure and what would be the data type and domain in RDBMS.

```xml
<?xml version="1.0" encoding="ISO-8859-1"?>

<bookstore>

<book category="COOKING">
 <title lang="en">Everyday Italian</title>
 <author>Giada De Laurentiis</author>
 <year>2005</year>
 <price>30.00</price>
</book>

<book category="CHILDREN">
 <title lang="en">Harry Potter</title>
 <author>J K. Rowling</author>
 <year>2005</year>
 <price>29.99</price>
</book>

<book category="WEB">
 <title lang="en">XQuery Kick Start</title>
 <author>James McGovern</author>
 <author>Per Bothner</author>
 <author>Kurt Cagle</author>
 <author>James Linn</author>
 <author>Vaidyanathan Nagarajan</author>
 <year>2003</year>
 <price>49.99</price>
</book>

<book category="WEB">
 <title lang="en">Learning XML</title>
 <author>Erik T. Ray</author>
 <year>2003</year>
 <price>39.95</price>
</book>

</bookstore>
```

The syntax for XPath is also hierarchical. This embeds both hierarchical structure and program logic into one syntactic unit. XPath includes over

100 built-in functions for strings, numerics, and temporal data comparisons. However, there are navigational functions for finding and manipulating nodes and sequences.

Here are some simple examples using our bookstore document. Slashes look like the directory trees in Linux and Windows, and square brackets hold functions that are applied at that level in the nesting.

`/bookstore/book[last()]`	Selects the last book element that is the child of the bookstore element
`/bookstore/book[last()-1]`	Selects the last but one book element that is the child of the bookstore element
`/bookstore/book[position()<3]`	Selects the first two book elements that are children of the bookstore element
`//title[@lang]`	Selects all the title elements that have an attribute named lang
`//title[@lang='eng']`	Selects all the title elements that have an attribute named lang with a value of 'eng'
`/bookstore/book[price>35.00]`	Selects all the book elements of the bookstore element that have a price element with a value greater than 35.00
`/bookstore/book[price>35.00]/title`	Selects all the title elements of the book elements of the bookstore element that have a price element with a value greater than 35.00

Nested Sets Model of Hierarchies

T REES ARE OFTEN drawn as "boxes-and-arrows" charts and that graphic tends to lock your mental image of a tree into a graph structure. Another way of representing trees is to show them as nested sets. It is strange that this approach was overlooked for so long among SQL programmers. Many of us are old enough to have used *The Art of Computer Programming* (Donald Knuth, 978-0321751041) in college as our textbook and we should remember this representation of trees in a chapter of his book. Younger programmers think of it as "counting tags" in XML, HTML, and other mark-up languages. Mathematical programmers can think of it as parentheses or as, well, nested sets.

Because SQL is a set-oriented language, this is a better model for the approach discussed here. Let us define an Organizational chart table to represent the hierarchy and people in our sample organization. The first column is the name of the member of this organization. I will explain the (lft, rgt) columns shortly, but for now, note that their names are abbreviations for "left" and "right," which are reserved words in Standard SQL.

```
CREATE TABLE OrgChart
(member CHAR(10) NOT NULL PRIMARY KEY,
 lft INTEGER NOT NULL,
 rgt INTEGER NOT NULL);
```

```
INSERT INTO OrgChart (member, lft, rgt)
VALUES ('Albert', 1, 12),
       ('Bert', 2, 3),
       ('Chuck', 4, 11),
       ('Donna', 5, 6),
       ('Eddie', 7, 10);
```

To show a tree as nested sets, replace the boxes with ovals and then nest subordinate ovals inside their parents. Containment represents subordination. The root will be the largest oval and will contain every other node. Leaf nodes will be the innermost ovals, with nothing else inside them, and nesting will show the hierarchical relationship. This is a natural way to model a parts explosion, since a final assembly is made of physically nested assemblies that finally break down into separate parts. This tree (Figure 4.1) translates into this nesting of sets (Figure 4.2).

Using this approach, we can model a tree with (lft, rgt) nested sets with number pairs. These number pairs will always contain the pairs of their subordinates so that a child node is within the bounds of its parent. This is a version of the nested sets, flattened onto a number line (Figure 4.3).

If that mental model does not work for you, then visualize the nested sets model as a little worm with a Bates automatic numbering stamp crawling along the "boxes-and-arrows" version of the tree. The worm

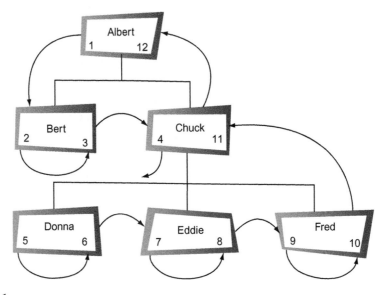

Figure 4.1

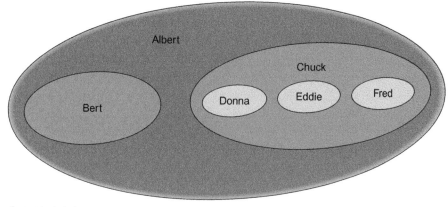

As nested circles

Figure 4.2

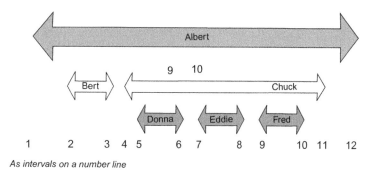

As intervals on a number line

Figure 4.3

starts at the top, the root, and makes a complete trip around the tree.
When he comes to a node, he puts a number in the cell on the side that
he is visiting and his numbering stamp increments itself. Each node will
get two numbers: one for the right (rgt) side and one for the left (lft) side.
Computer science majors will recognize this as a preorder (or depth-first)
tree traversal algorithm with a modification for numbering the nodes.
This numbering has some predictable results that can be used for building
queries (Figure 4.4).

4.1 Finding Root and Leaf Nodes

The root will always have a 1 in its lft column and twice the number of nodes
in its rgt column. This is easy to understand; because the worm has to visit
each node twice, once for the left side and once for the right side, the final

Figure 4.4 Bates numbering stamp

count has to be twice the number of nodes in the whole tree. The root of the tree is found with the query

```
SELECT *
  FROM Orgchart
 WHERE lft = 1;
```

This query will take advantage of an index on the left value. A leaf node is one that has no children under it. In an adjacency matrix model, it is not that easy to find all the leaf nodes because you have to use a correlated subquery:

```
SELECT *
  FROM OrgChart AS O1
 WHERE NOT EXISTS
       (SELECT *
          FROM OrgChart AS O2
         WHERE O1.member = O2.boss);
```

In the nested sets table, the difference between (lft, rgt) values of leaf nodes is always 1. Think of the little worm turning the corner as he crawls along the tree. That means you can find all leaf nodes with the extremely simple query

```
SELECT *
  FROM Orgchart
 WHERE (rgt - lft) = 1;
```

There is a further trick, to speed up queries. Build a unique index on either the left column or on the pair of columns (lft, rgt) and then you can rewrite the query to take advantage of the index. The previous query will also benefit.

```
SELECT *
  FROM Orgchart
 WHERE lft = (rgt - 1);
```

The reason this improves performance is that the SQL engine can use an index on the lft column when it does not appear in an expression. Do not use (rgt − lft) = 1, as it might prevent the index from being used unless your SQL allows indexing on expressions

4.2 Finding Subtrees

Trees have many special properties and those properties are very useful to us. A tree is a graph that has no cycles in it. That is, no path folds back on itself to catch you in an endless loop when you follow it. Another defining property is that there is always a path from the root to any other node in the tree.

Another useful property is that any node in the tree is the root of a subtree and certain properties of that subtree are immediately available from the (lft, rgt) pair. In the nested sets table, all the descendants of a node can be found by looking for nodes whose (lft, rgt) numbers are between the (lft, rgt) values of their parent node. This is the nesting expressed in number ranges instead of in a drawing of circles within circles.

Finally, a tree has exactly one node without a superior, the root. All other nodes can be reached by paths from the root. In the case of the nested sets model, it is the node where (rgt − lft + 1) = 2 * (SELECT COUNT(*) FROM TREE).

For example, to find out all subordinates of each boss in the organizational hierarchy, you would write:

```
SELECT Mgrs.member AS boss, Workers.member AS worker
  FROM Orgchart AS Mgrs, Orgchart AS Workers
 WHERE Workers.lft BETWEEN Mgrs.lft AND Mgrs.rgt
   AND Workers.rgt BETWEEN Mgrs.lft AND Mgrs.rgt;
```

Look at the way the numbering was done and you can convince yourself that this search condition is too strict. We can drop the last predicate and simply use:

```
SELECT Mgrs.member AS boss, Workers.member AS worker
  FROM Orgchart AS Mgrs, Orgchart AS Workers
 WHERE Workers.lft BETWEEN Mgrs.lft AND Mgrs.rgt;
```

This would tell you that everyone is also his own superior, so in some situations you would also add the predicate

```
.. AND Workers.lft <> Mgrs.lft
```

or change it to

```
WHERE Workers.lft > Mgrs.lft
  AND Workers.lft < Mgrs.rgt;
```

This simple self-join query is the basis for almost everything that follows in the nested sets model.

4.3 Finding Levels and Paths in a Tree

The level of a node in a tree is the number of edges between the node and the root, where the larger the depth number, the farther away the node is from the root. A path is a set of edges that connect two nodes directly.

The nested sets model uses the fact that each containing set is "wider" (where width = (rgt − lft)) than the sets it contains. Obviously, the root will always be the widest row in the table. The level function is the number of edges between two given nodes; it is fairly easy to calculate. For example, to find the level of each worker, you would use

```
SELECT O2.member, COUNT(O1.member) AS lvl
  FROM OrgChart AS O1, OrgChart AS O2
 WHERE O2.lft BETWEEN O1.lft AND O1.rgt
 GROUP BY O2.member;
```

The expression COUNT(O1.member) will count the node itself; if you prefer to start at zero, use (COUNT(O1.member) − 1). You will see it done both ways in the literature.

4.3.1 Finding the Height of a Tree

The height of a tree is the length of the longest path in the tree. Because we know that this path runs from the root to a leaf node, we can write a query to find like this:

```
SELECT MAX(level) AS height
  FROM (SELECT O2.member, (COUNT(O1.member) - 1)
          FROM OrgChart AS O1, OrgChart AS O2
         WHERE O2.lft BETWEEN O1.lft AND O1.rgt
         GROUP BY O2.member) AS L1(member, level);
```

Other queries can be built from this tabular subquery expression of the nodes and their level numbers. If you find yourself using this subquery expression often, you might consider creating a VIEW from this expression.

4.3.2 Finding Levels of Subordinates

The adjacency model allows you to find immediate subordinates of a node immediately; you simply look in the columns that give the parent of each child of each node in the tree. The real problem is finding a given generation or level in the tree.

This becomes complicated in the nested sets model. Immediate subordinates are defined as personnel who have no other employee between themselves and their boss.

```
CREATE VIEW Immediate_Subordinates (boss, worker, lft, rgt)
AS SELECT Mgrs.member, Workers.member, Workers.lft, Workers.rgt
     FROM OrgChart AS Mgrs, OrgChart AS Workers
    WHERE Workers.lft BETWEEN Mgrs.lft AND Mgrs.rgt
    AND NOT EXISTS -- no middle manager between the boss and us!
         (SELECT *
            FROM OrgChart AS MidMgr
           WHERE MidMgr.lft BETWEEN Mgrs.lft AND Mgrs.rgt
           AND Workers.lft BETWEEN MidMgr.lft AND MidMgr.rgt
           AND MidMgr.member NOT IN (Workers.member, Mgrs.member));
```

You also need to look at Section 4.9 (Converting Nested Sets Model to Adjacency List) for better answers for immediate subordinates. I am simply giving an elaborate query here to show a pattern. Likewise, Mgrs.member could be replaced with Workers.boss in the SELECT statement.

There is a reason for setting this up as a VIEW and including the (lft, rgt) numbers of the children. The (lft, rgt) numbers for the parent of each node can be reconstructed by

```
SELECT boss, MIN(lft) - 1, MAX(rgt) + 1
  FROM Immediate_Subordinates
 GROUP BY boss;
```

This query can be generalized to any distance (:n) in the hierarchy, thus:

```
SELECT Workers.member, ' is ', :n, ' levels down from ', :my_member
  FROM OrgChart AS Mgrs, OrgChart AS Workers
 WHERE Mgrs.member = :my_member
   AND Workers.lft BETWEEN Mgrs.lft
                    AND Mgrs.rgt
   AND :n = (SELECT COUNT(MidMgr.member) + 1
              FROM OrgChart AS MidMgr
             WHERE MidMgr.lft BETWEEN Mgrs.lft
                                AND Mgrs.rgt
               AND Workers.lft BETWEEN MidMgr.lft
                                  AND MidMgr.rgt
               AND MidMgr.member
                   NOT IN (Workers.member, Mgrs.member));
```

This query can be flattened out and probably runs faster without the subquery:

```
SELECT Workers.member, ' is ', :n, ' levels down from ', :my_member
  FROM OrgChart AS Mgrs, OrgChart AS Workers,
       OrgChart AS MidMgr
 WHERE Mgrs.member = :my_member
   AND Workers.lft BETWEEN Mgrs.lft AND Mgrs.rgt
   AND MidMgr.lft BETWEEN Mgrs.lft AND Mgrs.rgt
   AND Workers.lft BETWEEN MidMgr.lft AND MidMgr.rgt
   AND MidMgr.member NOT IN (Workers.member, Mgrs.member)
 GROUP BY Workers.member
HAVING :n = COUNT(MidMgr.member);
```

In the nested sets model, queries based on subtrees are usually easier to write than those for individual nodes or other subsets of the tree.

Switching to another hierarchy, let's look at a simple parts explosion (Figure 4.5). This table will be modified in later examples to include more information, but for now, just assume that it looks like this.

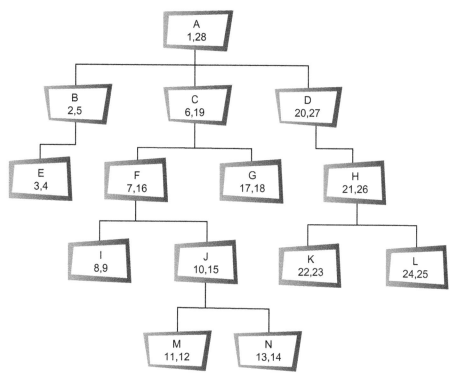

Figure 4.5

```
CREATE TABLE Assemblies
(part CHAR(2) NOT NULL
      REFERENCES Inventory(part) -- assume an inventory
      ON UPDATE CASCADE,
lft INTEGER NOT NULL,
rgt INTEGER NOT NULL,
 ...);

INSERT INTO Assemblies
VALUES ('A', 1, 28),
       ('B', 2, 5),
       ('C', 6, 19),
       ('D', 20, 27),
       ('E', 3, 4),
       ('F', 7, 16),
       ('G', 17, 18),
       ('H', 21, 26),
```

```
('I', 8, 9),
('J', 10, 15),
('K', 22, 23),
('L', 24, 25),
('M', 11, 12),
('N', 13, 14);
```

If you want, show levels as a single row, where NULLs are used to show that there is no part at that level:

```
CREATE VIEW Flat_Parts(part, level_0, level_1, level_2, level_3)
AS
SELECT A1.part,
       CASE WHEN COUNT(A3.part) = 2
            THEN A2.node
            ELSE NULL END AS lvl_0,
       CASE WHEN COUNT(A3.part) = 3
            THEN A2.node
            ELSE NULL END AS lvl_1,
       CASE WHEN COUNT(A3.part) = 4
            THEN A2.part
            ELSE NULL END AS lvl_2,
       CASE WHEN COUNT(A3.part) = 5
            THEN A2.part
            ELSE NULL END AS lvl_3
  FROM Assemblies AS A1, -- subordinates
       Assemblies AS A2, -- superiors
       Assemblies AS A3 -- items in between them
 WHERE A1.lft BETWEEN A2.lft AND A2.rgt
   AND A3.lft BETWEEN A2.lft AND A2.rgt
   AND A1.lft BETWEEN A3.lft AND A3.rgt
 GROUP BY A1.part, A2.part;
```

Now you can write a query to show the path from a node to the root of the tree horizontally:

```
SELECT part, MAX(level_0), MAX(level_1),
             MAX(level_2), MAX(level_3)
  FROM Flat_Parts
 GROUP BY part;
```

You could also fold all of this into one query, but the VIEW is useful for other reports. Another way to flatten the tree is credited to Richard Romley of Smith-Barney in New York City. He claims that the following query runs with half the I/O of the VIEW-based solution in SQL Server:

```
SELECT A1.part,
       (SELECT part
          FROM Assemblies
         WHERE lft = MAX(A2.lft)) AS lvl_0,
       (SELECT part
          FROM Assemblies
         WHERE lft = MAX(A3.lft)) AS lvl_1,
       (SELECT part
          FROM Assemblies
         WHERE lft = MAX(A4.lft)) AS lvl_2,
       (SELECT part
          FROM Assemblies
         WHERE lft = MAX(A5.lft)) AS lvl_3
  FROM Assemblies AS A1
       LEFT OUTER JOIN
       Assemblies AS A2
       ON A1.lft > A2.lft AND A1.rgt < A2.rgt
          LEFT OUTER JOIN
          Assemblies AS A3
          ON A2.lft > A3.lft AND A2.rgt < A3.rgt
             LEFT OUTER JOIN
             Assemblies AS A4
             ON A3.lft > A4.lft AND A3.rgt < A4.rgt
                LEFT OUTER JOIN
                Assemblies AS A5
                ON A4.lft > A5.lft AND A4.rgt < A5.rgt
GROUP BY A1.part;
```

This is a little tricky on two points. The use of an aggregate in a WHERE clause is generally not allowed, but because the MAX() is an outer reference in the scalar subqueries, it is valid Standard SQL. The nested LEFT OUTER JOINs reflect nesting of the (lft, rgt) ranges, but they will return NULLs when there is nothing at a particular level.

The result is as follows.

Result

part	level_0	level_1	level_2	level_3
'A'	NULL	NULL	NULL	NULL
'B'	'A'	NULL	NULL	NULL
'C'	'A'	NULL	NULL	NULL
'D'	'A'	NULL	NULL	NULL
'E'	'B'	'A'	NULL	NULL
'F'	'C'	'A'	NULL	NULL
'G'	'C'	'A'	NULL	NULL
'H'	'D'	'A'	NULL	NULL
'I'	'F'	'C'	'A'	NULL
'J'	'F'	'C'	'A'	NULL
'K'	'H'	'D'	'A'	NULL
'L'	'H'	'D'	'A'	NULL
'M'	'J'	'F'	'C'	'A'
'N'	'J'	'F'	'C'	'A'

Both approaches are compact, easy to follow, and easy to expand to as many levels as desired.

4.3.3 Finding Oldest and Youngest Subordinates

The nested sets model usually assumes that subordinates are ranked by age, seniority, or in some way from left to right among the immediate subordinates of a node. Because the adjacency model does not have a concept of such rankings, the following queries are not possible without extra columns to hold the rankings in the adjacency list model.

Most senior subordinates are found by this query:

```
SELECT Workers.member, ' is the most senior subordinate of ', :my_member
  FROM OrgChart AS Mgrs, OrgChart AS Workers
 WHERE Mgrs.member = :my_member

   AND Workers.lft = Mgrs.lft + 1; -- leftmost child
```

Most junior subordinates are found by this query:

```
SELECT Workers.member, ' is the least senior subordinate of ', :my_member
  FROM OrgChart AS Mgrs, OrgChart AS Workers
 WHERE Mgrs.member = :my_member
   AND Workers.rgt = Mgrs.rgt - 1; -- rightmost child
```

The real trick is to find the nth sibling of a parent in a tree. If you remember the old Charlie Chan movies, Detective Chan always referred to his sons by number, such as "Number One son," "Number Two son," and so forth. This becomes a self-join on the set of immediate subordinates of the parent under consideration, which is why I created a VIEW for telling us the immediate subordinates before introducing this problem. The query is much easier to read using the VIEW.

```
SELECT S1.worker, ' is the ', :n, '-th subordinate of ', S1.boss
  FROM Immediate_Subordinates AS S1
 WHERE S1.boss = :my_member
   AND :n = (SELECT COUNT(S2.lft) - 1
               FROM Immediate_Subordinates AS S2
              WHERE S2.boss = S1.boss
                AND S2.boss <> S1.worker
                AND S2.lft BETWEEN 1 AND S1.lft);
```

Note that you have to subtract one to avoid counting the parent as his own child. Here is another way to do this and get a complete ordered listing of siblings:

```
SELECT O1.member AS boss, S1.worker,
       COUNT(S2.lft) AS sibling_order
  FROM Immediate_Subordinates AS S1,
       Immediate_Subordinates AS S2,
       OrgChart AS O1
 WHERE S1.boss = O1.member
   AND S2.boss = S1.boss
   AND S1.worker <> S2.worker
   AND S2.lft <= S1.lft
 GROUP BY O1.member, S1.worker;
```

The siblings of a given node can be found by looking for a common parent and rows on the same level. Using the assemblies parts explosion tree, we can define a view with the level number in it as

```
CREATE VIEW Siblings (lvl, part, lft, rgt)
AS SELECT COUNT(A2.lft), A1.part, A1.lft, A1.rgt
     FROM Assemblies AS A1, Assemblies AS A2
    WHERE A1.lft BETWEEN A2.lft AND A2.rgt
    GROUP BY A1.part, A1.lft, A1.rgt;
```

This VIEW can then be used for

```
SELECT DISTINCT S2.part
  FROM Siblings AS S1, Siblings AS S2
 WHERE S1.part = :my_sibling_part
   AND EXISTS
       (SELECT *
          FROM Siblings AS S0
         WHERE S1.lft BETWEEN S0.lft AND S0.rgt
           AND S2.lft BETWEEN S0.lft AND S0.rgt
           AND S0.lvl = S1.lvl - 1
           AND A1.lvl = A2.lvl);
```

This says look at the parent of your current node (part) and then find all the immediate children of the parent node and they are your siblings.

4.3.4 Finding a Path

To find and number nodes in the path from a :start_node to a :finish_node, you can repeat the nested set "BETWEEN predicate trick" twice to form an upper and a lower boundary on the set.

```
SELECT A2.part,
       (SELECT COUNT(*)
          FROM Assemblies AS A4
         WHERE A4.lft BETWEEN A1.lft AND A1.rgt
           AND A2.lft BETWEEN A4.lft AND A4.rgt) AS path_nbr

  FROM Assemblies AS A1, Assemblies AS A2, Assemblies AS A3
 WHERE A1.part = :start_node
   AND A3.part = :finish_node
   AND A2.lft BETWEEN A1.lft AND A1.rgt
   AND A3.lft BETWEEN A2.lft AND A2.rgt;
```

Using the assemblies parts explosion tree, this query would return the following table for the path from 'C' to 'N', with 1 being the highest starting node and the other nodes numbered in the order they must be traversed.

node	path_nbr
C	1
F	2
J	3
N	4

However, if you just need a column to use in a sort for output to a host language, then replace the subquery expression with "(A2.rgt - A2.lft) AS sort_col" and use an "ORDER BY sort_col" clause in a cursor.

4.3.5 Finding Relative Position

Given two nodes, can you find their relative position in the hierarchy; that is, who is the subordinate of whom or are they in different subtrees of the hierarchy?

```
SELECT CASE WHEN :first_member = :second_member
            THEN :first_member || ' is ' || :second_member
            WHEN O1.lft BETWEEN O2.lft AND O2.rgt
            THEN :first_member || ' subordinate to ' || :second_member
            WHEN O2.lft BETWEEN O1.lft AND O1.rgt
            THEN :second_member || ' subordinate to ' || :first_member
            ELSE :first_member || 'no relation to ' || :second_member
       END
  FROM OrgChart AS O1, OrgChart AS O2
 WHERE O1.member = :first_member
   AND O2.member = :second_member;
```

Because this query will report all cases, if the same member holds various positions in the organizational chart, several rows can be returned. It also will report no relationship if one or both of the parameters is not in the table at all.

4.4 Functions in the Nested Sets Model

The level of a given node is a matter of counting how many (lft, rgt) groupings (superiors) this node's lft or rgt is within. You can get this by modifying the sense of the BETWEEN predicate in the query for subtrees:

```
SELECT :my_member, COUNT(Mgrs.member) AS lvl
  FROM OrgChart AS Mgrs, OrgChart AS Workers
 WHERE Workers.lft BETWEEN Mgrs.lft AND Mgrs.rgt
   AND Workers.member = :my_member;
```

Let's assume that this organization is involved in a pyramid sales operation and that a supervising member gets credit for the total sales of himself and all his subordinates. First, we need to have a table for the sales that each member made

```
CREATE TABLE Sales
(member CHAR(10) NOT NULL PRIMARY KEY,
 sale_amt DECIMAL(12,4) NOT NULL);

SELECT :my_member, SUM(S1.sale_amt) AS total_sales
  FROM OrgChart AS Mgrs, OrgChart AS Workers,
       Sales AS S1
 WHERE Workers.lft BETWEEN Mgrs.lft AND Mgrs.rgt
   AND P1.job_title = Workers.job_title
   AND Mgrs.member = :my_member;
```

A slightly trickier function involves using quantity columns in the nodes to compute an accumulated total. This usually occurs in parts explosions, where one assembly may contain several occurrences of subassemblies. Let's assume we have a table called "Blueprint" with the price and quantity for each part required for each subassembly; for example, an assembly might require 10 Number 5 machine screws at $0.07 each. The total cost of any given part would be:

```
SELECT :this_part, SUM(Subassem.qty * Subassem.price) AS totalcost
  FROM Blueprint AS Assembly, Blueprint AS Subassem
 WHERE Subassem.lft
       BETWEEN Assembly.lft AND Assembly.rgt
   AND Assembly.part = :this_part;
```

The use of AVG(), MIN(), and MAX() aggregate functions is possible, but you have to watch out for the meaning of the results in the context of your data model.

4.5 Deleting Nodes and Subtrees

Another interesting property of the nested sets model is that subtrees must fill from lft to rgt. In other tree representations, it is possible for a parent node to have a right child and no left child, but this can make traversals more complicated in exchange for being able to assign significance to the position of a node within a group of siblings.

Deleting a single node in the middle of the tree is conceptually harder than removing whole subtrees in the nested sets model. When you remove a node in the middle of the tree, you have to decide how to fill the hole. There are several basic ways. The first method is to connect the children to the parent of the original node—Mom dies and the kids are adopted by Grandma. In effect, the position itself is removed. This is a vertical promotion of an entire subtree.

Another vertical promotion is to move only a single child node to the deleted node's position—give the business to the oldest son. The problem is that when the son is promoted, this leaves a vacancy in his former position.

The second method is horizontal promotion. The sibling to the deleted node's right (i.e., Next most senior) moves over to the vacant position—Dad dies and his oldest brother takes over the business. This assumes that there is such a brother to take the vacant position.

In practice, you will find a mixture of these methods as vacancies are created in the hierarchy and have to be handled. As I said, single node deletion is not easy.

A Website with a demonstration program for the nested sets model in PHP written by Arne Klempert (arne@klempert.de) can be found at http://www.klempert.de/php/nested_sets/demo/. It is under the terms of the GNU Lesser General Public License. The demo allows you to add or delete nodes or subtrees with a simple interface.

4.5.1 Deleting Subtrees

This query will take the downsized employee as a parameter and remove the subtree rooted under him. The trick in this query is that we are using the node value, but we need to get the (lft, rgt) values to do the work. One answer is scalar subqueries:

```
DELETE FROM OrgChart
  WHERE lft BETWEEN
    (SELECT lft FROM OrgChart WHERE member = :downsized_guy)
    AND
    (SELECT rgt FROM OrgChart WHERE member = :downsized_guy);
```

The problem is that this will result in gaps in the sequence of nested set numbers. You can still do most tree queries on a table with such gaps, but you will lose the algebraic properties that let you easily find leaf nodes, the size of the subtrees, and other structural properties. Let's put the query and "housekeeping" into a single procedure instead:

```
CREATE PROCEDURE DropTree (IN downsized CHAR(10))
LANGUAGE SQL
DETERMINISTIC
BEGIN ATOMIC
DECLARE drop_member CHAR(10);
DECLARE drop_lft INTEGER;
DECLARE drop_rgt INTEGER;

-- save the dropped subtree data with a singleton SELECT
SELECT member, lft, rgt
  INTO drop_member, drop_lft, drop_rgt
  FROM OrgChart
 WHERE member = downsized;

-- subtree deletion is easy
DELETE FROM OrgChart
 WHERE lft BETWEEN drop_lft and drop_rgt;

-- close up the gap left by the subtree
UPDATE OrgChart
   SET lft = CASE
             WHEN lft > drop_lft
             THEN lft - (drop_rgt - drop_lft + 1)
             ELSE lft END,
       rgt = CASE
             WHEN rgt > drop_lft
             THEN rgt - (drop_rgt - drop_lft + 1)
             ELSE rgt END
 WHERE lft > drop_lft
    OR rgt > drop_lft;
END;
```

A complete procedure should have some error handling, but I am leaving that as an exercise for the reader. The expression (drop_rgt − drop_lft + 1) is the size of the gap and we renumber every node to the right of the gap by that amount. The WHERE clause makes the two ELSE clauses redundant, but because they make me feel safer, I write them anyway.

If you used only the original DELETE FROM statement instead of the procedure just given or build a table from several different sources, you could get multiple gaps that you wish to close. This requires a complete renumbering:

```
UPDATE OrgChart
   SET lft = (SELECT COUNT(*)
                    FROM (SELECT lft FROM OrgChart
                           UNION ALL
                           SELECT rgt FROM OrgChart) AS LftRgt (seq)
                   WHERE seq <= lft),
       rgt = (SELECT COUNT(*)
                    FROM (SELECT lft FROM OrgChart
                           UNION ALL
                           SELECT rgt FROM OrgChart) AS LftRgt (seq)
                   WHERE seq <= rgt);
```

Alternately, if the derived table LftRgt is a bit slow, you can use a VIEW, which has the actual replacement numbers for the whole table.

```
CREATE VIEW SeqLftRgt (old_seq, new_seq)
AS
SELECT old_seq, ROW_NUMBER() OVER (ORDER BY seq) AS new_seq
  FROM(SELECT lft FROM OrgChart
       UNION ALL
       SELECT rgt FROM OrgChart)
       AS X(old_seq, new_seq)
 WHERE old_seq <> new_seq;
```

Now the update can only be done if the VIEW is not empty.

```
IF EXISTS (SELECT * FROM SeqLftRgt)
THEN UPDATE
      SET lft
         = COALESCE ((SELECT new_seq
                       FROM SeqLftRgt AS S
                      WHERE lft = old_seq), lft),
          rgt
         = COALESCE ((SELECT new_seq
                       FROM SeqLftRgt AS S
                      WHERE rgt = old_seq), rgt);
END IF;
```

But you can now use a MERGE statement.

```
MERGE INTO OrgChart
USING (SELECT lft_rgt, ROW_NUMBER() OVER()ORDER BY lft_rgt AC)
        FROM (SELECT lft FROM Orgchart
             UNION ALL
             SELECT rgt FROM Orgchart)
           AS X(lft_rgt)
      )AS X(old_seq, new_seq)
   ON X2.old_seq IN (OrgChart.lft, OrgChart.rgt)
 WHEN MATCHED
 THEN UPDATE OrgChart
        SET lft = CASE WHEN lft = old_seq THEN new_seq ELSE lft END,
            rgt = CASE WHEN rgt = old_seq THEN new_seq ELSE rgt END;
```

As the optimizers get better, this single statement should be the best choice.

4.5.2 Deleting a Single Node

Deleting a single node in the middle of the tree is harder than removing whole subtrees. When you remove a node in the middle of the tree, you have to decide how to fill the hole. One approach is to put a "vacant position" marker in the organizational chart so that the structure does not change. This might be followed by moving existing personnel into the vacancies as they are created.

There are two basic ways to change the structure when a node is removed. One method is to connect the children to the parent of the original node—Mom dies and the kids are adopted by Grandma, as shown in Figure 4.6.

This happens automatically in the nested sets model; you just delete the node and its children are already contained in their ancestor nodes. Now you need to renumber nodes to the left of the deletion.

The second method is to promote one of the children to the original node's position—Dad dies and the oldest son takes over the business, as shown in Figure 4.7. The oldest child is always shown as the leftmost child node under its parent.

There is a problem with this operation, however. If the older child has children of his own, then you have to decide how to handle them and so on down the tree until you get to a leaf node.

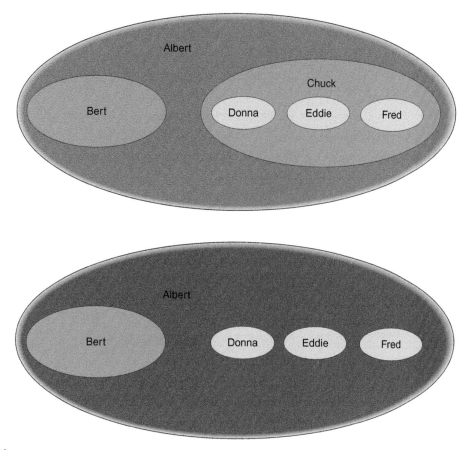

Figure 4.6

Let's use a '{vacant}' as a marker for the vacancy. That way we can promote the oldest subordinate to the vacant job and then decide if we want to fill his previous position with his oldest subordinate.

```
CREATE PROCEDURE Downsize(IN downsized_guy CHAR(10))
LANGUAGE SQL
DETERMINISTIC
UPDATE OrgChart
    SET member
        = CASE WHEN OrgChart.member = downsized_guy
                AND OrgChart.lft +1 = OrgChart.rgt -- leaf node
            THEN '{vacant}'
```

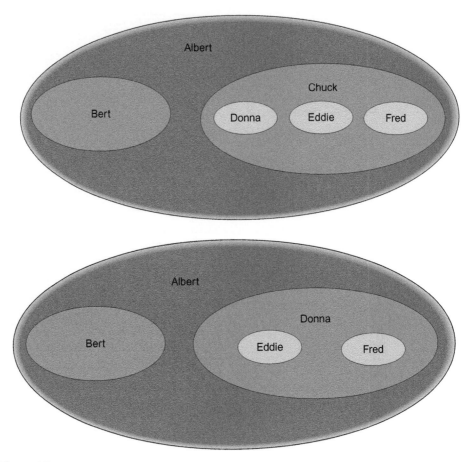

Figure 4.7

```
WHEN OrgChart.member = downsized_guy
     AND OrgChart.lft +1 <> OrgChart.rgt -- promote subordinate
THEN (SELECT O1.member
       FROM OrgChart AS O1
      WHERE OrgChart.lft + 1 = O1.lft)
WHEN OrgChart.member -- vacate subordinate position
     = (SELECT O1.member
         FROM OrgChart AS O1
        WHERE OrgChart.lft + 1 = O1.lft)
THEN '{vacant}'
ELSE member END;
```

This leads to cases:

1. A leaf node has no subordinates to promote, so the node becomes vacant.

2. If there are subordinates, then we have two steps:
   a. promote a subordinate
   b. vacate the subordinate's current position

4.5.3 Pruning a Set of Nodes from a Tree

An interesting version of this problem is displaying the tree with some of the subtrees pruned from the tree. This is usually a dynamic process used for displaying the tree structure in the front end. The most common example is clicking on the "+" and "−" boxes of a Windows directory display to open and close nested files.

First, build a table for the root nodes of the subtrees you wish to hide:

```
CREATE TABLE Cuts (node CHAR(5) NOT NULL PRIMARY KEY);
```

Next, use a VIEW to drop subtrees rooted at cut nodes:

```
CREATE VIEW PrunedTree (node, lft, rgt)
AS
SELECT T1.T1.part, T1.lft, T1.rgt
  FROM Tree AS T1, Tree AS T2, Cuts AS C1
 WHERE T1.lft
       NOT BETWEEN T2.lft +1
               AND T2.rgt -1
   AND C1.part = T2.part
 GROUP BY T1.part, T1.lft, T1.rgt
HAVING COUNT(*) = (SELECT COUNT(*) FROM Cuts);
```

These actions will not renumber the (lft, rgt) pairs, but we can do that if you need it. Otherwise, the "between" predicates for nesting are still valid and are all that is required for displaying the tree.

4.6 Closing Gaps in the Tree

The important thing is to preserve the nested subsets based on (lft, rgt) numbers. As you remove nodes from a tree, you create gaps in the nested sets numbers. These gaps do not destroy the subset property, but can present other problems and should be closed. This is like garbage collection in other languages. The easiest way to understand the code is to break it up into a series of meaningful VIEWs and then use VIEWs to UPDATE the tree table. This VIEW "flattens out" the whole tree into a list of nested sets numbers, regardless of whether they are lft or rgt numbers.

Let's start with a table of assemblies and add some constraints to it.

```
CREATE TABLE Assemblies
(part CHAR(2) PRIMARY KEY,
 lft INTEGER NOT NULL UNIQUE,
 rgt INTEGER NOT NULL UNIQUE,
 CONSTRAINT valid_lft CHECK (lft > 0),
 CONSTRAINT valid_rgt CHECK (rgt > 1),
 CONSTRAINT valid_range_pair CHECK (lft < rgt));

INSERT INTO Assemblies
VALUES ('A', 1, 28),
       ('B', 2, 5),
       ('C', 6, 19),
       ('D', 20, 27),
       ('E', 3, 4),
       ('F', 7, 16),
       ('G', 17, 18),
       ('H', 21, 26),
       ('I', 8, 9),
       ('J', 10, 15),
       ('K', 22, 23),
       ('L', 24, 25),
       ('M', 11, 12),
       ('N', 13, 14);
```

First, we can use a view with all the (lft, rgt) numbers in a single column.

```
CREATE VIEW LftRgt (visit)
AS SELECT lft FROM Assemblies
   UNION
   SELECT rgt FROM Assemblies;
```

This VIEW finds left numbers in gaps instead of in the tree.

```
CREATE VIEW Firstvisit (visit)
AS SELECT (visit + 1)
    FROM LftRgt
  WHERE (visit + 1) NOT IN (SELECT visit FROM LftRgt)
    AND (visit + 1) > 0;
```

The final predicate is to keep you from going past the leftmost limit of the root node, which is always 1. Likewise, this VIEW finds the right nested sets numbers in gaps instead of in the tree.

```
CREATE VIEW LastVisit (visit)
AS SELECT (visit - 1)
    FROM LftRgt
  WHERE (visit - 1) NOT IN (SELECT visit FROM LftRgt)
    AND (visit - 1) < 2 * (SELECT COUNT(*) FROM LftRgt);
```

The final predicate is to keep you from going past the rightmost limit of the root node, which is twice the number of nodes in the tree. You then use these two VIEWs to build a table of the gaps that have to be closed.

```
CREATE VIEW Gaps (commence, finish, spread)
AS SELECT A1.visit, L1.visit, ((L1.visit - A1.visit) + 1)
    FROM Firstvisit AS A1, LastVisit AS L1
  WHERE L1.visit = (SELECT MIN(L2.visit)
                      FROM LastVisit AS L2
                    WHERE A1.visit <= L2.visit);
CREATE PROCEDURE X1()
LANGUAGE SQL
DETERMINISTIC

WHILE EXISTS (SELECT * FROM Gaps)
  DO UPDATE Assemblies
      SET rgt = CASE
                  WHEN rgt > (SELECT MIN(commence) FROM Gaps)
                  THEN rgt - 1 ELSE rgt END,
          lft = CASE
                  WHEN lft > (SELECT MIN(commence) FROM Gaps)
                  THEN lft - 1 ELSE lft END;
END WHILE;
```

```
CREATE VIEW Gaps (commence, finish, spread)
AS SELECT A1.visit, L1.visit, ((L1.visit - A1.visit) + 1)
    FROM Firstvisit AS A1, LastVisit AS L1
   WHERE L1.visit = (SELECT MIN(L2.visit)
                       FROM LastVisit AS L2
                      WHERE A1.visit <= L2.visit);
```

This query will tell you the start and finish nested sets numbers of the gaps, as well as their spread. It makes a handy report in itself, which is why I have shown it with the redundant finish and spread columns. But that is not why we created it. It can be used to "slide" everything over to the left, thus:

```
CREATE PROCEDURE X2()
LANGUAGE SQL
DETERMINISTIC
-- This will have to be repeated until gaps disappear
WHILE EXISTS (SELECT * FROM Gaps)
DO UPDATE Assemblies
        SET rgt = CASE
                WHEN rgt > (SELECT MIN(commence) FROM Gaps)
                THEN rgt - 1 ELSE rgt END,
            lft = CASE
                WHEN lft > (SELECT MIN(commence) FROM Gaps)
                THEN lft - 1 ELSE lft END;
END WHILE;
```

The actual number of iterations is given by comparing the size of the original table and the final size after the gaps are closed. This method keeps the code fairly simple at this level, but the VIEWs under it are pretty tricky and could take a lot of execution time. It would seem reasonable to use the gap size to speed up the closure process, but that can get tricky when more than one node has been dropped.

4.7 Summary Functions on Trees

There are tree queries that deal strictly with the nodes themselves and have nothing to do with the tree structure at all. For example, what is the name of the president of the company? How many people are in the company? Are there two people with the same name working here? These queries are handled with the usual SQL queries and there are no surprises.

Other types of queries do depend on the tree structure. For example, what is the total weight of a finished assembly (i.e., the total of all of its subassembly weights)? Do Harry and John report to the same boss? And so forth.

Use of the BETWEEN predicate with a GROUP BY and aggregate functions lets us do basic hierarchical summaries, such as finding the total salaries of the subordinates of each employee.

```
SELECT O2.member, SUM(O1.salary) AS total_salary_budget
  FROM OrgChart AS O1, Personnel AS O2
 WHERE O1.lft BETWEEN O2.lft AND O2.rgt
 GROUP BY O2.member;
```

Any other aggregate function, such as MIN(), MAX(), AVG(), and COUNT(), can be used along with CASE expressions and function calls. You can be pretty creative here, but there is one serious problem to watch out for. This query format assumes that the structure within the subtree rooted at each node does not matter.

4.7.1 Iterative Parts Update

Let's consider a sample database that shows a parts explosion for a Frammis in a nested sets representation. A Frammis is the imaginary device that holds those widgets MBA students are always marketing in their textbooks. This is built from the assemblies table we have been using, with extra columns for the quantity and weights of the various assemblies. As an aside, constraint names in Standard SQL must be unique at the schema level, not the table level.

```
CREATE TABLE Frammis
(part CHAR(2) PRIMARY KEY,
 qty INTEGER NOT NULL
     CONSTRAINT positive_qty CHECK (qty > 0),
 wgt INTEGER DEFAULT 0 NOT NULL,
 CONSTRAINT non_negative_wgt
     CHECK ((wgt = 0 AND rgt-lft > 1) OR (wgt > 0 AND rgt-lft = 1)),
 lft INTEGER NOT NULL UNIQUE
     CONSTRAINT valid_lft CHECK (lft > 0),
 rgt INTEGER NOT NULL UNIQUE
     CONSTRAINT valid_rgt CHECK (rgt > 1),
 CONSTRAINT valid_range_pair CHECK (lft < rgt));
```

We initially load it with these data:

Frammis

part	qty	wgt	lft	rgt
'A'	1	0	1	28
'B'	1	0	2	5
'C'	2	0	6	19
'D'	2	0	20	27
'E'	2	12	3	4
'F'	5	0	7	16
'G'	2	6	17	18
'H'	3	0	21	26
'I'	4	8	8	9
'J'	1	0	10	15
'K'	5	3	22	23
'L'	1	4	24	25
'M'	2	7	11	12
'N'	3	2	13	14

Leaf nodes are the most basic parts, the root node is the final assembly, and the nodes in between are subassemblies. Each part or assembly has a unique catalog number (in this case one or two letters), a weight, and the quantity of this unit that is required to make the next unit above it.

The Frammis table is a convenient fiction to keep examples simple. In a real schema for a parts explosion, there should be other tables. One such table would be an Assembly table to describe the structural relationship of the assemblies. Another would be an Inventory or Parts table to describe each indivisible part of the assemblies. There would also be tables for suppliers, for estimated assembly times, and so forth. For example, parts data in the Frammis table might be split out and put into a table like this:

```
CREATE TABLE Parts
(part_id CHAR(2) NOT NULL PRIMARY KEY,
 part_name VARCHAR(15) NOT NULL,
 wgt INTEGER NOT NULL
     CHECK (wgt >= 0),
 supplier_nbr INTEGER NOT NULL
         REFERENCES Suppliers (supplier_nbr),
 ..);
```

The quantity has no meaning in the Parts table. If a part is an undividable piece of raw material it will have a weight and other physical attributes.

Thus we might have a wheel made from steel that we buy from an outside supplier that we later replace with a wheel made from aluminum that we buy from a different supplier and substitute into the assemblies that use wheels. It is a different wheel, but the same function and quantity as the old wheel.

Likewise, we might stop making our own motors and start buying them from a supplier. The motor assembly would still be in the tree and it would still be referred to by an assembly code, but its subordinates would disappear. In effect, the "blueprint" for the assemblies is shown in the nesting of the nodes of the assemblies table with quantities added.

The iterative procedure for calculating the weight of any part is fairly straightforward. If the part has no children, just use its own weight. For each of its children, if they have no children, then their contribution is their weight times their quantity. If they do have children, their contribution is the total of the quantity times the weight of all the children.

```
CREATE PROCEDURE WgtCalc_1 ()
LANGUAGE SQL
DETERMINISTIC
BEGIN
UPDATE Frammis -- clear out the weights
   SET wgt = 0
 WHERE lft < (rgt - 1);
WHILE EXISTS (SELECT * FROM Frammis WHERE wgt = 0)
DO UPDATE Frammis
      SET wgt =
            CASE -- all the children have a weight computed
            WHEN 0 < ALL (SELECT C.wgt
                           FROM Frammis AS C
                            LEFT OUTER JOIN
                            Frammis AS B
                            ON B.lft
                              = (SELECT MAX(S.lft)
                                   FROM Frammis AS S
                                  WHERE C.lft > S.lft
                                    AND C.lft < S.rgt)
                          WHERE B.part = Frammis.part)
            THEN (SELECT COALESCE (SUM(C.wgt * C.qty), Frammis.wgt)
                    FROM Frammis AS C
                     LEFT OUTER JOIN
```

```
                          Frammis AS B
                          ON B.lft
                             = (SELECT MAX(S.lft)
                                  FROM Frammis AS S
                                 WHERE C.lft > S.lft
                                   AND C.lft < S.rgt)
                     WHERE B.part = Frammis.part)
          ELSE Frammis.wgt END;
END WHILE;
END;
```

This will give us this result, after moving up the tree, one level at a time, as shown in Figures 4.8 thru 4.12.

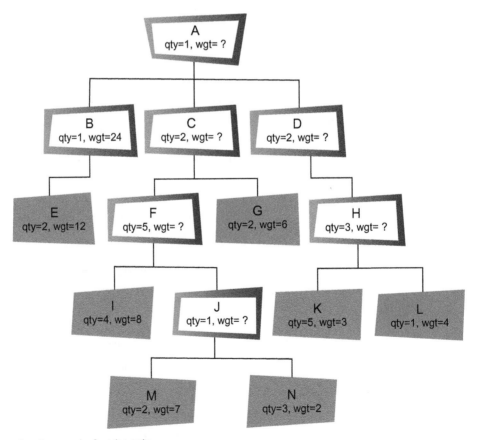

Iteration one, leaf nodes only

Figure 4.8

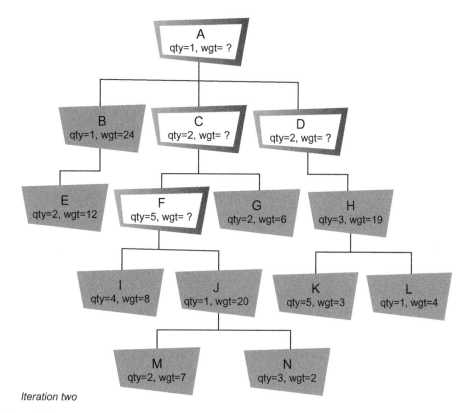

Iteration two

Figure 4.9

Frammis

part	qty	wgt	lft	rgt
A	1	682	1	28
B	1	24	2	5
C	2	272	6	19
D	2	57	20	27
E	2	12	3	4
F	5	52	7	16
G	2	6	17	18
H	3	19	21	26
I	4	8	8	9
J	1	20	10	15
K	5	3	22	23
L	1	4	24	25
M	2	7	11	12
N	3	2	13	14

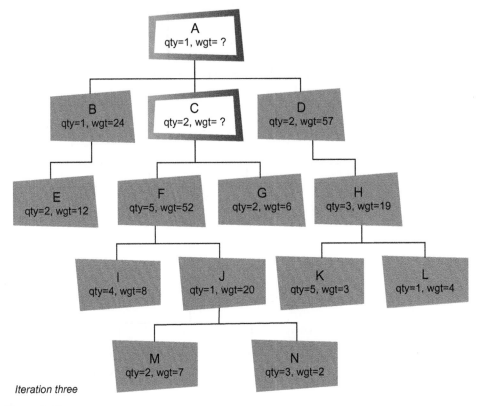

Iteration three

Figure 4.10

The weight of an assembly will be calculated as the total weight of all its subassemblies. Look at the M and N leaf nodes; the table says that we need two M units weighing 7 kilograms each, plus three N units weighing 2 kilograms each, to make one J Assembly. Therefore, a J assembly weighs $((2 * 7) + (3 * 2)) = 20$ kilograms. This process is iterated from the leaf nodes up the tree, one level at a time until the total weight appears in the root node.

4.7.2 Recursive Parts Update

Let's define a recursive function WgtCalc() that takes part as an input and returns the weight of that part. To compute the weight, the function assumes that the input is a parent node in the tree and sums the quantity times the weight for all the children.

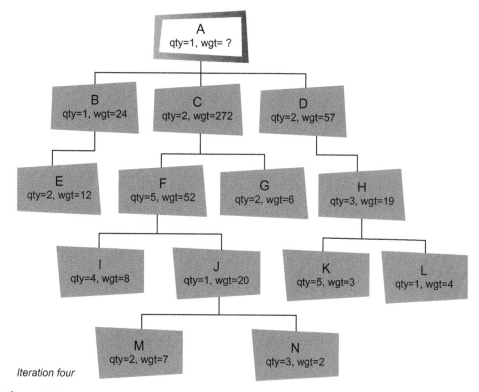

Iteration four

Figure 4.11

If there are no children, it returns just the parent's weight, which means the node was a leaf node. If any child is itself a parent, the function calls itself recursively to resolve that part's weight.

```
CREATE FUNCTION WgtCalc2 (IN my_part CHAR(2))
RETURNS INTEGER
LANGUAGE SQL
DETERMINISTIC
-- recursive function
RETURN
(SELECT COALESCE(SUM(Subassemblies.qty
            * CASE WHEN Subassemblies.lft + 1 = Subassemblies.rgt
                THEN Subassemblies.wgt
                ELSE WgtCalc (Subassemblies.part)
                END), MAX(Assemblies.wgt))
```

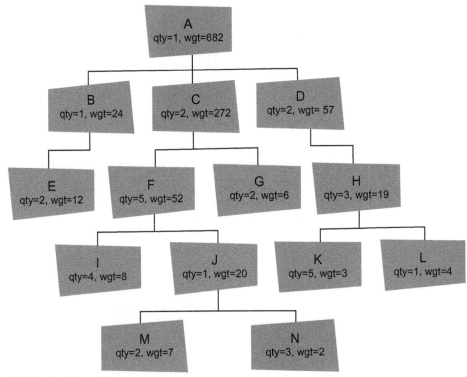

Iteration five, the root

Figure 4.12

```
FROM Frammis AS Assemblies
     LEFT OUTER JOIN
     Frammis AS Subassemblies
     ON Assemblies.lft < Subassemblies.lft
        AND Assemblies.rgt > Subassemblies.rgt
        AND NOT EXISTS
           (SELECT *
              FROM Frammis
             WHERE lft < Subassemblies.lft
               AND lft > Assemblies.lft
               AND rgt > Subassemblies.rgt
               AND rgt < Assemblies.rgt)
WHERE Assemblies.part = my_part);
```

We can use the function in a VIEW to get the total weight.

```
CREATE VIEW TotalWeight (part, qty, wgt, lft, rgt)
AS
SELECT part, qty, WgtCalc(part, lft, rgt)
  FROM Frammis;
```

Of course, the UPDATE is now trivial ...

```
UPDATE Frammis SET wgt = WgtCalc(part);
```

4.8 Inserting and Updating Trees

Updates to nodes are done by searching for the key of each node; there is nothing special about them. However, rearranging the structure of the tree is tricky because figuring out the (lft, rgt) nested sets numbers requires a good bit of algebra in a large tree. As a programming project, you might want to build a tool that takes a "boxes-and-arrows" graphic and converts it into a series of UPDATE and INSERT statements. Inserting a subtree or a new node involves finding a place in the tree for the new nodes, spreading the other nodes apart by incrementing their nested sets numbers, and then renumbering the subtree to fit into the gap created. This is basically the deletion procedure in reverse. First determine the parent for the node and then spread the nested sets numbers out two positions to the right.

```
CREATE PROCEDURE InsertNewNode
(IN new_part CHAR(2), IN parent_part CHAR(2),
 IN new_qty INTEGER, IN new_wgt INTEGER)
LANGUAGE SQL
DETERMINISTIC

BEGIN ATOMIC
DECLARE parent INTEGER;
SET parent = (SELECT rgt
                FROM Frammis
               WHERE part = parent_part);
UPDATE Frammis
   SET lft = CASE WHEN lft > parent
                  THEN lft + 2
                  ELSE lft END,
```

```
       rgt = CASE WHEN rgt >= parent
                  THEN rgt + 2
                  ELSE rgt END
WHERE rgt >= parent;

INSERT INTO Frammis (part, qty, wgt, lft, rgt)
VALUES (new_part, new_qty, new_wgt, parent, (parent + 1));
END;
```

This code is credited to Mark E. Barney. The idea is to spread the (lft, rgt) numbers after the youngest child of the parent, G in this case, over by two to make room for the new addition, G1. This procedure will add the new node to the rightmost child position, which helps preserve the idea of an age order among siblings.

A slightly different version of the same code will let you add a sibling to the right of a given sibling.

```
CREATE PROCEDURE InsertNewNode
(IN new_part CHAR(2), IN lft_sibling_part CHAR(2),
 IN new_qty INTEGER, IN new_wgt INTEGER)
LANGUAGE SQL
DETERMINISTIC
BEGIN ATOMIC
IF (SELECT lft -- the root has no siblings
      FROM Frammis
    WHERE part = lft_sibling_part) = 1
THEN LEAVE insert_on_lft;
ELSE BEGIN
    DECLARE lft_sibling INTEGER;
    SET lft_sibling
        = (SELECT rgt

              FROM Frammis
              WHERE part = lft_sibling_part);
    UPDATE Frammis
      SET lft = CASE WHEN lft < lft_sibling
                     THEN lft ELSE lft + 2 END,
          rgt = CASE WHEN rgt < lft_sibling
                     THEN rgt ELSE rgt + 2 END
      WHERE rgt > lft_sibling;
```

```
    INSERT INTO Frammis
    VALUES (new_part, new_qty, new_wgt, (lft_sibling + 1), (lft_sibling
+ 2));
    END;
END IF;
END;
```

The reason for giving both blocks of code is a note from Morgan Kelsey about some problems he found using a nested set model for a multithreaded message board. They were doing strange things with replies to posted messages.

For example, one would assume this was correct behavior, when there are multiple children:

```
--1 message 1
----2 - reply to 1
----3 - reply to 1
------ 5 - reply to 3
----4 - reply to 1
```

However, there are boards around doing this:

```
--1 message 1
----4 - reply to 1
----3 - reply to 1
------ 5 - reply to 3
----2 - reply to 1
```

Here's an example: http://boards.gamers.com/messages/overview.asp ?name=scstratboard.

When the tree structure is displayed, you have to go down to the right, but then up to read the new messages. Apparently, people had taken the first method (i.e., insert new guy as the rightmost sibling) as the way to do any insertions and implemented it blindly.

4.8.1 Moving a Subtree within a Tree

Yes, it is possible to move subtrees inside the nested sets model for hierarchies. But we need to get some preliminary things out of the way first. The nested sets model needs a few auxiliary tables to help it. The first is the usual LftRgt view.

```
CREATE VIEW LftRgt (seq)
AS SELECT lft FROM Tree
    UNION ALL
    SELECT rgt FROM Tree;
```

Yes, LftRgt can be written as a derived table inside queries, but there are advantages to using a VIEW. Self-joins are much easier to construct. Code is easier to read. If more than one user needs this table, it can be materialized only once by the SQL engine. The next table is a working table to hold subtrees that we extract from the original tree. This could be declared as a local temporary table.

```
CREATE LOCAL TEMPORARY TABLE WorkingTree
(root CHAR(2) NOT NULL,
 node CHAR(2) NOT NULL,
 lft INTEGER NOT NULL,
 rgt INTEGER NOT NULL,
 PRIMARY KEY (root, node))
ON COMMIT DELETE ROWS;
```

The root column is going to be the value of the root node of the extracted subtree. This gives us a fast way to find an entire subtree via part of the primary key. While this is not important for the stored procedure discussed here, it is useful for other operations that involve multiple extracted subtrees.

Let me move right to the commented code. Input parameters are the root node of the subtree being moved and the node that is to become its new parent. In this procedure, there is an assumption that new siblings are added on the right side of the existing siblings, in effect ordering them by their age.

```
CREATE PROCEDURE MoveSubtree
                (IN my_root CHAR(2),
                 IN new_parent CHAR(2))
LANGUAGE SQL
DETERMINISTIC
BEGIN ATOMIC
DECLARE right_most_sibling INTEGER;
DECLARE subtree_size INTEGER;
```

```
     -- Cannot move a subtree under itself
          DECLARE Self_reference CONDITION;
     -- No such subtree root node
          DECLARE No_such_subtree CONDITION;
     -- No such parent node in the tree
          DECLARE No_such_parent_node CONDITION;

body_of_proc:
BEGIN
IF my_root = new_parent
   OR new_parent
    IN (SELECT T1.node
          FROM Tree AS T1, Tree AS T2
        WHERE T2.node = my_root
            AND T1.lft BETWEEN T2.lft AND T2.rgt)
THEN SIGNAL Self_reference; -- error handler invoked here
     LEAVE body_of_proc; -- or leave the block
END IF;

IF NOT EXISTS
   (SELECT *
      FROM Tree
     WHERE node = my_root)
THEN SIGNAL No_such_subtree; -- error handler invoked here
     LEAVE body_of_proc; -- or leave the block
END IF;

IF NOT EXISTS
   (SELECT *
      FROM Tree
     WHERE node = new_parent)
THEN SIGNAL No_such_parent_node; -- error handler invoked here
     LEAVE body_of_proc; -- or leave the block
END IF;

-- put subtree into working table
INSERT INTO WorkingTree (root, node, lft, rgt)
SELECT my_root, T1.node,
```

```
              T1.lft - (SELECT MIN(lft)
                          FROM Tree
                        WHERE node = my_root),
              T1.rgt - (SELECT MIN(lft)
                          FROM Tree
                        WHERE node = my_root)
    FROM Tree AS T1, Tree AS T2
  WHERE T1.lft BETWEEN T2.lft AND T2.rgt
     AND T2.node = my_root;

-- remove the subtree from original tree
DELETE FROM Tree
 WHERE node IN (SELECT node FROM WorkingTree);

-- get the spread and location for inserting working tree into tree
SET right_most_sibling
    = (SELECT rgt
         FROM Tree
        WHERE node = new_parent);

SET subtree_size = (SELECT (MAX(rgt) +1) FROM WorkingTree);

-- make a gap in the tree
UPDATE Tree
   SET lft = CASE WHEN lft > right_most_sibling
                  THEN lft + subtree_size
                  ELSE lft END,
       rgt = CASE WHEN rgt >= right_most_sibling
                  THEN rgt + subtree_size
                  ELSE rgt END
 WHERE rgt >= right_most_sibling;

-- insert the subtree and renumber its rows
INSERT INTO Tree (node, lft, rgt)
SELECT node,
       lft + right_most_sibling,
       rgt + right_most_sibling
  FROM WorkingTree;

-- close gaps in tree
UPDATE Tree
```

```
      SET lft = (SELECT COUNT(*)
                    FROM LftRgt
                    WHERE LftRgt.i <= Tree.lft),
          rgt = (SELECT COUNT(*)
                    FROM LftRgt
                    WHERE LftRgt.i <= Tree.rgt);

-- clean out working tree table
DELETE FROM WorkingTree;
END body_of_proc;

END; -- of MoveSubtree
```

As a minor note, the variables right_most_sibling and subtree_size could have been replaced with their scalar subqueries in the UPDATE and INSERT INTO statements that follow their assignments, but that would make the code much harder to read at the cost of only a slight boost in performance.

The final UPDATE statement is a version of the standard self-join trick used to find the ordinal position of a value in a column.

I also used this code to show how error handling is done in the SQL/ PSM Standard language. You can declare error conditions and then use the SIGNAL statement to put their names into the diagnostics area when they are detected by a handler and some action is taken. The LEAVE command voids out the actions of the labeled block of code in which it appears and jumps control to the end of the block. In this sample code, LEAVE is never executed because the SIGNAL terminates execution immediately, and a SIGNAL that was caught and handled would determine whether the block's actions are "voided" or not.

This is one of the few times I will show you possible error handling or even the deferring of constraints. Each vendor's procedural language will be different and you will have to adjust this code to your product in the real world.

4.8.2 MoveSubtree Second Version

Another version of the MoveSubtree procedure that does not use the WorkingTree table looks like this:

```
CREATE PROCEDURE MoveSubtree
          (IN my_root CHAR(2), IN new_parent CHAR(2))
```

```
LANGUAGE SQL
DETERMINISTIC
BEGIN ATOMIC
DECLARE origlft INTEGER;
DECLARE origrgt INTEGER;
DECLARE new_parent_rgt INTEGER;

SELECT lft, rgt
  INTO origlft, origrgt
  FROM Tree
 WHERE node = my_root;

SET new_parent_rgt
    = (SELECT rgt
         FROM Tree
        WHERE node = new_parent);

UPDATE Tree
   SET lft
       = lft
         + CASE
           WHEN new_parent_rgt < origlft
           THEN CASE

               WHEN lft BETWEEN origlft AND origrgt
               THEN new_parent_rgt - origlft
               WHEN lft BETWEEN new_parent_rgt
                            AND origlft -1
               THEN origrgt - origlft + 1
               ELSE 0 END
           WHEN new_parent_rgt > origrgt
           THEN CASE
               WHEN lft BETWEEN origlft
                            AND origrgt
               THEN new_parent_rgt - origrgt -1
               WHEN lft BETWEEN origrgt + 1
                            AND new_parent_rgt -1
               THEN origlft - origrgt -1
               ELSE 0 END

         ELSE 0 END,
```

```
      rgt
      = rgt
        + CASE
          WHEN new_parent_rgt < origlft
          THEN CASE
               WHEN rgt BETWEEN origlft
                            AND origrgt
               THEN new_parent_rgt - origlft
               WHEN rgt BETWEEN new_parent_rgt AND origlft -1
               THEN origrgt - origlft + 1
               ELSE 0 END
          WHEN new_parent_rgt > origrgt
          THEN CASE
               WHEN rgt BETWEEN origlft
                            AND origrgt
               THEN new_parent_rgt - origrgt -1
               WHEN rgt BETWEEN origrgt + 1
                            AND new_parent_rgt -1
               THEN origlft - origrgt -1
               ELSE 0 END
          ELSE 0 END;
END; -- Movesubtree
```

This code is credited to Alejandro Izaguirre. It does not set a warning if the subtree is moved under itself, but leaves the tree unchanged. Again, the calculations for origlft, origrgt, and new_parent_rgt could be put into the UPDATE statement as scalar subquery expressions, but the code would be more difficult to read.

4.8.3 Insertion of an Immediate Subtree

Inserting a subtree can be done with a simple procedure in which we start with a subtree parent node and a varying number of mediate subordinates. Let's use a generic Tree table skeleton that can have up to 10 children under a parent node.

```
CREATE TABLE Tree
(node_name VARCHAR(15) NOT NULL,
lft INTEGER NOT NULL CHECK (lft > 0) UNIQUE,
```

```
rgt INTEGER NOT NULL CHECK (rgt > 1) UNIQUE,
CHECK (lft < rgt));
```

You will need a single node to start the tree.

```
INSERT INTO Tree VALUES ('Global', 1, 2);
```

The procedure uses a technique known as the long parameter list. While the SQL/PSM Standard is silent on the issue, most SQL procedural language implementations allow a large number of parameters. SQL Server 2008 allows 2K and IBM DB2 allows 32K parameters in the list.

```
CREATE PROCEDURE InsertChildrenIntoTree
(IN root_node VARCHAR(15),
IN child_01 VARCHAR(15),
IN child_02 VARCHAR(15),
IN child_03 VARCHAR(15),
IN child_04 VARCHAR(15),
IN child_05 VARCHAR(15),
IN child_06 VARCHAR(15),
IN child_07 VARCHAR(15),
IN child_08 VARCHAR(15),
IN child_09 VARCHAR(15),
IN child_10 VARCHAR(15) )
BEGIN
-- Find the parent node of the new subtree
DECLARE local_parent_rgt INTEGER;
SET local_parent_rgt
= (SELECT rgt
FROM Tree
WHERE node_name = root_node);

-- put the children into Kindergarten;
-- it is a local temporary table that clears on COMMIT

INSERT INTO Kindergarten
SELECT node_name,
(lft + local_parent_rgt -1) AS lft,
(rgt + local_parent_rgt -1) AS rgt
FROM (VALUES (child_01, 1, 2),
```

```
(child_02, 3, 4),
(child_03, 5, 6),
(child_04, 7, 8),
(child_05, 9, 10),
(child_06, 11, 12),
(child_07, 13, 14),
(child_08, 15, 16),
(child_09, 17, 18),
(child_10, 19, 20))
AS Kids (node_name, lft, rgt)
WHERE node_name IS NOT NULL;
--use the size of the Kindergarten to make a gap
UPDATE Tree
SET lft = CASE WHEN lft > local_parent_rgt
THEN lft + (2 * (SELECT COUNT(*) FROM Kindergarten))
ELSE lft END,
rgt = CASE WHEN rgt >= local_parent_rgt
THEN rgt + (2 * (SELECT COUNT(*) FROM Kindergarten))
ELSE lft END
WHERE lft > local_parent_rgt
OR rgt >= local_parent_rgt;
INSERT INTO Tree (node_name, lft, rgt)
SELECT node_name, lft, rgt
FROM Kindergarten;
END;
```

As examples, let me do a simple geographical hierarchy:

```
CALL InsertChildrenIntoTree ('Global', 'USA','Canada','Europe', 'Asia');
CALL InsertChildrenIntoTree ('USA', 'Texas', 'Georgia', 'Utah', 'New
York', 'Maine', 'Alabama');
```

4.8.4 Subtree Duplication

In many hierarchies, subtrees are repeated in different parts of the structure. The same subassembly might appear under many different assemblies. In the military, squads, platoons, divisions, and so forth are defined by a known collection of soldiers, each with particular military occupational skills. It would be nice to be able to copy the structure of a subtree under a different root node.

Consider a simple tree where we are going to duplicate node values in each copy of the structure. Obviously, duplicated nodes cannot be keys, so we have to use the (lft, rgt) pairs instead.

```
CREATE TABLE Tree
(node VARCHAR(5) NOT NULL,
 lft INTEGER NOT NULL,
 rgt INTEGER NOT NULL,
 PRIMARY KEY (lft, rgt));
```

Let's do this problem in steps with the calculations explained and then consolidate everything into one procedure.

1. We need to find the rightmost position of the node that will be the new parent of the copy of the subtree.

2. Find out how big the subtree is so that we can make a gap for it in the new parent's (lft, rgt) range.

3. Insert the copy, renumbering the (lft, rgt) pairs to fill the gap you just made. This is like moving a subtree, but the original subtree is not deleted in the process, nor do we need a working table to hold the subtree.

```
CREATE PROCEDURE CopyTree
      (IN new_parent VARCHAR(5),
       IN subtree_root VARCHAR(5))
LANGUAGE SQL
DETERMINISTIC
BEGIN ATOMIC
-- create the gap
UPDATE Tree
   SET lft = CASE WHEN lft > (SELECT rgt
                                FROM Tree
                               WHERE node = new_parent)
                  THEN lft + (SELECT (rgt - lft + 1)
                                FROM Tree
                               WHERE node = subtree_root)
                  ELSE lft END,
       rgt = CASE WHEN rgt >= (SELECT rgt
```

```
                                    FROM Tree
                                    WHERE node = new_parent)
                         THEN rgt + (SELECT (rgt - lft + 1)

                                    FROM Tree
                                    WHERE node = subtree_root)
                         ELSE rgt END
    WHERE rgt >= (SELECT rgt
                  FROM Tree
                  WHERE node = new_parent);

-- insert the copy
INSERT INTO Tree (node, lft, rgt)
SELECT T1.node || '2',
       T1.lft
       + (SELECT rgt - lft + 2
            FROM Tree
           WHERE node = subtree_root),
       T1.rgt
       + (SELECT rgt - lft + 2
            FROM Tree
           WHERE node = subtree_root)
  FROM Tree AS T1, Tree AS T2
 WHERE T2.node = subtree_root

   AND T1.lft BETWEEN T2.lft AND T2.rgt;

END;
```

I gave the new nodes a name with a digit '2' appended to them, but that is to make the results easier to read and is not required.

This little renaming trick also solved another problem you have to consider. If I try to copy a subtree under itself, I may have a recursive relationship that is infinite or impossible. Consider a parts explosion that has a subassembly 'X' in which one of the components is another 'X', in which this second 'X' in turn has to contain a third 'X' to work, and so forth.

You might want to add the predicate to assure that this does not happen.

```
CONSTRAINT new_parent
NOT BETWEEN (SELECT lft FROM Tree WERE node = subtree_root)
        AND (SELECT rgt FROM Tree WERE node = subtree_root)
```

4.8.5 Swapping Siblings

The following solution for swapping the positions of two siblings under the same parent node is due to Mr. Vanderghast and originally appeared in a posting on the MS-SQL Server Newsgroup.

If the leftmost sibling has its (lft, rgt) = (i0, i1) and the other subtree, the rightmost sibling, has (i2, i3), implicitly, we know that (i0 < i1 < i2 < i3).

With a little algebra, we can figure out that if (I) is a lft or rgt value in the table between i0 and i3, then

1.   If (i BETWEEN i0 AND i1) then (i) should be updated to (i + i3 − i1).

2.   If (i BETWEEN i2 AND i3) then (i) should be updated to (i + i0 − i2).

3.   If (i BETWEEN i1 + 1 AND i2 − 1), then (i) should be updated to (i0 + i3 + i − i2 − i1).

All of this becomes a single update statement, but we will put the (lft, rgt) pairs of the two siblings into local variables so that a human being can read the code.

```
CREATE PROCEDURE SwapSiblings
        (IN lft_sibling CHAR(2), IN rgt_sibling CHAR(2))
LANGUAGE SQL
DETERMINISTIC

BEGIN ATOMIC
DECLARE i0 INTEGER;
DECLARE i1 INTEGER;
DECLARE i2 INTEGER;
DECLARE i3 INTEGER;
SET i0 = (SELECT lft FROM Tree WHERE node = lft_sibling);
SET i1 = (SELECT rgt FROM Tree WHERE node = lft_sibling);
SET i2 = (SELECT lft FROM Tree WHERE node = rgt_sibling);
SET i3 = (SELECT rgt FROM Tree WHERE node = rgt_sibling);

UPDATE Tree
   SET lft = CASE WHEN lft BETWEEN i0 AND i1
                  THEN i3 + lft - i1
                  WHEN lft BETWEEN i2 AND i3
                  THEN i0 + lft - i2
                  ELSE i0 + i3 + lft - i1 - i2 END,
```

```
        rgt = CASE WHEN rgt BETWEEN i0 AND i1
                   THEN i3 + rgt - i1
                   WHEN rgt BETWEEN i2 AND i3
                   THEN i0 + rgt - i2
                   ELSE i0 + i3 + rgt - i1 - i2 END
WHERE lft BETWEEN i0 AND i3
  AND i0 < i1
  AND i1 < i2
  AND i2 < i3;
END;
```

4.9 Converting Nested Sets Model to Adjacency List Model

Most SQL databases have used the adjacency list model for two reasons. The first reason is that in the early days of the relational model, Dr. Codd published a paper using the adjacency list and he was the final authority. The second reason is that the adjacency list is a way of "faking" pointer chains, the traditional programming method in procedural languages for handling trees.

To convert a nested sets model into an adjacency list model, use this query:

```
SELECT B.member AS boss, P.member
 FROM OrgChart AS P
      LEFT OUTER JOIN
      Personnel AS B
      ON B.lft = (SELECT MAX(S.lft)
                    FROM OrgChart AS S
                   WHERE P.lft > S.lft
                     AND P.lft < S.rgt);
```

This single statement, originally written by Alejandro Izaguirre, replaces my own previous attempt that was based on a pushdown stack algorithm. Once more, we see that the best way to program SQL is to think in terms of sets and not procedures.

Another version of the same query is credited to Ben-Nes Michael of Italy.

```
SELECT B.member AS boss, P.member
  FROM OrgChart AS B, Personnel AS P
```

```
WHERE P.lft BETWEEN B.lft AND B.rgt
  AND B.member
     = (SELECT MAX(S.member)
          FROM OrgChart AS S
         WHERE S.lft < P.lft
           AND S.rgt > P.rgt);
```

He found that this was faster and simpler according to the EXPLAIN results in PostgreSQL. However, the Ben-Nes version does not produce a (NULL, <root>) row in the result set, only the edges of the graph.

4.10 Converting Adjacency List Model to Nested Sets Model

Because the adjacency list model is still more common, you can expect to have to convert it into a nested sets model. There are a few ways to do this.

4.10.1 Stack Algorithm

To convert an adjacency list model to a nested sets model, use this bit of SQL/PSM code. It is a simple pushdown stack algorithm and is shown without any error handling. The first step is to create tables for adjacency list data and one for the nested sets model.

```
-- Tree holds the adjacency model
CREATE TABLE Tree
(node CHAR(10) NOT NULL,
 parent CHAR(10));

-- Stack starts empty, will hold the nested set model
CREATE TABLE Stack
(stack_top INTEGER NOT NULL,
 node CHAR(10) NOT NULL,
 lft INTEGER,
 rgt INTEGER);
```

The Stack table will be used as a pushdown stack and will hold the final results. The extra column "stack_top" holds an integer that tells you what the current top of the stack is.

```
CREATE PROCEDURE AdjToNested()
LANGUAGE SQL
DETERMINISTIC
BEGIN ATOMIC

DECLARE lft_rgt INTEGER;
DECLARE max_lft_rgt INTEGER;
DECLARE current_top INTEGER;

SET lft_rgt = 2;
SET max_lft_rgt = 2 * (SELECT COUNT(*) FROM Tree);
SET current_top = 1;

--clear the stack
DELETE FROM Stack;

-- push the root
INSERT INTO Stack
SELECT 1, node, 1, max_lft_rgt
  FROM Tree
 WHERE parent IS NULL;

-- delete rows from tree as they are used
DELETE FROM Tree WHERE parent IS NULL;

WHILE lft_rgt <= max_lft_rgt - 1
DO IF EXISTS (SELECT *
                FROM Stack AS S1, Tree AS T1
               WHERE S1.node = T1.parent
                 AND S1.stack_top = current_top)
     THEN BEGIN -- push when top has subordinates and set lft value
       INSERT INTO Stack
       SELECT (current_top + 1), MIN(T1.node), lft_rgt, NULL

         FROM Stack AS S1, Tree AS T1
        WHERE S1.node = T1.parent
          AND S1.stack_top = current_top;

         -- delete rows from tree as they are used
         DELETE FROM Tree
          WHERE node = (SELECT node
```

```
                    FROM Stack
                    WHERE stack_top = current_top + 1);
         -- housekeeping of stack pointers and lft_rgt
       SET lft_rgt = lft_rgt + 1;
       SET current_top = current_top + 1;
     END;
     ELSE
     BEGIN -- pop the stack and set rgt value
       UPDATE Stack
          SET rgt = lft_rgt,
              stack_top = stack_top -- pops the stack
        WHERE stack_top = current_top;
       SET lft_rgt = lft_rgt + 1;
       SET current_top = current_top - 1;
     END;

   END IF;
END WHILE;
 -- stack top is not needed in final answer

IF EXISTS (SELECT * FROM Tree)
THEN << error handling for orphans in original tree >>
END IF;
END;
```

4.10.2 Ben-Gan's Recursive Common Table Expression (CTE)

This solution is credited to Itzak Ben-Gan. It uses a rather complicated recursive CTE to find the (lft, rgt) pairs and the level number, starting at a given root node.

```
CREATE TABLE Personnel_Orgchart
(emp_id INTEGER NOT NULL PRIMARY KEY,
 mgr_emp_id INTEGER NULL
   REFERENCES Personnel_OrgChart,
 UNIQUE (mgr_emp_id, emp_id),
 emp_name VARCHAR(25) NOT NULL,
 salary_amt DECIMAL (10,2) NOT NULL);
```

```
INSERT INTO Personnel_OrgChart(emp_id, mgr_emp_id, emp_name,
salary_amt)
VALUES(1, NULL, 'David', 10000.00);
      (2, 1, 'Eitan', 7000.00),
      (3, 1, 'Ina', 7500.00),
      (4, 2, 'Seraph', 5000.00),
      (5, 2, 'Jiru', 5500.00),
      (6, 2, 'Steve', 4500.00),
      (7, 3, 'Aaron', 5000.00),
      (8, 5, 'Lilach', 3500.00),
      (9, 7, 'Rita', 3000.00),
      (10, 5, 'Sean', 3000.00),
      (11, 7, 'Gabriel', 3000.00),
      (12, 9, 'Emilia', 2000.00),
      (13, 9, 'Michael', 2000.00),
      (14, 9, 'Didi', 1500.00);

BEGIN
DECLARE root_emp_id INTEGER;
SET root_emp_id = 1;

-- CTE with two numbers: 1 and 2
WITH TwoNumsCTE (n)
AS
(VALUES (1), (2))
--CTE with two binary sort paths for each node:
-- One smaller than descendants sort paths
-- One greater than descendants sort paths
Sort_pathCTE
AS
(SELECT emp_id, 0 AS lvl, n,
          CAST(n AS VARBINARY(MAX)) AS sort_path
   FROM Personnel_OrgChart
         CROSS JOIN
         TwoNumsCTE
  WHERE emp_id = root_emp_id
UNION ALL
```

```
SELECT C.emp_id, P.lvl + 1, TN.n,
        P.sort_path
          + CAST(ROW_NUMBER()
                  OVER(PARTITION BY C.mgr_emp_id -- order of siblings
                  ORDER BY C.emp_name, C.emp_id, TN.n)
              AS BINARY(4))
  FROM Sort_pathCTE AS P, Personnel_OrgChart AS C
 WHERE P.n = 1
   AND C.mgr_emp_id = P.emp_id
CROSS JOIN
TwoNumsCTE AS TN),

-- CTE with row numbers representing sort_path order
SortCTE
AS
(SELECT emp_id, lvl,
        ROW_NUMBER() OVER(ORDER BY sort_path) AS sortval
   FROM Sort_pathCTE),

-- CTE with lft and rgt values
NestedSetsCTE
AS
(SELECT emp_id, lvl,
        MIN(sortval) AS lft,
        MAX(sortval) AS rgt
    FROM SortCTE
  GROUP BY emp_id, lvl)

SELECT emp_id, lvl, lft, rgt
  FROM NestedSetsCTE;
```

This was written for the Microsoft SQL Server, so be careful when porting it.

4.11 Separation of Edges and Nodes

One of the most important features of a model for hierarchies is the separation of edges and nodes. The personnel of a company are entities, and the organizational chart for the company is a relationship among those entities. Because they are different kinds of things, they need to be in separate tables. Not only is this just good data modeling, but it has some very practical advantages.

4.11.1 Multiple Structures

As an example, a shoe company had two reporting hierarchies: one for the manufacturing side of the company, which was based on the physical construction of the footwear, and another volatile hierarchy for the marketing department. The marketing hierarchy was based on where and to whom the shoes were sold.

For example, steel-toed work boots were one category in the manufacturing reports. But at that time, there were two distinct groups of buyers of steel-toed work boots: construction workers with really big feet and teenaged girls into punk rock with really small feet. People with average-sized feet did not wear these things. For marketing, size was a vital factor, and for manufacturing, it was a few switches on a shoe-making machine.

```
CREATE TABLE Shoes
(shoe_nbr INTEGER NOT NULL PRIMARY KEY,
 ...);

CREATE TABLE ManufacturingReports
(shoe_nbr INTEGER NOT NULL
          REFERENCES Shoes(shoe_nbr),
 lft INTEGER NOT NULL,
 rgt INTEGER NOT NULL,
 ...);

CREATE TABLE MarketingReports
(shoe_nbr INTEGER NOT NULL
          REFERENCES Shoes(shoe_nbr),
 lft INTEGER NOT NULL,
 rgt INTEGER NOT NULL,
 ...);
```

4.11.2 Multiple Nodes

Aaron J. Mackey pointed out that you can attach a variable number of attributes to a node and then make queries based on searching for them. For example, given this general structure

```
CREATE TABLE Tree
(node INTEGER NOT NULL PRIMARY KEY,
 lft INTEGER NOT NULL UNIQUE,
 rgt INTEGER NOT NULL UNIQUE,
 ...);
```

Now attach various attributes to each node.

```
CREATE TABLE NodeProperty_1
(node INTEGER NOT NULL
        REFERENCES Tree (node)
        ON DELETE CASCADE
        ON UPDATE CASCADE,
 value CHAR(15) NOT NULL);

CREATE TABLE NodeProperty_2
(node INTEGER NOT NULL
        REFERENCES Tree (node)
        ON DELETE CASCADE
        ON UPDATE CASCADE,
 value CHAR(15) NOT NULL);
```

Each node may have 0 to (n) related properties, each of which has a value. This query gives all the parents of the set defined by nodes that have a particular property.

4.12 Comparing Nodes and Structure

There are really several kinds of equality comparisons when dealing with a hierarchy:

1. Same nodes in both tables.

2. Same structure in both tables, without regard to nodes.

3. Same nodes in the same positions in the structure in both tables—they are identical

Let me once more invoke my organization chart in the nested sets model.

```
CREATE TABLE OrgChart
(member CHAR(10) NOT NULL PRIMARY KEY,
 lft INTEGER NOT NULL UNIQUE CHECK (lft > 0),
 rgt INTEGER NOT NULL UNIQUE CHECK (rgt > 1),
 CONSTRAINT order_okay CHECK (lft < rgt));
```

and insert the usual sample data:

```
INSERT INTO OrgChart (member, lft, rgt)
VALUES ('Albert', 1, 12),
       ('Bert', 2, 3),
       ('Chuck', 4, 11),
       ('Donna', 5, 6),
       ('Eddie', 7, 8),
       ('Fred', 9, 10);
```

The organizational chart would look like this as a directed graph:

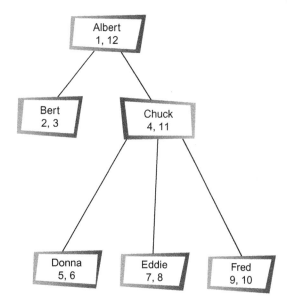

Figure 4.13

Let's create a second table with the same nodes, but with a different structure:

```
CREATE TABLE OrgChart_2
(member CHAR(10) NOT NULL PRIMARY KEY,
 lft INTEGER NOT NULL UNIQUE CHECK (lft > 0),
```

```
rgt INTEGER NOT NULL UNIQUE CHECK (rgt > 1),
CONSTRAINT order_okay CHECK (lft < rgt));
```

Insert this table's sample data:

```
INSERT INTO OrgChart_2 (member, lft, rgt)
VALUES ('Albert', 1, 12),
       ('Bert', 2, 3),
       ('Chuck', 4, 5),
       ('Donna', 6, 7),
       ('Eddie', 8, 9),
       ('Fred', 10, 11);
```

Now we can do queries based on the set of nodes and on the structure. Let's make a list of variations on such queries.

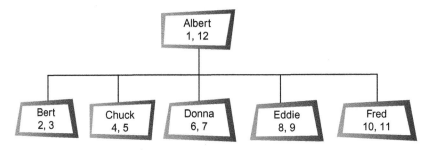

Figure 4.14

1. Do we have the same nodes, but in a different structure? One way to do this is with this query.

```
SELECT DISTINCT 'They have different sets of nodes'
  FROM (SELECT * FROM OrgChart
        UNION ALL
        SELECT * FROM OrgChart_2) AS PO (member, lft, rgt)
 GROUP BY PO.member
HAVING COUNT(*) <> 2;
```

But do they have to occur the same number of times? That is, if we were to put 'Albert' under 'Donna' in the first organizational chart, how do we count him—once or twice? This is the classic sets versus multisets argument that pops up in SQL all the time. The code given previously will reject duplicate multisets. If you want to accept them, then use this:

```
SELECT DISTINCT 'They have different multi-sets of nodes'
  FROM (SELECT DISTINCT *
          FROM OrgChart)
        UNION ALL
        (SELECT DISTINCT *
          FROM OrgChart_2) AS PO (member, lft, rgt)
 GROUP BY PO.member
HAVING COUNT(*) <> 2;
```

2. Do they have the same structure, but with different nodes? Let's present a table with sample data that has different people inside the same structure as the original personnel table.

```
INSERTN INT OrgChart_3(member, lft, rgt)
VALUES ('Amber', 1, 12),
       ('Bobby', 2, 3),
       ('Charles', 4, 11),
       ('Donald', 5, 6),
       ('Edward', 7, 8),
       ('Frank', 9, 10);
```

The structure is held in the (lft, rgt) pairs, so if they have identical structures, the (lft, rgt) pairs will exactly match each.

```
SELECT DISTINCT 'They have different structures'
  FROM (SELECT * FROM OrgChart)
        UNION ALL
        (SELECT * FROM OrgChart_3) AS PO (member, lft, rgt)
 GROUP BY PO.lft, PO.rgt
HAVING COUNT(*) <> 2;
```

3. Do they have the same nodes and same structure? That is, are the trees identical? The logical extension of the other two tests is simply:

```
SELECT DISTINCT 'They are not identical'
  FROM (SELECT * FROM OrgChart)
        UNION ALL
        (SELECT * FROM OrgChart_3) AS PO (member, lft, rgt)
 GROUP BY PO.lft, PO.rgt, PO.member
HAVING COUNT(*) <> 2;
```

More often than not, you will be comparing subtrees within the same tree. This is best handled by putting the two subtrees into a canonical form. First you need the root node and then you can renumber the (lft, rgt) pairs with a derived table of this form:

```
(SELECT O1.member,
        O1.lft - (SELECT MIN(lft)
                    FROM OrgChart
                  WHERE member = :my_member_1) +1,
        O1.rgt - (SELECT MIN(lft)
                    FROM OrgChart
                  WHERE member = :my_member_1) +1
   FROM OrgChart AS O1, OrgChart AS O2
  WHERE O1.lft BETWEEN O2.lft AND O2.rgt
    AND O2.member = :my_member_1) AS P0 (member, lft, rgt);
```

4.13 Nested Sets Code in Other Languages

Flavio Botelho (nuncanadaig.com.br) wrote code in MySQL for extracting an adjacency list model from a nested sets model. While the code depends on the fact that MySQL is not really a relational database, but does sequential processing behind a "near-SQL dialect" language, it is worth passing along. Mr. Botelho had seen the outer join query for the conversion (Section 4.9) and wanted to find a faster solution without subqueries, which were not supported in MySQL.

```
SELECT parent_lft = 33; //Change these to fit your needs
SELECT parent_rgt = 102;

SELECT next_brother := parent_lft;

SELECT next_brother :=
       CASE WHEN lft >= next_brother
            THEN rgt + 1
            ELSE next_brother END AS next_brother,
       name, rgt
  FROM Categories

 WHERE lft >= parent_lft
   AND rgt <= parent_rgt
HAVING next_brother = rgt + 1
 ORDER BY left;
```

Because the next_brother stores the right value from the last direct child, whatever is left comes immediately after this right value and is the next direct child.

So you update the next_brother to this new child and then the HAVING clause will filter to only those children that have the next_brother equal to their right-side sibling. It works in MySQL, but it requires that you are able to change next_brother's value inside the SELECT statement. Because that is impossible in Standard SQL, you would have to do this with cursors and a loop construct of some kind.

Those who like the nested sets model and work with MySQL and PHP may want to look at a PHP library Mr. Botelho made to handle nested sets tables in MySQL at http://dev.e-taller.net/dbtree/.

Although it is good to add, update, and delete records, he recommends writing your own queries to get data from a table instead of using the library function.

There is also a thread or two in the PostgreSQL newsgroups that give code for manipulating the nested sets model. You can start with this link and then explore on your own: http://archives.postgresql.org/pgsql-sql/2002-11/ msg00397.php.

Look for the names "Robert Treat" (xzillausers.sourceforge.net) and "Martin Crundall" (pgsqlac6rm.net) on postings. I do not know what will be out there by the time you read this book.

For a Java library, go to http://www.codebits.com/ntm/java.htm. This library was written by David Medinets, who cautions you that you might want to improve it for production work.

For ACCESS code, go to http://www.mvps.org/access/queries/qry0023.htm.

Frequent Insertion Trees

T HE PROBLEM IN a nested sets tree with frequent insertions is that the (lft, rgt) pairs have to be adjusted so often that locking the table, changing the rows, and unlocking the table again become a major overhead. The nested sets model does not require that the union of rgt and lft numbers be an unbroken sequence to show nesting. All you need is the condition that (lft < rgt), uniqueness of lft and rgt numbers, and that subordination is represented by containment of one (lft, rgt) pair within the ranges of the other (lft, rgt) pairs.

This means that we can put gaps into the initial design of the table and fill them without having to reorganize the table each time. The size of the gaps depends on the available physical implementation of exact numeric types and the expected depth of the tree. The other related factor is how much fill factor (free space) was allocated for the data pages so that new rows can be added without reorganizing the physical storage.

The most common example for computer people is trees in the forest of messages that make up a Newsgroup thread (Figure 5.1). A reply to a posting can be inserted anywhere and to almost any depth. The number of messages posting to a newsgroup can also be huge.

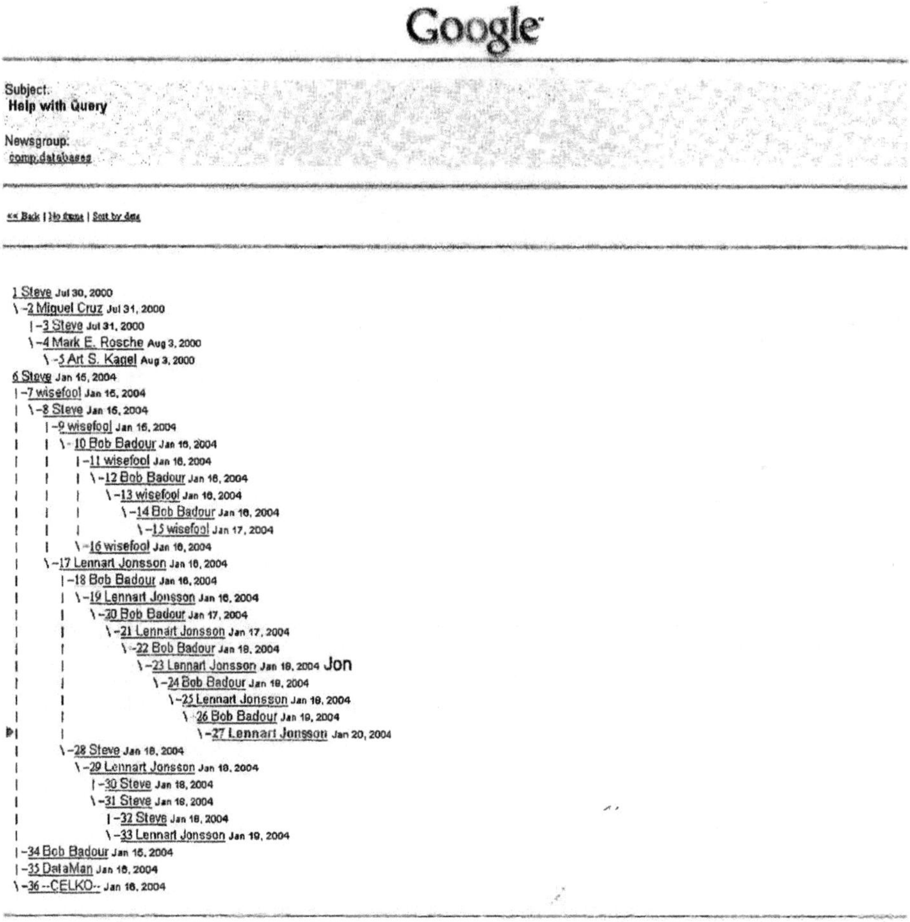

Figure 5.1

As a first attempt at this approach, let's renumber my little organizational chart by multiplying all the lft and rgt numbers by 100.

```
CREATE TABLE Personnel_Orgchart
(emp_id CHAR(10) NOT NULL PRIMARY KEY,
 lft INTEGER NOT NULL UNIQUE CHECK (lft > 0),
 rgt INTEGER NOT,
 CONSTRAINT order_okay CHECK (lft < rgt));
```

Personnel_Orgchart

emp_id	lft	rgt
'Albert'	100	1200
'Bert'	200	300
'Chuck'	400	1100
'Donna'	500	600
'Eddie'	700	800
'Fred'	900	1000

The term spread will mean the value of (rgt − lft) for one node, and the term gap will mean the distance between adjacent siblings under the same Parent node. To insert someone under 'Bert', say 'Betty', you look at the size of Bert's range (300 − 200 = 100) and pack the newcomer to the leftmost position, while leaving her node wide enough for more subordinates. One way of doing this is:

```
INSERT INTO Personnel_Orgchart VALUES ('Betty', 201, 210); -- spread of 9
```

To insert someone under 'Betty', you look at the size of Betty's range (210 − 201) and pack from the left:

```
INSERT INTO Personnel_Orgchart VALUES ('Bobby', 202, 203); --spread of 1
```

The new rows should be inserted in the table without locking the table for an update on multiple rows. Assuming you have a 32-bit integer, you can have a depth of 9 or 10 levels before you have to reorganize the tree. There are two tricks in this approach. First you must decide on the data type to use for the (lft, rgt) pairs and then get a formula for the spread size you want to use. You will see shortly that my simple multiplication is not the best way to achieve the goal.

5.1 The Data Type of (lft, rgt)

The (lft, rgt) pairs will obviously be an exact numeric data type. Because the goal is to get as wide a numeric range as you can, SMALLINT or TINYINT is obviously not going to be considered. Here are your three choices.

5.1.1 Exploiting the Full Range of Integers

If you do not mind negative numbers, you can use the full range of the integers, something like this on a typical 32-bit machine:

```
INSERT INTO Tree VALUES ('root', -4294967295, 4294967296);
```

I am obviously skipping some of the algebra for computing the spread size, but you get the basic idea. There are some other tricks that involve powers of two and binary trees, but that is another topic. If this is not enough, there is also a BIGINT data type in Standard SQL. The standards are deliberately vague on physical implementation details. The choice of binary versus decimal precision is implementation defined, but the same radix shall be chosen for all exact numeric data types. The precision of SMALLINT is less than or equal to the precision of INTEGER, and the precision of BIGINT is greater than or equal to the precision of INTEGER. Currently, this usually means an INTEGER is 32 bits, a BIGINT is 64 bits, and a SMALLINT is 16 bits. As a bit of history, some Algol implementations used the keywords LONG and SHORT to double or halve the number of bits as many times as physically possible on the hardware. That meant that if INTEGER was 16 bits, then SHORT INTEGER was 8 bits, SHORT SHORT INTEGER was 4 bits, LONG INTEGER was 32 bits, LONG LONG INTEGER was 64 bits, and LONG LONG LONG INTEGER was 128 bits.

5.1.2 FLOAT, REAL, or Double Precision Numbers

Floating point numbers just give the illusion that the spread can be almost infinite while truncation and rounding errors will, de facto, impose their own limitations. Two floating point numbers will be considered to be equal, if they are within an epsilon—a small quantity that allows for rounding error in computations.

I strongly recommend that you do not use FLOAT or REAL because they will fail when your tree is very deep because the math they use is not precise. Double precision has the same problems, but they will not show up as soon. This is the worst situation—failure occurs when the database is large and errors are harder to detect.

There is also the problem that many machines used for database applications do not have floating point hardware. Floating point math is seldom used in commercial applications on mainframes. This means that floating point math has to be done in software, which takes longer.

5.1.3 NUMERIC(p,s) or DECIMAL(p,s) Numbers

The DECIMAL(p,s) data type gives you a greater range than INTEGER in most database products and does not have the rounding problems of FLOAT. Precision of over 30 digits is typical, but consult your particular product.

The bad news is that math on DECIMAL(p,s) numbers is often slower than on either INTEGER or FLOAT. The reason is that most machines do not have hardware support for this data type like they do for INTEGER and FLOAT.

5.2 Computing the Spread to Use

There are any numbers of ways to compute the size of the spread that you want to use when you initialize the tree. In the nested sets model, sibling nodes have an order from left to right under their parent node. Given a parent node ('Parent', x, z), we can assume that the oldest (leftmost) child is of the form ('child_1', (x + 1), y), where $(x < (x + 1) < y < z)$. Likewise, in a fully packed nested sets model, we would also know the youngest (rightmost) child is of the form ('child_n', w, (z − 1)), where $(x < w < (z − 1) < z)$.

When we have to insert a new sibling and there is no room in the right gap under his parent, we want to push the existing siblings to the left and leave a gap on the right for the new sibling (Figures 5.2 and 5.3).

First let's construct a VIEW that will show us what numbers we have for the spread under each parent node.

```
CREATE VIEW Spreads (emp_id, commence, finish)
AS
SELECT O1.emp_id, MAX(O2.rgt), (O1.rgt-1)
  FROM Personnel_Orgchart AS O1, Personnel_Orgchart AS O2
 WHERE O2.lft BETWEEN O1.lft AND O1.rgt
   AND O1.emp_id <> O2.emp_id
 GROUP BY O1.emp_id, O1.rgt
```

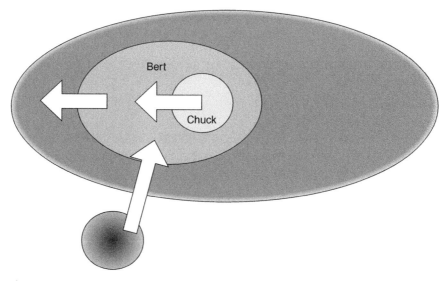

Figure 5.2

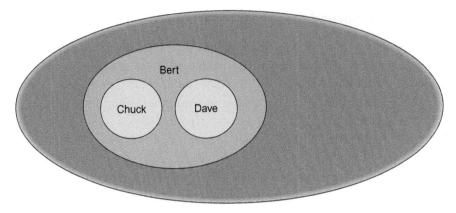

Figure 5.3

```
UNION ALL
SELECT O1.emp_id, (O1.lft +1), (O1.rgt-1)
  FROM Personnel_Orgchart AS O1
 WHERE NOT EXISTS
       (SELECT *
          FROM Personnel_Orgchart AS O2
         WHERE O2.lft BETWEEN O1.lft AND O1.rgt
           AND O1.emp_id < > O2.emp_id)
```

The reason for using a UNION-ed query is that the leaf nodes have no children and will not show up in the SELECT statement of the UNION. We do not need this VIEW, but it makes the code much easier to read than if we folded it into a single statement. Now, the real work.

```
CREATE PROCEDURE InsertNewGuy (IN parent CHAR(10), IN new_guy CHAR(10))
BEGIN ATOMIC
DECLARE commence INTEGER;
DECLARE finish INTEGER;
SET commence = (SELECT commence + 1 FROM Spreads WHERE emp_id = parent);
SET finish = (SELECT finish - 1 FROM Spreads WHERE emp_id = parent);
IF (finish - commence) <= 0 THEN LEAVE; -- error handling needed

-- give the new guy 1/10 of the remaining spread
INSERT INTO Personnel_Orgchart
VALUES (new_guy, commence,
        commence + CAST (((finish - commence)/ 10.0) AS INTEGER));
END;
```

What this procedure does is allocate a tenth of the remaining available spread space to each sibling. Perhaps a demonstration will make this easier to see. Using my organizational chart again:

```
DELETE FROM Personnel_Orgchart;
INSERT INTO Personnel_Orgchart VALUES ('Albert', 1, 10000000);
```

The maximum depth that a path in this tree can have is 7 because $10^7 =$ 10,000,000. A different choice of initial width and spread size would give different results. This series of calls will rebuild the original sample tree structure with different (lft, rgt) pairs.

```
CALL InsertNewGuy ('Albert', 'Bert');
CALL InsertNewGuy ('Albert', 'Chuck');
CALL InsertNewGuy ('Chuck', 'Donna');
CALL InsertNewGuy ('Chuck', 'Eddie');
CALL InsertNewGuy ('Chuck', 'Fred');

Here are some new rows

CALL InsertNewGuy ('Albert', 'Allen'); -- under the root
CALL InsertNewGuy ('Fred', 'George');
CALL InsertNewGuy ('George', 'Herman');
CALL InsertNewGuy ('Herman', 'Irving');
CALL InsertNewGuy ('Irving', 'Joseph');
CALL InsertNewGuy ('Joseph', 'Kirby'); -- failure!
```

The attempt to insert 'Kirby' fails because the maximum depth is exceeded and the "order_okay" constraint is violated. This is easier to see if we show the spread at each level size as (rgt − lft).

emp_id	lft	rgt	spread
Albert	1	10000000	9999999
Allen	1900003	2710002	809999
Bert	3	1000002	999999
Chuck	1000003	1900002	899999
Donna	1000005	1090004	89999
Eddie	1090005	1171004	80999
Fred	1171005	1243904	72899
George	1171007	1178296	7289
Herman	1171009	1171737	728
Irving	1171011	1171083	72
Joseph	1171013	1171019	6

When we insert 'Joseph', this node only has a range of seven positions, and attempting to divide that range into tenths causes a failure.

We need to consider other ways of determining the divisors and what to do if we need to reorganize the tree because we have nodes where (rgt − lft) = 1 and we wish to insert a new node under them.

5.2.1 Varying the Spread

If you know something about the general shape of the tree—if it is shallow and wide or deep and narrow—you can replace the constant divisor with a parameter in the procedure, a formula, or a table lookup subquery expression.

5.2.2 Divisor Parameter

This is a trivial change to the original procedure:

```
CREATE PROCEDURE InsertNewGuy
      (IN parent CHAR(10), IN new_guy CHAR(10),
       IN divisor INTEGER)
LANGUAGE SQL
DETERMINISTIC
BEGIN
DECLARE commence INTEGER;
DECLARE finish INTEGER;
DECLARE divisor INTEGER;
SET commence
    = (SELECT commence FROM Spreads WHERE emp_id = parent);
SET finish
    = (SELECT finish FROM Spreads WHERE emp_id = parent);
INSERT INTO Personnel_Orgchart
VALUES (new_guy, commence,
        commence + ((finish - commence)/ divisor));
END;
```

Note that the computation in the last INSERT INTO statement depends on the truncation and rounding rules of your particular product, as they are implementation defined in Standard SQL; you might want to use an explicit CAST() expression and perhaps truncation and rounding functions.

The actual procedure might want to call itself recursively with smaller and smaller spread sizes when it finds a failure due to an absurdly large spread size. Then, if we reach a spread size of one, call a reorganization procedure.

5.2.3 Divisor via Formula

The depth of a node in the tree is given by

```
CREATE VIEW DepthFormula (emp_id, depth)
AS
SELECT O1.emp_id, COUNT(O2.emp_id)
   FROM Personnel_Orgchart AS O1, Personnel_Orgchart AS O2
  WHERE O1.lft BETWEEN O2.lft AND O2.rgt
  GROUP BY O1.emp_id, O1.lft;
```

The root will be at (depth = 1), and the depth will increase as you traverse to the leaf nodes. The depth column in the VIEW can be used as part of a more complex formula to determine the divisors at each level in the tree. I have shown just the depth itself, but one possible example might be $(10^{\land}COUNT(*))$, or a CASE expression driven by the depth, such as

```
CASE depth
WHEN 1 THEN 5
WHEN 2 THEN 10
WHEN 3 THEN 25
ELSE 5 END;
```

I do not have any suggestions for the proper formula to use. That would require knowledge of the particular tree's shape.

5.2.4 Divisor via Table Lookup

You can also construct a table of the form:

```
CREATE TABLE DepthDivisors
(depth INTEGER NOT NULL PRIMARY KEY,
 divisor INTEGER NOT NULL);
```

or a table of the form:

```
CREATE TABLE EmpDivisors
(emp_id CHAR(10) NOT NULL PRIMARY KEY,
 divisor INTEGER NOT NULL);
```

The first version uses the depth to determine the divisor, so there is an assumption that all nodes at the same level behave approximately the same in regard to subordinates.

The second version uses the employee to determine the divisor, so there is an assumption that some nodes are expected to have more or fewer subordinates than other nodes.

5.2.5 Partial Reorganization

The traditional approach to return the table to the original nested sets model uses a simple UNION-ed VIEW that puts the lft and rgt values in a single column.

```
CREATE VIEW LftRgt (seq)
AS SELECT lft FROM Personnel_Orgchart
   UNION ALL
   SELECT rgt FROM Personnel_Orgchart;
```

Then we use that to update the table.

```
UPDATE Personnel_Orgchart
   SET lft = (SELECT COUNT(*)
                 FROM LftRgt AS LR
               WHERE LR.seq <= lft),
       rgt = (SELECT COUNT(*)
                 FROM LftRgt AS LR
               WHERE LR.seq <= rgt);
```

There is no need for a WHERE clause because all of the nodes will be changed. Unfortunately, we have also destroyed the "big spread" property. A better version uses the ordinal ROW_COUNT() function. This version will do sequential numbering once in the VIEW instead of repeating the COUNT(*) over and over.

```
CREATE VIEW LftRgt2(lr, seq)
AS
```

```
SELECT lr, ROW_COUNT() OVER (ORDER BY lr)
  FROM (SELECT lft FROM (Personnel_Orgchart
        UNION ALL
        SELECT rgt FROM Personnel_Orgchart)
        AS LR(lr));
```

Note that we could also write this as "<spread value or formula> * ROW_COUNT() OVER (ORDER BY lr)" in the VIEW.

```
UPDATE Personnel_Orgchart
  SET lft = (SELECT seq
              FROM LftRgt2 AS LR
             WHERE LR.lr = lft),
      rgt = (SELECT seq
              FROM LftRgt2 AS LR
             WHERE LR.lr = rgt);
```

There are several approaches to spreading the (lft, rgt) pairs apart in the usual nested sets model. We can write a query that converts the nested sets model into the adjacency list model, puts it into a temporary table, and then passes each (emp_id, boss) node pair to the InsertNewGuy() procedure, one pair one at a time. This is a lot of work, but you get complete control over the reorganization.

The most obvious method is simply to multiply each (lft, rgt) by a constant in the aforementioned UPDATE statement. There are trade-offs in this approach. The code is easy and will close up some of the gaps left by deletions. However, it creates new gaps between siblings. Consider the original Personnel_Orgchart table with a constant of 100 as the spread used at the start of this chapter.

Personnel_Orgchart

emp_id	lft	rgt
'Albert'	100	1200
'Bert'	200	300
'Chuck'	400	1100
'Donna'	500	600
'Eddie'	700	800
'Fred'	900	1000

We have lost the ranges 1 to 99, 101 to 199, 301 to 399, and so forth to give every node a larger spread of the same proportions. If the insertions are made randomly in the table, this is not a big problem. However, if insertions are made at the leaf nodes, or into one particular subtree, then we will be doing this again sooner than if we had planned better.

You will notice that there is a pattern to the gaps that we created. Because the gaps are all of size (spread constant −1), we can shift all of the nodes left by that amount, as long as we do not shift a node's (lft, rgt) pair outside the range of its parent or change the size of the node. This leads us to the next topic.

5.2.6 Rightward Spread Growth

A simpler approach is to increase the spread only to the right of the point where the failure occurred. This can be done by either "stretching" the tree to the right or "squeezing" some of the nodes to the left at the point of failure. Let's assume that we have captured the node where we failed to insert a new node.

```
UPDATE Personnel_Orgchart
   SET lft = lft + 100,
       rgt = rgt + 100
 WHERE lft > (SELECT rgt
                FROM Personnel_Orgchart
               WHERE emp_id = :failure_emp_id)
    OR rgt >= (SELECT rgt
                FROM Personnel_Orgchart
               WHERE emp_id = :failure_emp_id);
```

Use of a step of 100 is arbitrary and could be replaced by a computation of some sort. The constant is simply easier to code and I am assuming that the tree will not need reorganization very often.

The other approach is to pack subordinate nodes to the left to create a larger spread on the right side of the node where the insertion failed.

```
CREATE PROCEDURE ShiftLeft()
LANGUAGE SQL
DETERMINISTIC
BEGIN ATOMIC
```

```
DECLARE squeeze INTEGER;
SET squeeze
   = (SELECT CASE WHEN MIN(O2.lft - O1.rgt) - 1 > 1
                  THEN MIN(O2.lft - O1.rgt) - 1
                  ELSE 1 END
        FROM Personnel_Orgchart AS O1,
             Personnel_Orgchart AS O2
       WHERE O1.rgt < O2.lft
         AND O1.emp_id <> O2.emp_id);

UPDATE Personnel_Orgchart
   SET lft = (lft - squeeze),
       rgt = (rgt - squeeze)
 WHERE (lft - squeeze) > 0
   AND NOT EXISTS
       (SELECT *
          FROM Personnel_Orgchart AS O1
         WHERE O1.emp_id <> Personnel_Orgchart.emp_id
           AND (O1.lft
                BETWEEN (Personnel_Orgchart.lft - squeeze)
                    AND (Personnel_Orgchart.rgt - squeeze)
                OR O1.rgt
                BETWEEN (Personnel_Orgchart.lft - squeeze)
                    AND (Personnel_Orgchart.rgt - squeeze)));
END;
```

This routine can be executed over and over until all of the children of each node are packed to the left and the largest possible gap is on the right. The problem is that it "slows down" rather quickly and depends on the value of the squeeze parameter.

First call:

emp_id	lft	rgt
Albert	100	1200
Bert	101	201
Chuck	400	1100
Donna	401	501
Eddie	601	701
Fred	801	901

Second call:

emp_id	lft	rgt
Albert	100	1200
Bert	101	201
Chuck	400	1100
Donna	401	501
Eddie	502	602
Fred	702	802

Third call:

emp_id	lft	rgt
Albert	100	1200
Bert	101	201
Chuck	400	1100
Donna	401	501
Eddie	502	602
Fred	701	801

The rightmost node, 'Fred', will continue to shift to the left, but only one step at a time. Albert never gets to (1, 1101), Bert never gets to (2, 102), and so forth.

5.3 Total Reorganization

There may come a time when you need to reorganize the entire table rather than simply shifting part of the table structure. The goal will be to shift all of the nodes over to the left without changing their spread so as to give the largest possible gap on the right side of the siblings of every parent in the tree. If you need a physical analogy, think of a collection of various sized boxes nested inside each other. Pick up the outermost box and turn it on its left side so that all the boxes shift to the left.

5.3.1 Reorganization with Lookup Table

The following solution is credited to Heinz Huber. Let's start with the original table given in Section 5 and decide what we want it to look like after reorganization.

Personnel_Orgchart—reorganized

emp_id	lft	rgt
Albert	1	1101
Bert	2	102
Chuck	103	803
Donna	104	204
Eddie	205	305
Fred	306	406

The structure and the spreads have remained the same, but the gaps between the employees have been closed by shifting them to the right. This leaves larger gaps on the right side of each row of siblings, for example, 'Fred' has a gap of (803 − 406) = 397 to his right, which is room for three more additions to his family, as the spread is 100 at this level.

The problem is that there is no "universal" shift factor. Instead, the shift is different for each employee, based on the gaps at their level in the tree. Let's assume that we do not want to implement a cursor solution, we can add another column to the table to hold the shift factor for each node and fourth column for the preorder traversal order. The problem with a cursor solution is that you need a stack for the rgt column values of all the parents so that you can traverse the tree. This is expensive and not very portable because every product has slightly different cursor implementations.

```
CREATE TABLE Personnel_Orgchart
(emp_id CHAR(10) NOT NULL PRIMARY KEY,
 lft INTEGER NOT NULL UNIQUE CHECK (lft > 0),
 rgt INTEGER NOT NULL UNIQUE CHECK (rgt > 1),
 CONSTRAINT order_okay CHECK (lft < rgt));
 shift INTEGER, -- null means not yet computed
 traversal_nbr INTEGER -- null means not yet computed);
```

Yes, this could all be done with a temporary table or a second table that joins to the original Personnel_Orgchart. However, these attributes are part of the tree structure and having them all in one place makes sense. Let's begin by initializing the table.

```
UPDATE Personnel_Orgchart
 SET shift = NULL,
     traversal_nbr = NULL;
```

The NULLs act as markers for the computations.

```
-- Calculate shift factor within a parent node.
-- Leftmost siblings are computed later.
UPDATE Personnel_Orgchart
   SET shift
       = lft - 1
         - (SELECT MAX(Siblings.rgt)
                FROM Personnel_Orgchart AS Siblings
                WHERE Siblings.rgt < Personnel_Orgchart.lft)
 WHERE shift IS NULL
   AND EXISTS -- has sibling on left side
       (SELECT *
           FROM Personnel_Orgchart AS Siblings
           WHERE Siblings.rgt < Personnel_Orgchart.lft);
```

That gives us this result at the leaf nodes.

Personnel_Orgchart—step 1

emp_id	lft	rgt	shift	traversal_nbr
Albert	100	1200	NULL	NULL
Bert	101	201	NULL	NULL
Chuck	400	1100	198	NULL
Donna	401	501	199	NULL
Eddie	601	701	99	NULL
Fred	801	901	99	NULL

Now it is time to look at the parents and shift them and their family.

```
UPDATE Personnel_Orgchart
   SET shift
       = lft - 1
         - (SELECT MAX(Parents.lft)
                FROM Personnel_Orgchart AS Parents
                WHERE Parents.lft < Personnel_Orgchart.lft
                  AND Parents.rgt > Personnel_Orgchart.rgt)
```

```
WHERE shift IS NULL
   OR (lft - shift)
      < (SELECT MAX(Parents.lft)
            FROM Personnel_Orgchart AS Parents
           WHERE Parents.lft < Personnel_Orgchart.lft
             AND Parents.rgt > Personnel_Orgchart.rgt);
```

Personnel_Orgchart—step 2

emp_id	lft	rgt	shift	traversal_nbr
Albert	100	1200	NULL	NULL
Bert	101	201	0	NULL
Chuck	400	1100	198	NULL
Donna	401	501	0	NULL
Eddie	601	701	99	NULL
Fred	801	901	99	NULL

At this point, only the root is still NULL. Shifting it will shift every node in the tree leftward.

```
UPDATE Personnel_Orgchart
   SET shift = lft - 1
 WHERE shift IS NULL;
```

Personnel_Orgchart—step 3

emp_id	ft	rgt	shift	traversal_nbr
Albert	100	1200	99	NULL
Bert	101	201	0	NULL
Chuck	400	1100	198	NULL
Donna	401	501	0	NULL
Eddie	601	701	99	NULL
Fred	801	901	99	NULL

Processing each level of the tree still does not give us the final results. We have not yet applied the shift values. For the shift itself, you need another additional column that contains the preorder traversal sequence.

```
UPDATE Personnel_Orgchart
   SET traversal_nbr
      = (SELECT COUNT(*)
            FROM Personnel_Orgchart AS Original_Personnel_Orgchart
           WHERE Original_Personnel_Orgchart.lft <= Personnel_Orgchart.lft);
```

Personnel_Orgchart—step 4

emp_id	lft	rgt	shift	traversal_nbr
Albert	100	1200	99	1
Bert	101	201	0	2
Chuck	400	1100	198	3
Donna	401	501	0	4
Eddie	601	701	99	5
Fred	801	901	99	6

Now it is time to do the big shift. Each node is moved leftward by the sum of the gaps to its left, and the order of execution is governed by the preorder traversal.

```
UPDATE Personnel_Orgchart
   SET lft
      = lft
        - (SELECT SUM(shift)
              FROM Personnel_Orgchart AS Original_Personnel_Orgchart
             WHERE Original_Personnel_Orgchart.traversal_nbr
                   <= Personnel_Orgchart.traversal_nbr),
       rgt
      = rgt
        - (SELECT SUM(shift)
              FROM Personnel_Orgchart AS Original_Personnel_Orgchart
             WHERE Original_Personnel_Orgchart.traversal_nbr
                   <= Personnel_Orgchart.traversal_nbr);
```

You are now ready to reset the shift and traversal_nbr columns to NULLs. The final answer is what we wanted.

```
UPDATE Personnel_Orgchart
   SET shift = NULL,
       traversal_nbr = NULL;
```

Personnel_Orgchart—step 5

emp_id	lft	rgt	shift	traversal_nbr
Albert	1	1101	NULL	NULL
Bert	2	102	NULL	NULL
Chuck	103	803	NULL	NULL
Donna	104	204	NULL	NULL
Eddie	205	305	NULL	NULL
Fred	306	406	NULL	NULL

It is hoped that this procedure will not be called very often. It will be expensive to run on a large deep tree and will probably lock the table while it is running. If you have a tree that is being dynamically altered this much, you might try using the quick but inadequate shift by a constant method first and then call this routine when you can take the application off line.

5.3.2 Reorganization with Recursion

This solution is credited to Richard Romley. Instead of using a table to hold the shifts, they are computed recursively inside a user-defined function.

```
CREATE FUNCTION LeftShift (IN my_emp_id CHAR(10))
RETURNS INTEGER
LANGUAGE SQL
DETERMINISTIC
--recursive
RETURN
  (SELECT CASE WHEN MAX(Par.emp_id) IS NULL
              THEN 0
              ELSE LeftShift (MAX(Par.emp_id)) END
          + COALESCE (SUM(Sib.rgt - Sib.lft), 0)
          + COUNT(Sib.emp_id) + 1
     FROM Personnel_Orgchart AS E1
          INNER JOIN
          Personnel_Orgchart AS Par
          ON E1.lft > Par.lft
             AND E1.rgt < Par.rgt
               AND NOT EXISTS
```

```
               (SELECT *
                  FROM Personnel_Orgchart
                 WHERE lft < E1.lft
                   AND lft > Par.lft
                   AND rgt > E1.rgt
                   AND rgt < Par.rgt)
            LEFT OUTER JOIN
       Personnel_Orgchart AS Sib
       ON Par.lft < Sib.lft
          AND Par.rgt > Sib.rgt
          AND Sib.lft < E1.lft
   WHERE E1.emp_id = my_emp_id);
```

A node can have only zero or one parent. The only node without a parent is the root. There can be many siblings to the left of a node, but all result rows will always have the same value for their parent. The MAX(Par.emp_id) in the SELECT list returns the value for parent and eliminates the need to do a GROUP BY.

The algorithm says that the new lft value for each employee node equals its parent's new lft value plus the sum of the spreads of all its older siblings (Sib.rgt − Sib.lft + 1)(which is the same as SUM(Sib.rgt − Sib.lft) + COUNT(Sib)) plus one. Because the spreads will be the same for the new values as they were for the old values, they can be calculated from the old values. But the parent's new lft value must be determined, which is done with a recursive function call.

So if a parent exists, the function calls itself to get the parent's new lft value, and this process will continue all the way up the tree until the root is found. Tree navigation takes place via recursive function calls.

5.4 Rational Numbers and Nested Intervals Model

Vadim Tropashko showed that it is possible to use rational numbers [for those of you who have forgotten your math, these are numbers of the form (a/b), where a and b are both integers]. This would avoid problems of floating point rounding errors, but it would require a library of functions for this new data type. Although nearly every programming language today implements IEEE floating point numbers, there are some—notably, computational algebra systems, such as Maple and Mathematica—that have internal formats for rational or even algebraic and irrational numbers, such as the square root of 2 and e.

Rational numbers and the use of half-open intervals, which are the basis for the temporal model in SQL, are all we would need. Suppose we want to insert a new child of the root node [0, 1)(or if you prefer [0/5, 5/5) to make the math cleaner) between the children bracketed by [1/5, 2/5) and [3/5, 4/5). You can insert new intervals with the gaps on each side. New members can be fit at any position there. For example, looking at 4/5 and 5/5, I can fit in a node at [21/25, 23/25) and still have plenty of room for more nodes. Given that my integers in most SQL products can go into the billions, I have a pretty big range of values to use before I would have to reorganize. The algebra for rational numbers is well known. You can find greatest common divisor (GCD) algorithms in any textbook and use them to keep the numerators and denominators as small as possible.

```
CREATE FUNCTION gcd(IN x INTEGER, IN y INTEGER) RETURNS INTEGER
LANGUAGE SQL
DETERMINISTIC
BEGIN
WHILE x < > y
   DO IF x > y THEN SET x = x – y; END IF;
      IF y > x THEN SET y = y – x; END IF;
END WHILE;
RETURN (x);
END;
```

This is known as the nested intervals model and it generalizes nested sets. A child node [clft, crgt] is a (indirect) descendant of a parent node [plft, prgt] if

```
((plft <= clft) AND (crgt <= prgt))
```

Now adding a child node is never a problem. You use an unoccupied segment [lft1, rgt1] within a parent interval [plft, prgt] and insert the new child node at [(2 * lft1 + rgt1)/3, (lft1 + 2 * rgt1)/3](Figure 5.4).

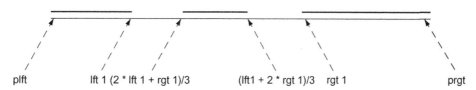

Figure 5.4

After insertion, we still have two more unoccupied segments [lft1, (2 * lft1 + rgt1)/3] and [(rgt1 + 2 * lft1)/3, rgt1] to add more children to the parent node.

The problem is that SQL would have to represent rational (lft, rgt) pairs as pairs of pairs, and the user will have to provide a complete math library for them. If your product supports SQL-99 style user-defined data types and functions, this is much easier.

Now we can easily see why nested sets cannot model arbitrary directed acyclic graphs; two dimensions are just not enough for representing any partial order.

IBM provides DECFLOAT in DB2. It is a floating point number without the precision issues of floating point. DECFLOAT is compliant with the industry standard IEEE754r specification. SQL Standards do not prohibit their use as implementation for REAL numerics.

Still, users may want to avoid using DECFLOAT because they are not widely supported in programming languages yet (e.g. there is no support for it in COBOL and other programming languages).

5.4.1 Partial Order Mappings

Let's introduce a path enumeration model of a tree (see Chapter 8). You will also recognize it as the way that the book you are reading is organized. The path column contains a string of the edges that make up a path from the root ('King') to each node, numbering them from left to right at each level in the tree. This sample organizational chart is from Tropashko and we are using it because it is a bit larger and deeper than the examples we have used before; this will help explain the calculations more easily.

Personnel_Orgchart

emp_id_name	path
'King'	'1'
'Jones'	'1.1'
'Scott'	'1.1.1'
'Adams'	'1.1.1.1'
'Ford'	'1.1.2'
'Smith'	'1.1.2.1'
'Blake'	'1.2'
'Allen'	'1.2.1'
'Ward'	'1.2.2'
'Clark'	'1.3'
'Miller'	'1.3.1'

For example, 'Ford' is the second child of the first child ('Jones') of the root ('King'). We are going to turn these directions into numbers shortly, so please be patient.

Let's look at the two-dimensional picture of nested intervals and assume that rgt is a horizontal axis x, and lft is a vertical axis y. Then, the nested intervals tree looks like Figure 5.5.

Each node [lft, rgt] has its descendants bounded within the two-dimensional cone ((y >= lft) AND (x <= rgt)). Because the right interval boundary is always less than the left one, none of the nodes are allowed above the main diagonal, x = y.

The other way to look at Figure 5.5 is to note that a child node is a descendant of the parent node whenever a set of all points defined by the child cone ((y >= clft) AND (x <= crgt)) is a subset of the parent cone (y >= plft) AND (x <= prgt). A subset relationship between the cones on the plane is a partial order (Figure 5.6).

We now need to assign pairs of points in the x–y plane that conform to these two constraints.

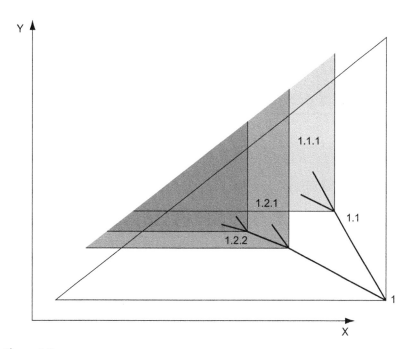

Figure 5.5

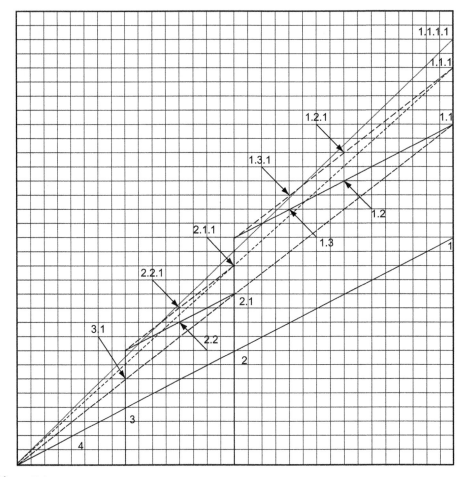

Figure 5.6

Because the choice of a root for the tree is arbitrary, let's start with the interval [0, 1]. In our geometrical interpretation, all tree nodes belong to the lower triangle of the unit square on the x–y plane.

For each node of the tree, let's first define two important points at the x–y plane. The depth-first convergence point is an intersection between the diagonal and the vertical line through the node. For example, the depth-first convergence point for (x = 1, y = 1/2) is (x = 1, y = 1). The breadth-first convergence point is an intersection between the diagonal (x = y) and the horizontal line through the point. For example, the breadth-first convergence point for (x = 1, y = 1/2) is (x = 1/2, y = 1/2). Refer to Figure 5.2 if this is hard to see in your head.

For each parent node, we define the position of the first child as a midpoint halfway between the parent point and depth-first convergence point. You draw a straight line from the parent's point and the depth-first convergence point and then find the midpoint of that line. Each sibling is defined as a midpoint halfway between the previous sibling point and breadth-first convergence point:

For example, node 2.1 of the Personnel_Orgchart tree is positioned at the point (x = 1/2, y = 3/8).

Now that the transformation is defined, it is clear which dense domain we are using: it's not rational or real numbers, but binary fractions. As an aside, the descendant subtree for the parent node "1.2" is a scaled-down replica of the subtree at node "1.1" and the subtree at node 1.1 is a scaled-down replica of the tree at node "1" so we have a little fractal.

5.4.2 Summation of Coordinates

Note that x and y are not completely independent; we can find both x and y if we know their sum. We will store two INTEGER numbers—numerator and denominator of the sum of the coordinates x and y—as an encoded node path. Given the numerator and denominator of the rational number representing the sum of the node coordinates, we can calculate (x, y) coordinates back with this function.

```
CREATE FUNCTION Find_x_numer (IN numer INTEGER, IN denom INTEGER)
RETURNS INTEGER
BEGIN
DECLARE ret_num INTEGER;
DECLARE ret_den INTEGER;
   SET ret_num = numer + 1;
   SET ret_den = 2 * denom;
   WHILE FLOOR(ret_num/2) = ret_num/2
      DO SET ret_num = ret_num/2;
         SET ret_den = ret_den/2;
   END WHILE;
   RETURN ret_num;
END;
```

Likewise, there is a function for the denominator of x.

```
CREATE FUNCTION Find_x_denom (IN numer INTEGER, IN denom INTEGER)
RETURNS INTEGER
BEGIN
DECLARE ret_num INTEGER;
```

```
DECLARE ret_den INTEGER;
   SET ret_num = numer + 1;
   SET ret_den = 2 * denom;
   WHILE FLOOR(ret_num/2) = ret_num/2
      DO SET ret_num = ret_num/2;
         SET ret_den = ret_den/2;
   END WHILE;
   RETURN ret_den;
END;
```

The two functions differ from each other by which variable is in the final RETURN statement. Informally, numer + 1 increment would move the ret_num/ret_den point vertically up to the diagonal; the x coordinate is half of the value, so we just multiplied the denominator by two. Next, we reduce both numerator and denominator by the common power of two.

Naturally, the y coordinate is defined as a complement to the sum:

```
CREATE FUNCTION y_numer (IN numer INTEGER, IN denom INTEGER)
RETURNS INTEGER
LANGUAGE SQL
DETERMINISTIC
BEGIN
DECLARE num INTEGER;
DECLARE den INTEGER;
   SET num = x_numer(numer, denom);
   SET den = x_denom(numer, denom);
   WHILE den < denom
     DO SET num = 2 * num;
        SET den = 2 * den;
   END WHILE;
   SET num = numer - num;
   WHILE FLOOR(num/2) = num/2
     DO SET num = num/2;
        SET den = den/2;
   END WHILE;
   RETURN num;
END;

CREATE FUNCTION y_denom(IN numer INTEGER, IN denom INTEGER)
LANGUAGE SQL
```

```
DETERMINISTIC
BEGIN
DECLARE num INTEGER;
DECLARE den INTEGER;
  SET num = x_numer(numer, denom);
  SET den = x_denom(numer, denom);
  WHILE den < denom
     DO SET num = 2 * num;
        SET den = 2 * den;
  END WHILE;
  SET num = numer - num;
  WHILE FLOOR(num/2) = num/2
    DO SET num = num/2;
       SET den = den/2;
  END WHILE;

   RETURN (den);
END;
```

Now, the test (where 39/32 is the node 1.3.1), using a dummy table for now.

```
SELECT x_numer(39, 32)||'/'||x_denom(39, 32),
       y_numer(39, 32)||'/'||y_denom(39, 32)
  FROM Dummy;
```

Results

5/8   19/32


```
SELECT 5/8 + 19/32, 39/32
  FROM Dummy;
```

Results

1.21875   1.21875

Note that we did not use floating points to represent rational numbers and wrote all the functions with INTEGER arithmetic instead. In the last test, however, we used a floating point just to verify that 5/8 and 19/32, returned by the previous query, do indeed add to 39/32.

We'll store two INTEGER numbers—numerator and denominator of the sum of the coordinates x and y—as an encoded node path. Unlike the pair of integers in the nested sets model, this mapping is stable. The nested intervals model is essentially an enumerated path encoded as a rational number. This is why the Personnel_Orgchart table was shown as an enumerated path model.

5.4.3 Finding Parent Encoding and Sibling Number

Given the (numer, denom) pair of a child node, we can find the node's parent with these functions.

```
CREATE FUNCTION parent_numer (IN numer INTEGER, IN denom INTEGER)
RETURNS INTEGER
LANGUAGE SQL
DETERMINISTIC
BEGIN
DECLARE ret_num INTEGER;
DECLARE ret_den INTEGER;
   IF numer = 3
   THEN RETURN CAST(NULL AS INTEGER);
   END IF;
   SET ret_num = (numer-1)/2;
   SET ret_den = denom/2;
   WHILE FLOOR((ret_num-1)/4) = (ret_num-1)/4
      DO SET ret_num = (ret_num + 1)/2;
         SET ret_den = ret_den/2;
   END WHILE;
   RETURN ret_num;
END;

CREATE FUNCTION parent_denom (IN numer INTEGER, IN denom INTEGER)
LANGUAGE SQL
DETERMINISTIC
BEGIN
BEGIN
DECLARE ret_num INTEGER;
DECLARE ret_den INTEGER;
   IF numer = 3
```

```
        THEN RETURN CAST(NULL AS INTEGER);

        END IF;
        SET ret_num = (numer-1)/2;
        SET ret_den = denom/2;
        WHILE FLOOR((ret_num-1)/4) = (ret_num-1)/4
            DO SET ret_num = (ret_num + 1)/2;
                SET ret_den = ret_den/2;
        END WHILE;
        RETURN ret_den;
END;
```

If the node is the root node, then it has a numerator of 3 and has no parent. Otherwise, we must move vertically down the x–y plane at a distance equal to the distance from the depth-first convergence point. If the node happens to be the first child, then that is the answer.

Otherwise, we must move horizontally at a distance equal to the distance from the breadth-first convergence point until we meet the parent node. Here is the test of the method in which (27/32) is the node '2.1.2' and (7/8) is '2.1'.

```
SELECT parent_numer(27, 32)||'/'||parent_denom(27, 32)
    FROM Dummy;
```

Results

```
7/8
```

In the previous method, counting the steps when navigating horizontally would give the sibling number with this function.

```
CREATE FUNCTION sibling_number (IN numer INTEGER, IN denom INTEGER)
RETURNS INTEGER
LANGUAGE SQL
DETERMINISTIC
BEGIN
DECLARE ret_num INTEGER;
DECLARE ret_den INTEGER;
DECLARE ret INTEGER;
    IF numer = 3
    THEN RETURN CAST(NULL AS INTEGER);
    END IF;
```

```
SET ret_num = (numer - 1)/2;
SET ret_den = denom/2;
SET ret = 1;
WHILE FLOOR((ret_num-1)/4) = (ret_num-1)/4
    DO IF ret_num = 1
        AND ret_den = 1
      THEN RETURN ret;
      END IF;
SET ret_num = (ret_num + 1)/2;
SET ret_den = ret_den/2;
SET ret = ret + 1;
END WHILE;
RETURN ret;
END;
```

The root node is a special stop condition, ret_num = 1 and ret_den = 1, which we can test with:

```
SELECT sibling_number(7, 8) FROM Dummy;
```

Results

```
1
```

5.4.4 Calculating the Enumerated Path and Distance between Nodes

Strictly speaking, we do not have to use an enumerated path, as our encoding is an alternative. However, because an enumerated path provides a much more intuitive visualization of the node position in the hierarchy, we can use the materialized path for input and output of data if we provide mapping to our model.

Implementation is a simple application of the methods from the previous sections. We print the sibling number, jump to the parent, and then repeat these two steps until we reach the root:

```
CREATE FUNCTION Path (IN numer INTEGER, IN denom INTEGER)
RETURNS VARCHAR (30)
LANGUAGE SQL
DETERMINISTIC
```

```
IF numer IS NULL
THEN RETURN ('?');
ELSE
RETURN Path(parent_numer(numer, denom),
            parent_denom(numer, denom))
  || '.' || sibling_number(numer, denom);
END IF;
```

Now we are ready to write a function that takes two nodes, P and C, and tells us when P is the parent of C. A more general query would return the number of levels between P and C, if C is reachable from P, and some exception indicator.

```
CREATE FUNCTION Distance (IN num1 INTEGER, IN den1 INTEGER,
                          IN num2 INTEGER, IN den2 INTEGER)
RETURNS INTEGER
LANGUAGE SQL
DETERMINISTIC
RETURN CASE
       WHEN num1 = num2 AND den1 = den2 -- same node
       THEN 0
       WHEN num1 IS NULL -- missing data
       THEN CAST (NULL AS INTEGER)
       ELSE (1 + Distance(parent_numer(num1, den1),
                          parent_denom(num1, den1), num2, den2))
       END;
```

Test it.

```
SELECT Distance (27, 32, 3, 4) FROM Dummy;
```

Results

```
2
```

Negative numbers are interpreted as exceptions. If the (num1/den1) node is not reachable from (num2/den2), then the navigation converges to the root. The alternative way to answer whether two nodes are connected is by simply calculating the (x, y) coordinates and checking if the parent interval encloses the child. A more thorough implementation of the method would involve a domain of integers and rational numbers with an unlimited range, such as those kinds of numbers supported by computer algebra systems, so that a comparison operation would be part of the compiler.

Our system would not be complete without a function inverse to the path, which returns a node's (numer/denom) value once the path is provided. Let's introduce two auxiliary functions, first:

```
CREATE FUNCTION Child_Numerator
(IN num INTEGER, IN den INTEGER, IN child INTEGER)
RETURNS INTEGER
LANGUAGE SQL
DETERMINISTIC
RETURN (num * (child * child) + 3 - (child * child));
```

and likewise, the matching function:

```
CREATE FUNCTION Child_Denominator
(IN num INTEGER, IN den INTEGER, IN child INTEGER)
RETURNS INTEGER
LANGUAGE SQL
DETERMINISTIC
RETURN den * (child * child);
```

For example, the third child of the node '1' (encoded as 3/2) is the node '1.3' (encoded as 19/16). The path encoding function is:

```
CREATE FUNCTION Path_Numer(path VARCHAR)
RETURNS INTEGER
LANGUAGE SQL
DETERMINISTIC
BEGIN
DECLARE num INTEGER;
DECLARE den INTEGER;
DECLARE postfix VARCHAR(1000);
DECLARE sibling VARCHAR(100);
    SET num = 1;
    SET den = 1;
    SET postfix = '.' || path || '.';
    WHILE CHAR_LENGTH(postfix) > 1
```

```
        DO SET sibling = SUBSTRING(postfix FROM 2 FOR INSTR(postfix, '.',
2)-2);
        SET postfix = SUBSTRING(postfix FROM INSTR(postfix, '.', 2) FOR
CHAR_LENGTH(postfix) - INSTR(postfix, '.', 2) + 1);
        SET num = Child_Numer(num, den, CAST(sibling AS INTEGER));
        SET den = Child_Denom(num, den, CAST(sibling AS INTEGER));
END WHILE;
RETURN num;
END;
```

The function INSTR() is a version of the POSITION() function that returns the nth occurrence of the second parameter string within the first parameter string. Again, the corresponding function for the denominator is

```
CREATE FUNCTION Path_Denom(path VARCHAR)
LANGUAGE SQL
DETERMINISTIC
BEGIN
DECLARE num INTEGER;
DECLARE den INTEGER;
DECLARE postfix VARCHAR(1000);
DECLARE sibling VARCHAR(100);
    SET num = 1;
    SET den = 1;
    SET postfix = '.' || path || '.';
    WHILE CHAR_LENGTH(postfix) > 1
        DO SET sibling = SUBSTRING(postfix FROM 2 FOR INSTR(postfix, '.',
    2)-2);
        SET postfix = SUBSTRING(postfix FROM INSTR(postfix, '.', 2) FOR
    CHAR_LENGTH(postfix) - INSTR(postfix, '.', 2) + 1);
        SET num = Child_Numer(num, den, CAST(sibling AS INTEGER));
        SET den = Child_Denom(num, den, CAST(sibling AS INTEGER));
END WHILE;
RETURN den;
END;

SELECT Path_Numer('2.1.3') || '/' ||
        Path_Denom('2.1.3')
    FROM Dummy;
```

Results

51/64

5.4.5 Building a Hierarchy

Let's create the Personnel_Orgchart hierarchy in this table.

```
CREATE TABLE Personnel_Orgchart
(name VARCHAR(30) NOT NULL UNIQUE,
 numer INTEGER NOT NULL,
 denom INTEGER NOT NULL,
 UNIQUE (numer, denom));

INSERT INTO Personnel_Orgchart
VALUES ('King', Path_Numer('1'), Path_Denom('1')),
      ('Jones', Path_Numer('1.1'), Path_Denom('1.1')),
      ('Scott', Path_Numer('1.1.1'), Path_Denom('1.1.1')),
      ('Adams', Path_Numer('1.1.1.1'), Path_Denom('1.1.1.1')),
      ('Ford', Path_Numer('1.1.2'), Path_Denom('1.1.2')),
      ('Smith', Path_Numer('1.1.2.1'), Path_Denom('1.1.2.1')),
      ('Blake', Path_Numer('1.2'), Path_Denom('1.2')),
      ('Allen', Path_Numer('1.2.1'), Path_Denom('1.2.1')),
      ('Ward', Path_Numer('1.2.2'), Path_Denom('1.2.2')),
      ('Martin', Path_Numer('1.2.3'), Path_Denom('1.2.3')),
      ('Turner', Path_Numer('1.2.4'), Path_Denom('1.2.4')),
      ('Clark', Path_Numer('1.3'), Path_Denom('1.3')),
      ('Miller', Path_Numer('1.3.1'), Path_Denom('1.3.1'));
```

All the functions written in the previous sections are combined conveniently in a single view:

```
CREATE VIEW Hierarchy (name, numer, denom,
                        numer_lft, denom_lft,
                        numer_rgt, denom_rgt,
                         path, depth)
AS SELECT name, numer, denom,
        y_numer(numer, denom),
        y_denom(numer, denom),
        x_numer(numer, denom),
```

```
        x_denom(numer, denom),
        path (numer, denom),
        Distance(numer, denom, 3, 2)
    FROM Personnel_Orgchart;
```

Finally, we can create the hierarchical reports.

5.4.6 Depth-first Enumeration by Left Interval Boundary

This is a depth-first enumeration by the left interval boundary.

```
SELECT depth, name, (numer_lft/denom_lft) AS indentation
  FROM Hierarchy

 ORDER BY indentation;
```

Results

depth	name
0	'King'
1	'Clark'
2	'Miller'
1	'Blake'
2	'Turner'
2	'Martin'
2	'Ward'
2	'Allen'
1	'Jones'
2	'Ford'
3	'Smith'
2	'Scott'
3	'Adams'

5.4.7 Depth-first Enumeration by Right Interval boundary

Depth-first enumeration, ordering by right interval boundary:

```
SELECT depth, name,
       (numer_rgt/denom_rgt) AS indentation
  FROM Hierarchy
 ORDER BY indentation DESC;
```

Results

depth	name
0	'King'
1	'Jones'
2	'Scott'
3	'Adams'
2	'Ford'
3	'Smith'
1	'Blake'
2	'Allen'
2	'Ward'
2	'Martin'
2	'Turner'
1	'Clark'
2	'Miller'

You can get the same results by ordering by path.

```
SELECT depth, name, path
  FROM Hierarchy
 ORDER BY path;
```

5.4.8 All Descendants of a Node

Using 'Ford' as the ancestor in question and excluding him, the query is

```
SELECT H2.name
  FROM Hierarchy AS H1, Hierarchy AS H2
 WHERE H1.name = 'Ford'
   AND Distance (H1.numer, H1.denom, H2.numer, H2.denom) > 0;
```

Results

name
'King'
'Jones'

You can change the "> 0" to ">= 0" in the predicate if you wish to get the entire subtree rooted at the 'Ford' node.

5.5 Egyptian Fractions

As an aside, before modern notation for fractions, the Egyptians and early Europeans used a sum of positive (usually) distinct unit fractions (i.e., fractions of the form 1/n). An Egyptian fraction is a sum of positive (usually) distinct unit fractions. Instead of writing 2/5, they wrote 1/3 + 1/15. For 2/7, they wrote 1/4 + 1/28. Some of the fractions were very complicated. For 2/29, they wrote 1/24 + 1/58 + 1/174 + 1/232.

The math is hard enough that you have to use lookup tables for them. The Rhind papyrus (circa 1650 BCE) is the first such lookup table for fractions of the form 2/n for odd values of n between 5 and 101. The Egyptians also had a special symbol for 2/3.

Any rational number has an Egyptian fraction representation with arbitrarily many terms and with arbitrarily large denominators. An infinite chain of unit fractions can be constructed using the identity

```
1/n = 1/(n + 1)+ 1/(n(n + 1)).
```

There are algorithms such as the binary remainder method, continued fraction unit fraction algorithm, generalized remainder method, greedy algorithm, reverse greedy algorithm, small multiple method, and splitting algorithm for decomposing an arbitrary fraction into unit fractions. However, we have no algorithm for finding unit fraction representations having either a minimum number of terms or smallest possible denominator.

In short, it is a nice math problem but of no practical use for representing rational numbers in a computer.

Linear Version of the Nested Sets Model

IF YOU LOOK at the diagram that shows the left and right numbers on a number line, you will realize that this diagram can be used directly to represent a tree in a nested sets model. The (lft, rgt) numbers each appear once, but the nodes of the tree appear exactly twice—once with the lft number and once with their rgt number. The table can be defined like this:

```
CREATE TABLE Personnel_Orgchart
(emp_id CHAR(10) NOT NULL,
 emp_seq INTEGER NOT NULL UNIQUE,
 CONSTRAINT natural_numbers
      CHECK(emp_seq > 0),
 CONSTRAINT got_all_numbers
 CHECK ((SELECT COUNT(*) FROM Personnel_Orgchart)
        = (SELECT MAX(emp_seq) FROM Personnel_Orgchart)),
 CONSTRAINT exactly_twice
 CHECK (NOT EXISTS
        (SELECT *
           FROM Personnel_Orgchart
          GROUP BY emp_id
         HAVING COUNT(*) <> 2)),
 PRIMARY KEY (emp_id, emp_seq));
```

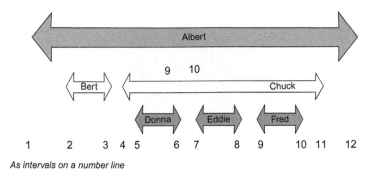

As intervals on a number line

Figure 6.1

In fairness, the "got_all_numbers" and "exactly_twice" constraints will be hard to implement in most SQL products today, but they are legal in full Standard SQL. Our Personnel_Orgchart tree is represented by these data.

Personnel_Orgchart

emp_id mp_	seq
'Albert'	1
'Bert'	2
'Bert'	3
'Chuck'	4
'Donna'	5
'Donna'	6
'Eddie'	7
'Eddie'	8
'Fred'	9
'Fred'	10
'Chuck'	11
'Albert'	12

The standard nested sets model can be constructed using this nonupdatable VIEW for queries:

```
CREATE VIEW Personnel_Orgchart_NS (emp_id, lft, rgt)
AS
SELECT emp_id, MIN(emp_seq), MAX(emp_seq)
  FROM Personnel_Orgchart
 GROUP BY emp_id;
```

Why bother with this approach? It can be handy for parsing markup language data into a relational table. You add a row for every begin tag and every end tag that you find as you read the text from left to right. It is also handy for groupings whose data are gathered in a linear fashion; more on that later.

6.1 Insertion and Deletion

Insertion and deletion are just modifications of the routines used in the standard nested sets model. For example, to remove a subtree rooted at :my_employee, you would use:

```
CREATE PROCEDURE RemoveSubtree (IN my_employee CHAR(10))
LANGUAGE SQL
DETERMINISTIC
BEGIN ATOMIC
 DECLARE leftmost INTEGER;
 DECLARE rightmost INTEGER;
 -- remember where the subtree root was
 SET leftmost = (SELECT MIN(emp_seq)
                    FROM Personnel_Orgchart
                   WHERE emp_id = my_employee);
 SET rightmost = (SELECT MAX(emp_seq)
                     FROM Personnel_Orgchart
                    WHERE emp_id = my_employee);
 -- remove the subtree
 DELETE FROM Personnel_Orgchart
  WHERE emp_seq BETWEEN leftmost AND rightmost;
 -- compute the size of the subtree & close the gap
 UPDATE Personnel_Orgchart
    SET emp_seq = emp_seq - (rightmost - leftmost + 1) / 2
  WHERE emp_seq > leftmost;
END;
```

Insertion is the reverse of this operation. You must create a gap and then add the new subtree to the table.

```
CREATE PROCEDURE InsertSubtree (IN my_boss CHAR(10))
LANGUAGE SQL
DETERMINISTIC
BEGIN ATOMIC
```

```
-- assume that the new subtree is held in NewTree
-- and is in linear nested set format
 DECLARE tree_size INTEGER;
 DECLARE boss_right INTEGER;
 -- get size of the subtree
 SET tree_size = (SELECT COUNT(*) FROM NewTree);
 -- place new tree to right of siblings
 SET boss_right = (SELECT MAX(emp_seq)
                      FROM Personnel_Orgchart
                    WHERE emp_id = my_boss);
 -- move everyone over to the right
 UPDATE Personnel_Orgchart
    SET emp_seq = emp_seq + tree_size
  WHERE emp_seq >= boss_right;
 -- re-number the subtree and insert it
 INSERT INTO Personnel_Orgchart
 SELECT emp_id, (emp_seq + boss_right) FROM NewTree;
 -- clear out subtree table
 DELETE FROM Subtrees;
END;
```

6.2 Finding Paths

The path from anode to root can be found by first looking for the emp_seq number, which would represent the lft number of the node in the nested sets model, and then returning emp_seq numbers lower than that value.

```
SELECT P1.emp_id
  FROM Personnel_Orgchart AS P1
  WHERE P1.emp_seq <= (SELECT MIN(P2.emp_seq) -- left parentheses
                      FROM Personnel_Orgchart AS P2
                      WHERE P2.emp_id = :my_guy)
 GROUP BY emp_id
HAVING COUNT(*) = 1;
```

This is a "flatten" version of the BETWEEN predicate in the nested sets model. The HAVING clause will remove pairs of siblings, leaving only the path.

6.3 Finding Levels

Getting the level is a little trickier. You count the "parentheses" (i.e., emp_seq) and then count the number of distinct things inside the parentheses (emp_id); every pair of parentheses moves you up a level. Then you do some algebra and come up with this answer.

```
SELECT :my_guy,
       2 * COUNT(DISTINCT P2.emp_id)
       - COUNT(DISTINCT P2.emp_seq) AS lvl
  FROM Personnel_Orgchart AS P1, Personnel_Orgchart AS P2
 WHERE P1.emp_id = :my_guy
   AND P2.emp_seq <= (SELECT MIN(emp_seq)
                        FROM Personnel_Orgchart
                       WHERE emp_id = :my_guy);
```

6.4 Cash Register Tape Problem

Data collected by cash registers and other devices will often produce a file that has a sequential number, an item type, and the item. For example,

```
CREATE TABLE Meals
(register_emp_seq INTEGER NOT NULL PRIMARY KEY
 item_type CHAR(5) NOT NULL
    CHECK (item_type IN ('MEAL', 'FOOD', 'DRINK')),
 item_name VARCHAR(15) NOT NULL);
```

with data such as

```
INSERT INTO Meals
VALUES
(1, 'MEAL', 'Fat Boy Box'),
(2, 'FOOD', 'Fat Burger'),
(3, 'FOOD', 'Fries'),
(4, 'DRINK', 'Coke'),
(5, 'MEAL', 'fountain item'),
(6, 'DRINK', 'Diet Coke'),
(7, 'MEAL', 'a la carte'),
(8, 'FOOD', 'Fat Burger'),
```

```
(9, 'FOOD', 'Burger'),
(10, 'MEAL', 'Fish Sandwich')
 etc
```

The hierarchy is that food and drink are subordinates of a meal. The first step is to find the bracketing MEAL register sequence numbers. In this example, the first meal includes all items between (1, 4), the second meal is (5, 6), and the third meal is (7, 9); we do not have enough data for the fourth meal, which is incomplete in this table (hence the use of the OUTER LEFT JOIN).

```
CREATE TABLE Meal_tree
(item_name VARCHAR(15) NOT NULL,
 rgt INTEGER NOTN NULL,
 lft INTEGER NOT NULL
 PRIMARY KEY (rgt, lft));
```

Is first loaded with query:

```
INSERT INTO Meal_Tree
SELECT M1.item_name,
       M1.register_seq AS rgt, MAX(M2.register_seq)-1 AS lft
  FROM Meals AS M1
       LEFT OUTER JOIN
       Meals AS M2
       ON M1.item_type = 'MEAL'
          AND M2.item_type = 'MEAL'
          AND M1.register_seq < M2.register_seq
 GROUP BY M1.item_name, M1.register_seq;
```

You can then insert the food and drinks with

```
INSERT INTO Meal_Tree
SELECT m1.item_name, M1.register_seq, M1.register_seq
  FROM Meals AS M1;
```

which gives us:

```
('Fat Boy Box', 1, 4),
('Fat Burger', 2, 2),
('Fries', 3, 3),
('Coke', 4, 4),
```

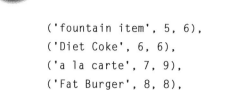

```
('fountain item', 5, 6),
('Diet Coke', 6, 6),
('a la carte', 7, 9),
('Fat Burger', 8, 8),
('Burger', 9, 9),
('Fish Sandwich', 10, NULL)
 Etc.
```

This is a "crunched" version of a nested sets model that can produce a meal with the usual BETWEEN lft AND rgt search conditions. If you wished to have the item type at the second level of the hierarchy and the item_name at the third level, then first create leaf nodes with the same (rgt, lft) values, create a 'DRINK' node and a 'FOOD' node, and finally subordinate them to a 'MEAL' node.

Binary Trees

BINARY TREES ARE a special case of trees in which each parent can have at most only two children that are ordered. There are no children, a left child, a right child, or both a left and a right child at each node. Binary trees are the subject of many chapters in data structures books because they have such nice mathematical properties. For example, the number of distinct binary trees with (n) nodes is called a Catalan number and is given by the formula $((2n)!/((n + 1)!n!))$. Let's stop and define some terms before we go any further.

Complete binary tree: a binary tree in which all leaf nodes are at level (n) or (n − 1), and all leaves at level (n) are toward the left, with "holes" on the right. There are between $(2^{(n - 1)})$ and $((2^n) - 1)$ nodes, inclusively, in a complete binary tree. A complete binary tree is efficiently implemented as an array, where a node at location (i) has children at indexes (2*i) and ((2*i) + 1) and a parent at location (i/2). This is also known as heap and is used in the HeapSort algorithm; we will get to that in a little while.

Perfect binary tree: a binary tree in which each node has exactly zero or two children and all leaf nodes are at the same level. A perfect binary tree has exactly $((2^h) - 1)$ nodes, where (h) is the height. Every perfect binary tree is a full binary tree and a complete binary tree.

Balanced binary tree: a binary tree where no leaf is more than a certain amount farther from the root than any other leaf. See also AVL tree, red-black tree, height-balanced tree, weight-balanced tree, and B-tree.

Balanced binary search tree: a binary tree used for searching for values in nodes. It is usually an index structure. Nodes in the right subtree are all less than or equal to the value at the root node. Nodes in the left subtree are all greater than or equal to the value at the root node. This is usually done with pointer chains so that a search for a value is a simple navigation algorithm.

AVL tree: a balanced binary tree where the heights of the two subtrees rooted at a node differ from each other by at most one. The structure is named for the inventors, Adelson-Velskii and Landis (1962).

Height-balanced tree: a tree whose subtrees differ in height by no more than one and the subtrees are height balanced, too. An empty tree is height balanced. A binary tree can be skewed to one side or the other. As an extreme example, imagine a binary tree with only left children, all in a straight line. The ideal situation is to have a balanced binary tree—one that is as shallow as possible because at each subtree the left and right children are the same size or no more than one node different. This will give us a worst search time of LOG2(n) tries for a set of (n) nodes.

Fibonacci tree: a variant of a binary tree where a tree of order (n) where (n > 1) has a left subtree of order $n - 1$ and a right subtree of order $(n - 2)$. An order 0 Fibonacci tree has no nodes, and an order 1 tree has one node. A Fibonacci tree of order (n) has $(F(n + 2) - 1)$ nodes, where F(n) is the nth Fibonacci number. A Fibonacci tree is the most unbalanced AVL tree possible.

In this example, 'b' is the left son of 'a' and 'c' is the right son of 'a'. Because all the locations have a value, this is called a complete binary tree (Figure 7.1).

In procedural programming languages, binary trees are usually represented with pointer chains or in a one-dimensional array, where the array subscript determines the relationship the node holds within the tree structure. The array location is determined by the rule that if a node has an array location of (n), then its left child has an array location of (2*n) and its right child has an array location of ((2*n) + 1). With a little algebra, you can see that the parent of a node is FLOOR(n/2).

A binary tree is used for searching by placing data in the nodes in such a way that for every node in the tree, all nodes in its left subtree are less than the parent node's value and all nodes in its right are greater than the parent

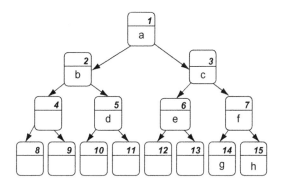

Figure 7.1

node's value. You locate a value by starting at the root of the tree and turning left or right as required until you find the value or that the value is not in the tree. All tree indexing schemes, such as B-trees and B+-trees, generalize this idea to a traversal in a multiway tree.

7.1 Binary Tree Traversals

One of the standard programs you have to write in freshman computer science is a traversal for a binary tree. A traversal is an orderly way of visiting every node so that you can perform some operation on it. There are three ways to traverse a binary tree, starting at the root.

1. Postorder traversal
    a. Recursively traverse the left son's subtree
    b. Recursively traverse the right son's subtree
    c. Visit the root of the current subtree

In this sample tree, you would get the list ('B', 'E', 'D', 'F', 'G', 'C', 'A'). This algorithm can be generalized to nonbinary trees and is called a depth-first search. If you were given the parse tree for an infixed arithmetic expression, as shown in Figure 7.2, the postorder traversal would give you the reverse Polish notation equivalent of the expression.

This algorithm can be generalized to nonbinary trees and is called a breadth-first search.

2. Preorder traversal
    a. Visit the root of the current subtree
    b. Recursively traverse the left son's subtree
    c. Recursively traverse the right son's subtree

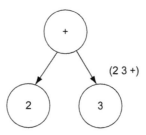

(2 3 +)

Figure 7.2

In this sample tree, you would get the list ('A', 'B', 'D', 'E', 'C', 'F', 'G'). This algorithm can be generalized to nonbinary trees and is called a depth-first search. If you were given the parse tree for an infixed arithmetic expression, as Figure 7.2 shows, the preorder traversal would give you the Polish notation equivalent of the expression.

This algorithm can be generalized to nonbinary trees and is called a breadth-first search.

3. Inorder traversal:
    a. Recursively traverse the left son's subtree
    b. Visit the root of the current subtree
    c. Recursively traverse the right son's subtree

In this sample tree, you would get the list ('D', 'B', 'E', 'A', 'F', 'C', 'G'). If you were given the parse tree for an arithmetic expression, as shown in Figure 7.2, the inorder traversal would give you the standard infixed notation equivalent of the expression.

This algorithm does not generalize to nonbinary trees. Damjan S. Vujnovic points out that preorder and postorder representations work because at most one tree exists that matches a given set of values. The inorder traversal situation is somewhat different. Consider the following two trees (nodes 'b' and 'c' are left children of node 'a'; node d is the right child of node 'a', and so on. Nodes having a "/" above are left children, and nodes having a "\" are right children:

MultiTree A (Figure 7.3):

MultiTree B (Figure 7.4):

If we try to represent these trees using an inorder traversal, we find that they share the same representation; note node 'X' in the diagrams. Inorder traversal works only with binary trees.

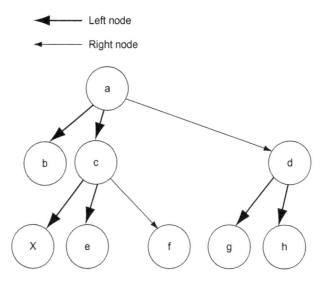

Figure 7.3

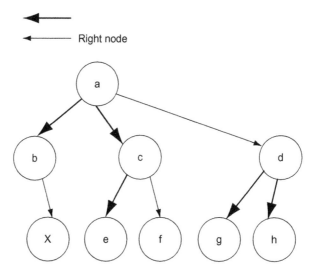

Figure 7.4

7.2 Binary Tree Queries

Damjan S. Vujnovic (damjan@galeb.etf.bg.ac.yu) worked out the details of the following queries against a binary tree. Let's construct a binary tree and load it with some sample data from (Figure 7.1).

```
CREATE TABLE BinTree
(node CHAR(10) NOT NULL,
 location INTEGER NOT NULL PRIMARY KEY);
INSERT INTO BinTree(node, location)
VALUES ('a', 1), ('b', 2), ('c', 3), ('d', 5),
    ('e', 6), ('f', 7), ('g', 14), ('h', 15);
```

The following table is useful for doing queries on the Heap table.

```
CREATE TABLE PowersOfTwo
(exponent INTEGER NOT NULL PRIMARY KEY
        CHECK(exponent >= 0),
 pwr_two INTEGER NOT NULL UNIQUE
        CHECK(pwr_two >= 1)
--, CHECK(2^exponent = pwr_two), but this is not standard SQL
);

INSERT INTO PowersOfTwo
VALUES (0, 1), (1, 2), (2, 4), (3, 8),
    (4, 16), (5, 32), (6, 64), (7, 128),
    (8, 256);
```

Most SQL implementations have base 10 or natural logarithm functions, and LOG2() can be expressed using either of them. The general formulas, carried to more precision than most computers can handle, are:

```
LOG10(x)/LOG10(2) = LOG10(x)/0.301029995663981195213738889472449

LN(x)/LN(2) = LN(x)/0.693147180559945309417232121458118
```

7.2.1 Find Parent of a Node

Getting the parent of a given child is trivial:

```
SELECT BinTree.*, :my_child
 FROM BinTree
 WHERE location
 =(SELECT FLOOR(location/2) AS parent
      FROM BinTree T1
      WHERE T1.node = :my_child)
```

Likewise, we know that the root of the whole tree is always at location one.

7.2.2 Find Subtree at a Node—Recursive Common Table Expression (CTE)

The recursive definition of a binary tree can be put directly into a recursive CTE:

```
WITH RECURSIVE Subtree(node_nbr)
AS
(SELECT T1.node_nbr
   FROM Binary_Tree AS T1
  WHERE T1.node_nbr = :in_root_nbr
 UNION
 SELECT T2.node_nbr
   FROM Binary_Tree AS T2, Subtree AS S1
  WHERE T2.node_nbr IN ((2*S1.node_nbr), (2*S1.node_nbr +1))
SELECT ..
   FROM Subtree AS S2
  WHERE ..;
```

This is a simple enough CTE, but recursion is always expensive. You need to compare it to the next version.

7.2.3 Find Subtree at a Node—Data Driven

Finding a subtree rooted at a particular node is a little bit complicated. Note that the locations of the children of a node with location (n) are:

```
(2*n), (2*n) + 1
(4*n), ..., (4*n) + 3
(8*n), ..., (8*n) + 7
(16*n), ..., (16*n) + 15
  ...
```

The node with location (s) is a subordinate of a node with location (n) if and only if (k) exists such that:

```
(2^k) * n <= s < (2^k) * (n + 1)
```

We know that (k) exists, therefore k = FLOOR (LOG2(s/n))

In other words, if

```
s < (2^FLOOR(LOG2(s/n))) *(n + 1)
```

then the node with location (s) is a subordinate of a node with location (n). This is easier to see with an example:

Example one:

```
n = 3, s = 13
13 < (2^2)* 4
13 < 16
TRUE
```

Example two:

```
n = 2, s = 12
12 < (2^2)* 3
12 < 12
FALSE
```

Thus we have the subordinates query:

```
SELECT :my_root, T1.*
  FROM BinTree AS T1, BinTree AS T2
 WHERE T2.node = :my_root
   AND T1.location
       <(FLOOR(LOG2(T1.location/T2.location))^2) *(n + 1);
```

This predicate lets you test a location number, (j), and see if it is a descendant of the node with location number (k) at level (i).

```
 j BETWEEN((2^i) * k) AND((2^i) * k + i)
```

To get all of the descendants, you could use a table of sequential integers that includes an integer from one to at least the depth of the tree.

This method can be generalized for n-ary tree with a bit of algebra. If the value of (n) is known in advance, we could improve its performance by adding the node level as another column.

7.3 Deletion from a Binary Tree

Deletion of a leaf node from the binary tree is easy. Remove the row with the target node and leave the rest of the tree alone. Deleting a subtree requires using the subordinates query, thus

```
DELETE FROM BinTree
  WHERE node = :my_root
    AND location
        IN (SELECT T1.location
              FROM BinTree AS T1
             WHERE T1.location
                   < (FLOOR (LOG2(T1.location/BinTree.location))^2) *(n + 1));
```

Deleting a node with subordinates requires a business rule about promotion of the subordinates, as every node must have a parent. This depends on the individual case and I cannot give a general statement about it.

7.4 Insertion into a Binary Tree

Insertion into the binary tree is easy if there is a vacant position in the tree. In general, new nodes are added as the left child and then the right child of the target parent node. If all child positions are full, then the tree must be reorganized according to some business rule.

7.5 Heaps

One of the nice things about a binary tree is that its predictable growth pattern allows you to assign a single number to locate each node. Sequentially number the nodes across the levels in the tree from left to right. This structure is also known as a heap when it is presented in an array and is the basis for the HeapSort algorithm.

Therefore, given a root node located at location (1), you know that its sons are at locations (2) and (3). Likewise, using integer division, the parent of a node is at location (n/2), and therefore the grandparent is at ((n/2)/2) = (n/4). This leads to a recurrence relation based on powers of two.

```
CREATE TABLE Heap
(node CHAR(10) NOT NULL,
 location INTEGER NOT NULL PRIMARY KEY);

INSERT INTO Heap
VALUES ('A', 1),
       ('B', 2),
       ('C', 3),
       ('D', 4),
       ('E', 5),
       ('F', 6),
       ('G', 7),
       ('H', 8);
```

The following table is useful for doing queries on the Heap table.

```
CREATE TABLE PowersOfTwo
(exponent INTEGER NOT NULL PRIMARY KEY
         CHECK(exponent >= 0),
```

```
pwr_two INTEGER NOT NULL UNIQUE
        CHECK (pwr_two >= 1)
--, CHECK (2^exponent = pwr_two), but this is not standard SQL
);
INSERT INTO PowersOfTwo
VALUES (0, 1), (1, 2), (2, 4), (3, 8),
       (4, 16), (5, 32), (6, 64), (7, 128),
       (8, 256);
```

In actual SQL products, you might want to use base two logarithms ($LOG2(n) = LOG(n)/LOG(2.0) = LOG(n)/0.69314718055994529$) or user-defined functions to check that the PowersOfTwo rows are correct. The LOG() and FLOOR() functions are not actually part of Standard SQL, but are common enough to be portable.

Given a table with powers of two, we can find all the ancestors of a node with this query, which depends on integer division.

```
SELECT H1.node, H1.location
  FROM Heap AS H1
 WHERE H1.location
   IN (SELECT :in_node/pwr_two
       FROM PowersOfTwo
      WHERE pwr_two <= :my_location);
```

The level of a node is easy, as each level starts with a power of two on the left side (remember that "Level" is a reserved word in SQL-99).

```
SELECT location,
   CAST (FLOOR(LOG(location)/LOG(2.0)) AS INTEGER) AS lvl
   FROM Heap;
```

The depth of the heap is much the same, but because it must include the incomplete level, it is the maximum level or the maximum level plus one.

```
(SELECT CAST (FLOOR(LOG(MAX(location))/LOG(2.0)) + 1.0 AS INTEGER)
   FROM Heap) AS depth;
```

Finding the descendants is much harder. Here is a solution from John Gilson, who also provided the two previous queries.

```
CREATE VIEW HeapDescendants
(node, location, descendant, dscnt_loc)
AS
SELECT H1.node, H1.location,
```

```
        H2.node AS dscnt,
        H2.location AS dscnt_loc
  FROM (SELECT FLOOR(LOG(MAX(location))/LOG(2.0)) + 1.0
          FROM Heap) AS D(depth)
       CROSS JOIN
       (SELECT location, FLOOR(LOG(location)/LOG(2.0))
         FROM Heap) AS L(location, lvl)
       INNER JOIN
       Heap AS H1
       ON H1.location = L.location
       INNER JOIN
       PowersOfTwo AS T
       ON T.exponent >= 0
          AND T.exponent < D.depth - L.lvl
       INNER JOIN
       Heap AS H2
       ON H2.location >= H1.location * pwr_two
          AND H2.location < H1.location * pwr_two + pwr_two;
```

Given the sample table, we would get this result.

Results

node	location	dscnt	dscnt_loc
'A'	1	'A'	1
'A'	1	'B'	2
'A'	1	'C'	3
'A'	1	'D'	4
'A'	1	'E'	5
'A'	1	'F'	6
'A'	1	'G'	7
'A'	1	'H'	8
'B'	2	'B'	2
'B'	2	'D'	4
'B'	2	'E'	5
'B'	2	'H'	8
'C'	3	'C'	3
'C'	3	'F'	6
'C'	3	'G'	7
'D'	4	'D'	4

Results—Cont'd

node	location	dscnt	dscnt_loc
'D'	4	'H'	8
'E'	5	'E'	5
'F'	6	'F'	6
'G'	7	'G'	7
'H'	8	'H'	8

7.6 Binary Tree Representation of Multiway Trees

There is a simple way to represent a multiway tree as a binary tree. The algorithm is given in Knuth's *Art of Programming* (Vol. 1, Section 2.3.2, Page 234, ISBN 978-0201485417). Binary tree representation of a multiway tree is based on first child–next sibling representation of the tree. In this representation, every node is linked with its leftmost child and its next (right nearest) sibling.

Informally, you take the original tree and traverse the nodes by going down a level and then across siblings. The leftmost sibling (if any) becomes the left child in the binary tree. The sibling in the second position (if any) becomes the right child in the binary, and the third and younger siblings become right children under the second child. The algorithm is applied recursively down the tree.

If you see one example, you will understand the idea. Let's start with this multiway tree (Figure 7.5).

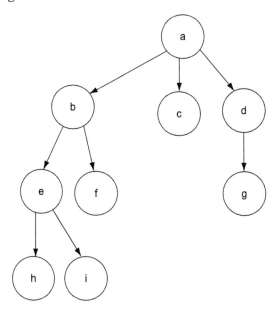

Figure 7.5

This tree can be represented in the first child–next sibling manner as shown in Figure 7.6.

Now grab this graph and pull it up a little so that things flop down 45° (Figure 7.7). Yes, that is not a very scientific description but it makes good visual sense, doesn't it?

Behold! A binary tree! [This example is credited to Paul E. Black (paul .black@nist.gov) and is part of the dictionary of algorithms from NIST http:// www.nist.gov/dads/HTML/binaryBinTreeRepofBinTree.html.]

The left child of a node is its immediate oldest subordinate, and the chain of right children from this root node are other subordinates in order by age (i.e., left to right).

NIST, the National Institute of Standards and Technology, was known between 1901 and 1988 as the National Bureau of Standards (NBS) and was the "Office of Weights and Measures" under John Quincy Adams. It is a federal government agency in charges of maintaining measurement standards laboratories. It does not have regulatory powers, however, it sets up tests for enforcement agencies.

Most Americans are effected in daily life by Handbook 44 that provides the "Specifications, Tolerances, and Other Technical Requirements for Weighing and Measuring Devices" used in the United States. We computer people care about Information Technology Laboratory (ITL). NIST are also active in ANSI (American National Standards Institute) ISO (International Organization for Standards), and other organizations that deal with IT.

7.7 Stern–Brocot Numbers

This is a method for constructing the set of all nonnegative fractions, (m/n), where m and n are relatively prime. It also represents any binary tree by assigning a unique fraction to each node.

The process begins with a pair of fractions $(0/1, 1/0)$ (Figure 7.8) and then the fraction $(m1 + m2)/(n1 + n2)$ is inserted between each pair of fractions $(m1/n1, m2/n2)$. For example, the first steps in the process give us:

```
(0/1, 1/0)
(0/1, 1/1, 1/0)
(0/1, 1/2, 1/1, 2/1, 1/0)
(0/1, 1/3, 1/2, 2/3, 1/1, 3/2, 2/1, 3/1, 1/0)
```

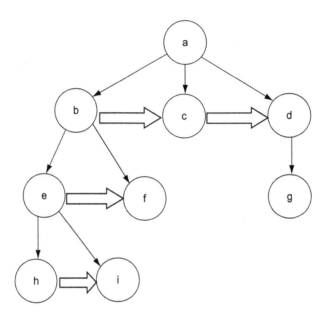

Figure 7.6

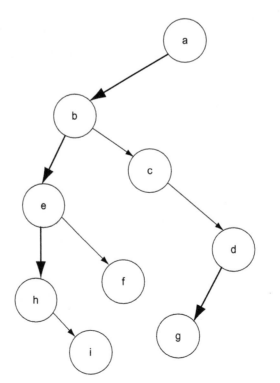

Figure 7.7

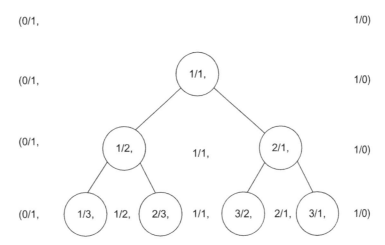

Figure 7.8

Remove (0/1) (i.e., zero) and (1/0) (i.e., infinity) and leave (1/1) (i.e., one) as the root of a binary tree. This maps every rational number into a set of left–right paths. For example, we can arrive at (5/7) by traversing the tree (left, right, right, left). It is a bit of algebra and programming, but you can map any tree into a binary tree and then use Stern–Brocot numbering to identify the nodes. Unfortunately, finding relationships in such a representation also requires bit of algebra and programming.

Other Models for Trees

THE MODELS FOR trees and hierarchies discussed so far are not the only ones. Others use different approaches and properties of trees, some of which are hybrids of other models.

8.1 Adjacency List with Self-References

A slight modification of the usual adjacency list model is to include an edge that loops back to the same node.

```
CREATE TABLE Personnel_OrgChart
(boss_emp_name VARCHAR(20) NOT NULL,
 emp_name VARCHAR(20) NOT NULL,
 PRIMARY KEY (boss_emp_name, emp_name));
```

Personnel_OrgChart

boss_emp_name	emp_name
'Albert'	'Albert'
'Albert'	'Bert'
'Albert'	'Chuck'
'Bert'	'Bert'
'Chuck'	'Chuck'
'Chuck'	'Donna'
'Chuck'	'Eddie'
'Chuck'	'Fred'
'Donna'	'Donna'
'Eddie'	'Eddie'
'Fred'	'Fred'

This makes the table longer, but avoids a NULL in the boss_emp_name column of the root. The query for finding the leaf nodes is

```
SELECT boss_emp_name
  FROM Personnel_OrgChart
 GROUP BY boss_emp_name
HAVING COUNT (boss_emp_name) = 1;
```

Other queries for the adjacency list still work in a modified form, but produce slightly different results.

8.2 Subordinate Adjacency List

Another modification of the usual adjacency list model is to show edges of the graph as oriented from the superior to the subordinate. Nodes without a subordinate are leaf nodes and have a NULL.

```
CREATE TABLE Personnel_OrgChart
(boss_emp_name VARCHAR(20) NOT NULL,
 emp_name VARCHAR(20), -- null means leaf node
 PRIMARY KEY (boss_emp_name, emp_name));
```

Personnel_OrgChart

boss_emp_name	emp_name
'Albert'	'Bert'
'Bert'	NULL
'Albert'	'Chuck'
'Chuck'	'Donna'
'Chuck'	'Eddie'
'Chuck'	'Fred'
'Donna'	NULL
'Eddie'	NULL
'Fred'	NULL

This avoids a NULL in the root, but gives you more NULLs in the table. Finding all the leaf nodes is easy:

```
SELECT P1.emp_name
  FROM Personnel_OrgChart AS P1
 WHERE P1.subordinate_emp_name IS NULL;
```

Queries for the adjacency list model still work, but they need modifications.

8.3 Hybrid Models

It is possible to mix the models we have discussed. The idea is to gain the advantages of each in one table, but the price can be increased for overhead and storage.

8.3.1 Adjacency and Nested Sets Model

This approach retains the parent node column in each row of a nested sets model. The problem is that you cannot include the constraints on the (lft, rgt) pairs that assure the tree structure, thus:

```
CREATE TABLE Tree
(node CHAR(5) NOT NULL,
 parent_node CHAR(5),
```

```
lft INTEGER DEFAULT 0 NOT NULL,
rgt INTEGER DEFAULT 0 NOT NULL);

INSERT INTO Tree
VALUES ('A', NULL, 1, 18),
       ('B', 'A', 2, 3),
       ('C', 'A', 4, 11),
       ('D', 'C', 5, 6),
       ('E', 'C', 7, 8),
       ('F', 'C', 9, 10),
       ('G', 'A', 12, 17),
       ('H', 'G', 13, 14),
       ('I', 'G', 15, 16);
```

The advantage of this model is that you can insert nodes using this statement and let the default values take effect.

```
INSERT INTO Tree (node, parent)
VALUES (:my_node, :my_parent);
```

The clean-up procedure has to detect any (0, 0) pairs in the tree table. If there is at least one such pair, we know nodes have been added, so the procedure needs to perform a complete rebuild of the tree from the (child, parent) columns. If there is no such pair we know that nodes might have been deleted, so the procedure needs to rerenumber the (lft, rgt) columns.

8.3.2 Nested Sets with Depth Model

This approach retains the level or depth in each row of a nested sets model, disregarding constraints, thus:

```
CREATE TABLE Tree
(node CHAR(5) NOT NULL,
 "depth" INTEGER NOT NULL, -- depth is reserved in Standard SQL
 lft INTEGER NOT NULL,
 rgt INTEGER NOT NULL);

INSERT INTO Tree
VALUES ('A', 1, 1, 18),
       ('B', 2, 2, 3),
       ('C', 2, 4, 11),
```

```
('D', 3, 5, 6),
('E', 3, 7, 8),
('F', 3, 9, 10),
('G', 2, 12, 17),
('H', 3, 13, 14),
('I', 3, 15, 16);
```

While the level number can be generated from the nested sets model in a VIEW, the query involves an expensive self-join. The advantage is in bill of materials ("B.O.M." or BOM) problems where subassembly data have to be computed up the tree from the leaf nodes (parts).

8.3.3 Adjacency and Depth Model

This model adds a column for the depth of the node to the adjacency list, thus:

```
CREATE TABLE Tree
(node CHAR(5) NOT NULL PRIMARY KEY,
 parent CHAR(5),
 "depth" INTEGER NOT NULL, -- depth is reserved in Standard SQL
 CHECK (...), -- constraints for tree structure
);
```

Adding a node is easy:

```
CREATE PROCEDURE AddChildNode (IN c INTEGER, IN p INTEGER)
DETERMINISTIC
LANGUAGE SQL
INSERT INTO Tree
SELECT c, p, ("depth" + 1)
  FROM Tree
 WHERE node = p;
```

However, this is a bad hybrid if you need to change the tree structure. When you delete a node, the elements of its subtree all have to be raised one level. Likewise, the depth has to be recalculated if a node is moved to a new parent. Tracing the path down the tree can be expensive in the adjacency list model because you need procedural code.

8.3.4 Computed Hybrid Models

John Gilson (jag@acm.org) came up with this set of VIEWs. For a given node N and a depth-first (preorder) traversal, each ancestor's sequence number is the greatest number on that level that is less than N's sequence number. For a given node N and breadth-first (postorder) traversal, each ancestor's sequence number is the least number on that level that is greater than N's sequence number. We can use these relationships directly to define the following views:

```
CREATE TABLE PreorderTree
(node VARCHAR(10) NOT NULL PRIMARY KEY,
 postorder_nbr INTEGER NOT NULL CHECK (postorder_nbr > 0),
 lvl INTEGER NOT NULL CHECK (lvl > 0),
UNIQUE (lvl, postorder_nbr));

-- Preorder
INSERT INTO PreorderTree
VALUES ('A', 1, 1),
       ('B', 2, 2),
       ('C', 3, 2),
       ('D', 4, 3),
       ('E', 5, 3),
       ('F', 6, 3),
       ('G', 7, 2),
       ('H', 8, 3),
       ('I', 9, 3);

CREATE VIEW PreorderRelationships
AS
SELECT T1.node AS descendant,
       T1.lvl AS descendant_lvl,
       T1.postorder_nbr AS descendant_postorder_nbr,
       T2.node AS ancestor,
       T2.lvl AS ancestor_lvl,
       T2.postorder_nbr AS ancestor_postorder_nbr
  FROM PreorderTree AS T1
       INNER JOIN
       PreorderTree AS T2
     ON T2.lvl < T1.lvl
```

```
            AND T2.postorder_nbr < T1.postorder_nbr
         LEFT OUTER JOIN
         PreorderTree AS T3
         ON T3.lvl = T2.lvl
            AND T3.postorder_nbr > T2.postorder_nbr
            AND T3.postorder_nbr < T1.postorder_nbr
  WHERE T3.postorder_nbr IS NULL;
```

And likewise for a postorder traversal.

```
CREATE TABLE PostorderTree
(node VARCHAR(10) NOT NULL PRIMARY KEY,
 postorder_nbr INTEGER NOT NULL CHECK (postorder_nbr > 0),
 lvl INTEGER NOT NULL CHECK (lvl > 0),
 UNIQUE (lvl, postorder_nbr));
-- Postorder
INSERT INTO PostorderTree
VALUES ('A', 9, 1),
       ('B', 1, 2),
       ('C', 5, 2),
       ('D', 2, 3),
       ('E', 3, 3),
       ('F', 4, 3),
       ('G', 8, 2),
       ('H', 6, 3),
       ('I', 7, 3);
CREATE VIEW PostorderRelationships
AS
SELECT T1.node AS descendant,
       T1.lvl AS descendant_lvl,
       T1.postorder_nbr AS descendant_postorder_nbr,
       T2.node AS ancestor,
       T2.lvl AS ancestor_lvl,
       T2.postorder_nbr AS ancestor_postorder_nbr
  FROM PostorderTree AS T1
       INNER JOIN
       PostorderTree AS T2
       ON T2.lvl < T1.lvl
          AND T2.postorder_nbr > T1.postorder_nbr
```

```
LEFT OUTER JOIN
PostorderTree AS T3
ON T3.lvl = T2.lvl
    AND T3.postorder_nbr < T2.postorder_nbr
    AND T3.postorder_nbr > T1.postorder_nbr
WHERE T3.postorder_nbr IS NULL;
```

We can then write some of the standard queries easily. Using the preorder tree, get all ancestors of a given node.

```
SELECT *
  FROM PreorderRelationships
 WHERE descendant = :my_guy;
```

Using postorder, get all descendants of C

```
SELECT *
  FROM PostorderRelationships
 WHERE ancestor = :my_ancestor;
```

8.4 Path Enumeration Using Prime Number Products

This model is credited to P. Thomas Roji. It uses a prime number table and basic mathematical operations to do basic hierarchy operations. Having said that, the disadvantage is that the product of prime numbers gets big very fast.

This model depends on two mathematical properties.

1. There is a unique path to every node in a tree from the root node.
2. The prime numbers that can be a divisor of the product of a set of prime numbers are only the prime numbers in the set.

That is, let the product of prime numbers be $\Pi(p(n))$, then the factors of $\Pi(p(n))$ can only be the prime numbers, $p(n)$ that participated in the multiplication, or the subproducts. Maple and other mathematical software tools have a built-in function for finding the ith prime. We are not so lucky in SQL and will use a one column table of primes, PrimeNumbers(prime).

The following is the table used in the examples.

```
CREATE TABLE Personnel_Orgchart
(emp_name VARCHAR(15) NOT NULL PRIMARY KEY,
 node_prime BIGINT NOT NULL
   REFERENCES PrimeNumbers(prime,
 path_product BIGINT NOT NULL);
```

Here are sample data for my five-node organizational chart.

```
INSERT INTO Personnel_Orgchart (emp_name, node_prime, path_product)
VALUES
('Albert', 2, 2),
('Bert', 3, 6),
('Chuck', 5, 10),
('Donna', 7, 70),
('Eddie', 11, 110),
('Fred', 13, 130);
```

The column node_prime is a unique prime number assigned to each employee. The column path_product holds the product of the node_prime values from the root to the current node.

We can also create a VIEW or CTE of the next available prime number with

```
REATE VIEW NextPrime(prime)
AS
SELECT MIN(prime)
FROM (SELECT prime FROM PrimeNumbers
EXCEPT
SELECT FROM node_prime FROM Personnel_Orgchart);
```

8.4.1 Find the Subordinates of a Node

The logic is simple. We get the prime number of the parameter node and find all the multiples of it.

```
CREATE PROCEDURE Find_Subordinates(IN in_emp_name VARCHAR(15))
LANGUAGE SQL
DETERMINISTIC

SELECT P1.emp_name, P2.emp_name AS manager_emp_name
FROM Personnel_Orgchart AS P1,
Personnel_Orgchart AS P2
WHERE in_emp_name = P1.emp_name
AND MOD(P2.path_product, P1.path_product) = 0;
```

8.4.2 Find the Superiors of a Node

The logic is simple. We get the path product of the parameter node and find all the divisors of it.

```
CREATE PROCEDURE Find_Superiors(IN in_emp_name VARCHAR(15))
LANGUAGE SQL
DETERMINISTIC

SELECT P1.emp_name, P2.emp_name AS manager_emp_name
FROM Personnel_Orgchart AS P1,
Personnel_Orgchart AS P2
WHERE in_emp_name = P1.emp_name
AND MOD(P1.path_product, P2.path_product) = 0
```

8.4.3 Hierarchy with Levels

This requires a table of prime numbers and the assumption that prime numbers are assigned to nodes in ascending order

```
CREATE PROCEDURE Find_Level(IN in_emp_name VARCHAR(15))
LANGUAGE SQL
DETERMINISTIC
SELECT P1.emp_name,
       SUM (CASE WHEN MOD(P1.path_product, N.prime) = 0
                 THEN 1 ELSE 0 END) AS lvl
  FROM Personnel_Orgchart AS P1,
       PrimeNumbers AS N
 WHERE in_emp_name = P1.emp_name
   AND N.prime < = MAX(P1.node_prime) OVER()
 GROUP BY P1.emp_name;
```

The CASE expression counts the divisors at the parameter. The root is at level one, and then we count down to the leaf nodes.

8.4.4 Insert New Employee under a Boss

This is done in one statement in full SQLs that support the use of scalar subquery expression in a VALUES() list.

```
CREATE PROCEDURE Insert_New_Employee
       (IN in_new_emp_name VARCHAR(15),
        IN in_boss_emp_id VARCHAR(15))
```

```
LANGUAGE SQL
DETERMINISTIC
INSERT INTO Personnel_Orgchart (emp_name, node_prime, path_product)
VALUES (in_new_emp_name,
       (SELECT prime FROM NextPrime),
       (SELECT prime FROM NextPrime)
       * (SELECT P1.path_product
            FROM Personnel_Orgchart AS P1
          WHERE P1.emp_name = in_boss_emp_id));
```

If your SQL has problems with this, then declare local variables and load them with the node_prime and path_product computation.

8.4.5 Delete an Employee

The first rule is that you cannot ever delete the root node. The tree would fall apart without a root. The next problem is what to do with the subordinates. In this case, we have opted to move the subordinates to the immediate superior.

The approach is simple. Given an employee, find the node_prime, and we are done with that row, so we delete it. We then factor out the delete_prime from all the subordinates.

```
CREATE PROCEDURE Delete_Employee
       (IN in_emp_name VARCHAR(15))
LANGUAGE SQL
DETERMINISTIC
BEGIN ATOMIC
--- find the prime of the deletion node
DECLARE delete_prime INTEGER;
SET delete_prime
  = (SELECT P1.node_prime
       FROM Personnel_Orgchart AS P1
     WHERE P1.emp_name = in_emp_name);

--- delete the node
DELETE FROM Personnel_Orgchart
 WHERE emp_name = in_emp_name;
```

```
--- delete the prime from the products
UPDATE Personnel_Orgchart
   SET path_product
     = CASE WHEN MOD(path_product, delete_prime) = 0
        THEN (path_product / delete_prime)
        ELSE path_product END
 WHERE node_prime > 2;
END;
```

8.4.6 Decomposing a Path

The product paths in this model are made up of single occurrences of primes. We assume that there is a table of primes, but we don't want to test all of them if we can help it. The WHERE clause tells us that the root is always at 2 and that the product we are testing could itself be a prime at the second level of the tree.

```
CREATE PROCEDURE Prime_Path_List(IN @in_path_product INTEGER)
LANGUAGE SQL
DETERMINISTIC
SELECT N.prime
  FROM PrimeNumbers AS N
 WHERE MOD(@in_path_product, N.prime) = 0
   AND N.prime BETWEEN 2 AND @in_path_product;
```

8.4.7 Helpful Functions

Because this method is based on factoring and products, it can be handy to have a small library of useful integer math functions.

8.4.7.1 Greatest Common Divisor

The greatest common divisor or GCD(a, b) is a classic algorithm in procedural programming language. The name describes the results. Because it has been around for millennia, there are several ways to do it. Here are three. The first is iterative and relatively fast.

```
CREATE FUNCTION GCD(IN a INTEGER, IN b INTEGER)
RETURNS INTEGER
LANGUAGE SQL
DETERMINISTIC
BEGIN
```

```
DECLARE tINTEGER;
   WHILE b < > 0
      DO SET t = b;
      SET b = MOD (a, b);
      SET a = t;
   END WHILE;
RETURN a;
END;
```

The next iterative version comes from Euclid, the remainder calculation (b = MOD (a, b)) is replaced by repeated subtraction.

```
CREATE FUNCTION GCD(IN a INTEGER, IN b INTEGER)
RETURNS INTEGER
LANGUAGE SQL
DETERMINISTIC
BEGIN
IF a = 0
THEN RETURN b;
ELSE WHILE b <> 0
      DO IF a > b
         THEN SET a = a - b;
         ELSE SET b = b - a;
         END IF;
   END WHILE;
RETURN a;
END IF;
END;
```

The recursive version is based on the equality of the GCDs of successive remainders and the halting condition GCD(n, 0) = n.

```
CREATE FUNCTION GCD(IN a INTEGER, IN b INTEGER)
RETURNS INTEGER
LANGUAGE SQL
DETERMINISTIC
IF b = 0
THEN RETURN a;
ELSE RETURN GCD(b, MOD (a, b));
END IF;
```

8.4.7.2 Least Common Multiple

The LCM(a,b), least common multiple, function is the other side of the GCD(). Again, its name explains the function. The easy way to compute is to use the formula:

```
LCM(a,b) = ABS(a*b) / GCD(a,b);
```

Proprietary Extensions for Trees

A S YOU CAN see from the examples given earlier in this book, you very quickly get into recursive or procedural code to handle trees. Because the single-table adjacency list model is popular, several vendors have added extensions and academics have proposals to handle tree traversal in SELECT statements.

9.1 Oracle Tree Extensions

Oracle has CONNECT BY PRIOR and START WITH clauses in the SELECT statement to provide partial support for reachability and path enumeration queries. The START WITH clause tells the engine which value the root of the tree has. The CONNECT BY PRIOR clause establishes the edges of the graph. The function LEVEL gives the distance from the root to the current node, starting at 1 for the root. Let us use a list of parts and subcomponents as the example database table. The query "Show all subcomponents of part A1, including the substructure" can be handled by the following Oracle PLSQL statement:

```
SELECT LEVEL AS path_length, assembly_nbr, subassembly_nbr
  FROM Blueprint
  START WITH assembly_nbr = 'A1'
CONNECT BY PRIOR subassembly_nbr = assembly_nbr;
```

The query produces the following result:

Result1

path_length	assembly_nbr	subassembly_nbr
1	'A1'	'A2'
2	'A2'	'A5'
2	'A2'	'A6'
3	'A6'	'A8'
3	'A6'	'A9'
1	'A1'	'A3'
2	'A3'	'A6'
3	'A6'	'A8'
3	'A6'	'A9'
2	'A3'	'A7'
1	'A1'	'A4'

The output is an adequate representation of the query result because it is possible to construct the path enumeration tree of Figure 9.1 from it. The CONNECT BY ... PRIOR clause provides traversal but not support for recursive functions before version 9.0 (check the status of the product at the time you are reading this chapter). For example, it is not possible to sum the weights of all subcomponents of part A1 to find the weight of A1. The only recursive function supported by the CONNECT BY ... PRIOR clause is the LEVEL function. Another limitation of the CONNECT BY ... PRIOR clause is that it does not permit the use of joins. The reason for disallowing joins

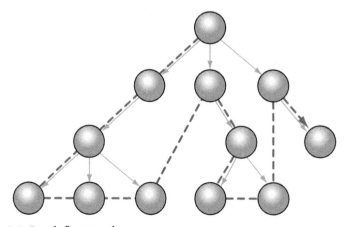

Figure 9.1 Depth-first search.

is that the order in which the rows are returned in the result is important. Because parent nodes appear before their children, you know that if the path length increases, these are children; if it does not, they are new nodes at a higher level.

This also means that an ORDER BY can destroy any meaning in the results. This means, moreover, that the CONNECT BY... PRIOR result is not a true table, as a table by definition does not have an internal ordering. In addition, this means that it is not always possible to use the result of a CONNECT BY query in another query. A trick for working around this limitation, which makes indirect use of the CONNECT BY ... PRIOR clause, is to hide it in a subquery that is used to make a JOIN at the higher level. For example, to attach a product category description, form another table to the parts explosion.

```
SELECT part_nbr, category_name
  FROM Parts, ProductCategories
 WHERE Parts.category_id = ProductCategories.category_id
   AND part_nbr IN (SELECT subassembly_nbr
                      FROM Blueprint
                     START WITH assembly_nbr = 'A1'
                    CONNECT BY PRIOR subassembly_nbr = assembly_nbr);
```

The main query involves a JOIN of two tables, which would not be possible with direct use of the CONNECT BY ... PRIOR clause. Another query that cannot be processed by direct use of the CONNECT BY ... PRIOR clause is one that displays all parent–child relationships at all levels. A technique to process this query is illustrated by the following SQL:

```
SELECT DISTINCT PX.part_nbr, PX.pname, PY.part_nbr, PY.pname
  FROM Parts AS PX, Parts AS PY
 WHERE PY.part_nbr
       IN (SELECT Blueprint.subassembly_nbr
             FROM Blueprint
            START WITH assembly_nbr = PX.part_nbr
           CONNECT BY PRIOR subassembly_nbr = assembly_nbr)
 ORDER BY PX.part_nbr, PY.part_nbr;
```

Again, the outer query includes a JOIN, which is not allowed with the CONNECT BY ... PRIOR clause in the inner query used in the IN() predicate. Note that the correlated subquery references PX.part_nbr.

9.1.1 Related Tree Extensions

Other vendors have done things similar to the Oracle approach to things, all based on establishing a root and a relationship to JOIN the original table to a correlated copy of itself. Indexing can help, but such queries are still very expensive.

XD was a SQL product that runs on PC platforms and was fully compatible with DB2. The company, XDB Systems, was founded by Dr. S. Bing Yao, who was known for his research in query optimization. Micro Focus bought XDB in 1998 and made it part of tehir COBOL Product line as the DB2 Optrion. The product had a set of extensions similar to those in Oracle, but this product uses functions instead of clauses to hide the recursion. The PREVIOUS (<column>) function finds rent node value of the child column for the row being currently processed by a query. The keyword LEVEL is a system value computed for each row, which gives its path length from the root; the root is at LEVEL = 0. There is a special value for the path length of a leaf node, called BOTTOM. For example, to find all of the subcomponents of A1, you would write this query:

```
SELECT assembly_nbr
  FROM Blueprint
 WHERE PREVIOUS (subassembly_nbr) = assembly_nbr
   AND assembly_nbr='A1'
   AND LEVEL  <= BOTTOM:
```

9.2 DB2 and the WITH Operator

IBM added the WITH operator from the SQL-99 Standard to their DB2 product line to handle the need to factor out common subquery expressions and give them a name for the duration of the query. Other alternatives have been to repeat the code (hoping that the optimizer would do the factoring) or to create a VIEW and use it. However, the VIEW will be persistent in the schema after the query is done unless you drop it explicitly.

However, instead of being a simple temporary VIEW mechanism, IBM made the WITH clause handle recursive queries by allowing self-references. This is useful for tree structures in particular. You define a special form of the temporary hidden table that has an initial subquery and a recursive subquery. These two parts have to be connected by a UNION ALL operator—no other set operation will do. The hidden table is initialized with results of the initial subquery and then the result of the recursive subquery is added to the hidden table over and over as it is used.

This might be easier to explain with an example taken from the usual adjacency list model OrgChart table. To find the immediate subordinates of Boss 'Albert' you would write:

```
SELECT *
  FROM OrgChart
 WHERE boss = 'Albert';
```

To find all of his subordinates, you add this WITH clause to the query:

```
WITH Subordinates (emp, salary)
  AS (SELECT emp, salary
        FROM OrgChart AS P0
       WHERE boss = 'Albert') -- initial set
       UNION ALL
      (SELECT emp, salary
         FROM OrgChart AS P1, Subordinates AS S1
        WHERE P1.boss = S1.emp) -- recursive set
SELECT emp
  FROM Subordinates;
```

Each time you fetch a row from Subordinates, the WITH clause is executed using the current rows of the temporary hidden table. First you fetch 'Albert' and his immediate subordinates. You then do a UNION ALL for personnel who have those subordinates as bosses and so forth until the subquery is empty. Then the hidden table is passed to the main SELECT clause to which the WITH clause is attached.

9.3 Date's EXPLODE Operator

In his book *Relational Database: Selected Writings*, Chris Date proposed an EXPLODE(<table-name>) table-valued function that would take an input table in the adjacency list model and return another table with four columns: level number, current node, subordinate node, and sequence number. The sequence number was included to get around the problem of the ordering having meaning in the hierarchy. EXPLODE results are derived from simple tree-traversal rules.

It is possible to write such a function in the current version of products that have a table-valued function feature. You can also write a procedure that will write the result set to a global or local temporary table that the rest of the session can use.

9.4 Tillquist and Kuo's Proposals

(John Tillquist and Feng-Yang Kuo, 1989) proposed an extension wherein a tree in an adjacency list model is viewed as a special kind of GROUP BY clause. They would add a GROUP BY LEAVES (major, minor) that can be approximated with the query:

```
SELECT *
  FROM Tree AS T1
 WHERE NOT EXISTS (SELECT *
                     FROM Tree AS T2
                    WHERE T1.major = T2.minor)
 GROUP BY T1.major;
```

The idea is that you get groups of leaf nodes, with their immediate parent as the single grouping column. Other extensions in Tillquist and Kuo's paper include a GROUP BY NODES (<parent node>, <child node>), which would use each node only once to prevent problems with cycles in the graph and would find all of the descendants of a given parent node. They then extend the aggregate functions with a COMPOUND function modifier (along the lines of DISTINCT) that carries the aggregation up the tree.

9.5 Microsoft Extensions

Microsoft added the HIERARCHYID data type in the SQL Server 2008 release as a proprietary version of a variable length, encoded path enumeration data type. Columns of this type are supposed to represent the position of its row in a hierarchy, but they do not have to represent a tree automatically. It is up to the application to generate and assign HIERARCHYID values in such a way that the desired relationship between rows is reflected in the values.

Given two HIERARCHYID values a and b, (a < b) means a comes before b in a depth-first traversal of the tree—a simple string search. The encoding used in the HIERARCHYID type is limited to 892 bytes. Consequently, nodes that have too many levels in their representation to fit into 892 bytes cannot be represented by the HIERARCHYID type.

In total violation of the SQL data integrity principles, the application has to manage concurrency in generating and assigning HIERARCHYID values. There is no guarantee that HIERARCHYID values in a column are unique unless the application uses a UNIQUE constraint. Hierarchical relationships represented by HIERARCHYID values are not enforced like a foreign key relationship. It is possible A has a subordinate B, and then A is deleted leaving B orphaned, that is, with a relationship to a nonexistent row.

This is a proprietary OO implementation that uses Methods rather than an SQL extension. They can be called by external programs. Here is a quick list of them.

1. ToString() method converts the HIERARCHYID value to the logical representation as a NVARCHAR(4000) data type.

2. Read () and Write () convert HIERARCHYID to VARBINARY.

3. Conversion from HIERARCHYID to XML is not supported. To transmit HIERARCHYID parameters through SOAP, first cast them as strings. A query with the FOR XML clause will fail on a table with HIERARCHYID unless the column is first converted to a character data type.

4. GetAncestor

5. GetDescendant

6. GetLevel

7. GetRoot

8. IsDescendantOf

9. Parse

10. Read

11. GetReparentedValue

12. ToString

13. Write

9.6 Other Methods

Looking at the literature, most of the attempts to add a tree structure operation to SQL have been based on the assumption that adjacency list representation was the only possible way to model a tree structure. But as we can see in this book, that simply is not true.

Perhaps the influence of decades of procedural languages is hard to overcome or it might be all of those "Boxes and Arrows" charts we have seen on the walls even before there were computers.

References

Date, C.J., 1986. Relational Database: Selected Writings. Addison Wesley. ISBN 978-0201141962.

Tillquist, J., Kuo, F.-Y., 1989. An approach to the recursive retrieval problem in the relational database. CACM 32 (2), 239–245.

Hierarchies in Data Modeling

T YPE HIERARCHIES ARE useful when trying to model entities for a database. How this hierarchy is mapped into SQL DDL is another issue. Many years ago, at an ANSI X3H2 Database Standards Committee meeting in Rapid City, South Dakota, Bjarne Stroustrup gave a lecture on C++ and object-oriented (OO) programming research at Bell Labs. When asked about using OO concepts in databases, he replied that the people at Bell Labs had experimented with it, tried several approaches, and came to the conclusion that while OO was good for programming, it was a bad idea for data. The most recent model of OO also seems to have gone back to a separation of data and procedures.

However, programmers who come into SQL from OO languages and models insist on trying to model class or type hierarchies in SQL. This is not a new phenomenon. When SQL first came out, COBOL programmers tried to force their mental model on SQL. Old files were converted directly into tables, each field became a column, and each record became a row. Then the application program could simply replace the file reads with a cursor and the programmer never had to learn the relational model. The performance stank, of course.

The usual attempts by OO programmers to force their model into SQL involve building a metadata model in SQL, where tables use a proprietary, nonrelational autoincrementing feature of some kind to replace a global OID (object identifier) and have columns that contain the names of attributes, their values, and something to establish class hierarchy.

Vendors such as SQL Server and DB2 have had this ?feature? for years, in slightly different versions.

The SQL:2011 draft standard now has an IDENTITY which is based on a table level SEQUENCE generator column. As expected, it has to be an exact numeric with scale zero only one such column is allowed per table. The basic BNF is:

```
<IDENTITY column specification> ::=
GENERATED {ALWAYS | BY DEFAULT} AS IDENTITY
AS <data type>
START WITH <signed numeric literal>
INCREMENT BY <signed numeric literal>
MAXVALUE <signed numeric literal> | NO MAXVALUE
MINVALUE <signed numeric literal> | NO MINVALUE
CYCLE | NO CYCLE
```

However, physically contiguous storage is only one way of building a relational database and is not always the best one. One of the basic ideas of a relational database is that the user is not supposed to know how things are stored at all, much less write code that depends on the particular physical representation in a particular release of a particular product. Because every underlying file system was different and there was no standard, every vendor came with a proprietary and nonportable scheme for autonumbering.

Let's look at the logical problems. First try to create a table with two columns and try to make them both autonumbered. This makes no sense; because the autonumber has to be at the row level within a table. Many products, such as the Sybase/SQL Server family and DB2, have an optional IDENTITY column on each table in the schema. Technically, it is a table property and not a column at all. It is a count of the physical insertion attempts (not necessarily successful) and has nothing to do with a *logical* data model.

As proof that this is a nonrelational feature, create a table with one column and declare it as autonumbered. Now try to insert, update, and delete different numbers from it. If you cannot insert, update, and delete rows from a table, then it is not a table by definition.

It gets worse; create a simple table with one autonumbered column and a few other columns. Insert a few rows into the table, thus letting the autonumber column, which is not shown in the list, default to its automatic values.

```
INSERT INTO Foobar (a, b, c) VALUES ('a1', 'b1', 'c1');
INSERT INTO Foobar (a, b, c) VALUES ('a2', 'b2', 'c2');
INSERT INTO Foobar (a, b, c) VALUES ('a3', 'b3', 'c3');
```

You will note that the autonumbering is sequential and in the order the INSERT INTO statements were presented. If you delete a row, the gap in the sequence is not filled in and the sequence continues from the highest number that has ever been used in that column in that particular table.

Now use an INSERT INTO statement with a query expression in it, like this:

```
INSERT INTO Foobar (a, b, c)
SELECT x, y, z
  FROM Floob;
```

Because a query result is a table, and a table is a set which has no ordering, what should the autonumbers be? The entire, whole completed set is presented to Foobar all at once, not a row at a time. There are (n!) ways to number (n) rows, so which one do you pick? The answer has been to use whatever the *physical* order of the result set happened to be. But it is actually worse than that. If the same query is executed again, but with new statistics or after an index has been dropped or added, the new execution plan could bring the result set back in a different *physical* order. Can you explain from a *logical modeling* viewpoint why the same rows in the second query get different autonumbers?

Using autonumbered as a PRIMARY KEY is a sign that there is no data model, only an imitation of a sequential file system. Because this number exists only as a result of the state of a particular piece of hardware at a particular time in a particular release of a particular version of an SQL product, how do you verify such a number in the reality you are modeling?

To quote from Dr. Codd: "… Database users may cause the system to generate or delete a surrogate, but they have no control over its value, nor is its value ever displayed to them …" (Dr. Codd in *ACM Transactions on Database Systems*, pp. 409–410 and Codd, E. (1979). Extending the database relational model to capture more meaning. *ACM Transactions on Database*

Systems, 4(4), pp. 397–434). This means that a surrogate should act like an index, hash, or other access method; created by the user; managed by the system; and *never* seen by a user. Dr. Codd also wrote the following:

> *There are three difficulties in employing user-controlled keys as permanent surrogates for entities.*
>
> *(1) The actual values of user-controlled keys are determined by users and must therefore be subject to change by them (e.g., if two companies merge, the two employee databases might be combined with the result that some or all of the serial numbers might be changed).*
>
> *(2) Two relations may have user-controlled keys defined on distinct domains (e.g., one uses social security, while the other uses employee serial numbers) and yet the entities denoted are the same.*
>
> *(3) It may be necessary to carry information about an entity either before it has been assigned a user-controlled key value or after it has ceased to have one (e.g., an applicant for a job and a retiree).*
>
> *These difficulties have the important consequence that an equi-join on common key values may not yield the same result as a join on common entities. A solution—proposed in part [4] and more fully in [14]—is to introduce entity domains which contain system-assigned surrogates. Database users may cause the system to generate or delete a surrogate, but they have no control over its value, nor is its value ever displayed to them. . . . (Codd in ACM Transactions on Database Systems, pp. 409–410; Codd, E. (1979). Extending the database relational model to capture more meaning. ACM Transactions on Database Systems 4(4), pp. 397–434).*

Such schemas usually fail in a short time in actual use in an organization and then become unmanageable. To make this more concrete, let's model "vehicles" and the subclasses "automobiles," "SUV," and so forth in a table like this:

```
CREATE TABLE VehicleClass
(id INTEGER NOT NULL AUTO_INCREMENT, -- not standard SQL
 attribute VARCHAR(255) NOT NULL,
 value VARCHAR(255) NOT NULL,
 subclass VARCHAR(255) NOT NULL,
 ..);
```

You will see this design referred to as an EAV model ("entity-attribute-value") in some of the literature. All the columns tend to be declared as the same long VARCHAR(n) or NVARCHAR(n) for a large value of (n) so that they can support strings that contain any numeric value, any temporal value, or any string that might hold the value of the entity's attribute. This now gives you overhead and possible errors of perpetual data type conversions. You need to be sure that everyone uses the same formats for all data types. Just think of all the ways that people enter date and time information and you have a rough idea how bad this is going to be.

To find an entity, you must assemble it from the pieces in the class table. Because some members of a class might not have exactly the same attributes as other members, you will tend to use a lot of expensive self OUTER JOINs in the queries.

Any typographical error becomes a new attribute. Consider adding a color attribute to the data model for a class of objects. The American programmer types in "color," the British programmer types in "colour," and the guy who is in a hurry types in "cloor" instead. Nobody dares remove any of the attributes, even if they can find them all, because those attributes might belong to someone's object. A data dictionary and careful data modeling can mitigate some of these data integrity problems, but performance will continue to degrade as the database size increases.

Perhaps even worse, the names of such columns tend to become attempts to pass along class hierarchy, physical storage, and usage information. The "color" attribute might be put into a table with column names such as "color_code_id," "color_code_id_value," or worse. Likewise, you will see "i_color_code" if the code is an INTEGER. A data dictionary becomes almost impossible. (For details on how to name a data element, consult the ISO-11179.6 Metadata Standards naming conventions.)

The use of NVARCHAR(n) has all these problems and the possibility that an entire Buddhist sutra in Chinese Unicode characters or a weird collation can be inserted as the value of an attribute.

It is extremely difficult to put constraints on such tables. Just consider the simple requirement that an employee be over 18 years of age. The birth date and hire date of each employee has to be found, converted from VARCHAR(n) to a temporal data type, math performed, and the candidate rejected with a useful error code. You then need to decide what to do if one or both of those attributes are missing.

In short, you are using a high-level tool to try to build an OO database from the ground up and it is an insane waste of time and resources. Does this mean that the idea of classes and relationships have no place in an SQL database? No, but they need to be implemented properly. There are some OO extensions in the SQL-99 Standard, but they are still not common in products and might not match the OO host language you are using.

In class hierarchies, we are looking for sets of entities defined by common attributes, and then within that set we look for subsets with unique attributes. For example, personnel within a company all have job titles, tax identification numbers, and salaries. Within the personnel set, the subset of salesmen also have a commission, the subset of executives also have stock options, and so forth.

The idea is to move from the general to the particular. This lets you handle the sets of entities at the appropriate level, based on the shared common attributes at that level.

10.1 Types of Hierarchies

A generalization hierarchy can be either overlapping or disjoint. In an overlapping hierarchy, an entity can be a member of several subclasses. For example, people at a university could be broken into three subclasses: faculty, staff, and students. But there is nothing to prevent the same person from belonging to two or more of these subclasses. A student could be on staff as part of a co-op program, a professor can take a class as a student, and so forth.

In a disjoint hierarchy, an entity can be in one and only one subclass. For example, students at a university could be broken into three subclasses: foreign, in state, and out of state.

For the OO-minded reader, disjoint hierarchies are rather like single-inheritance type hierarchies, whereas overlapping hierarchies are like multiple-inheritance type hierarchies.

10.2 Data Definition Language Constraints

This is a nice set of definitions, but how do we code it in SQL? Here the hierarchy is not in one table, but it is in the relationships among several tables.

10.2.1 Uniqueness Constraints

One of the basic tricks in SQL is representing a one-to-many relationship by creating a third table that references the two tables involved by their primary keys. This third table has quite a few popular names, such as "junction table" or "join table," but I know that it is a relationship. People tell you this and then leave you on your own to figure out the rest.

For example, here are two entity tables and a relationship table (assume single-parent households)

```
CREATE TABLE Mothers
(mother_name VARCHAR(30) NOT NULL PRIMARY KEY
 ...);

CREATE TABLE Children
(child_name VARCHAR(30) NOT NULL PRIMARY KEY,
 ...);

CREATE TABLE Families - wrong!
(mother_name VARCHAR(30) NOT NULL
        REFERENCES Mothers (mother_name),
 child_name VARCHAR(30) NOT NULL,
        REFERENCES Children (child_name));
```

The "Families" does not have its own key, so I can have redundant duplicate rows. This mistake is easy to make. What is worse is that too often a new programmer will try to correct the error by adding a key column to the table, often with some kind of proprietary autonumbering feature. This actually makes the problem worse because redundant duplicates can hide behind the autonumber and look like they are different instances of an entity.

There is a natural key in the form of PRIMARY KEY (mother_name, child_name) that needs to be enforced.

However, the only restriction on the Families that these constraints give us is that each (mother_name, child_name) pair appears only once. Every mother can be paired with every child, which is not what we wanted. Now, I want to make a rule that Mothers can have as many children as they want, but the children have to stick to one mother, the biological rule.

The way I do this is to use a NOT NULL UNIQUE constraint on the child_name column, which makes it a key. It's a simple key because it is only one column, but it is also a nested key because it appears as a subset of the compound PRIMARY KEY.

"Families" is a proper table, without duplicated (mother_name, child_name) pairs, but it also enforces the condition that a child has a unique parent.

```
CREATE TABLE Families
(mother_name VARCHAR(30) NOT NULL
        REFERENCES Mothers (mother_name),
 child_name VARCHAR(30) NOT NULL UNIQUE, -- nested key
        REFERENCES Children (child_name),
PRIMARY KEY (mother_name, child_name)); -- compound key
```

Note that (mother_name, child_name) is actually a super-key since child_name is a key. You usually like to avoid such redundancies, but because SQL can only reference columns in UNIQUE() and PRIMARY KEY() constraints in the referencing table, let me leave the code this way to help explain the purpose of the table.

Generalizing this schema is a bit complicated. Let's add a pet to the family and say that a pet belongs to one and only one child, but kids can have several pets. Another rule is that orphans cannot have pets. If orphans were allowed to have pets, then we would model the mother–children relationship with one table (Families) and model the child–pets relationship with a second table. They would be distinct relationships, described by separate relationship tables.

Clearly I need to start with a Pets table.

```
CREATE TABLE Pets
(pet_name VARCHAR(30) NOT NULL PRIMARY KEY,
 ...);
```

My primary key is the full length of the type hierarchy and the lowest subclass has to be unique.

```
CREATE TABLE Families -- wrong!
(mother_name VARCHAR(30) NOT NULL
        REFERENCES Mothers (mother_name),
 child_name VARCHAR(30) NOT NULL,
        REFERENCES Children (child_name),
 pet_name VARCHAR(30) NOT NULL
```

```
              REFERENCES Pets(pet_name),
  PRIMARY KEY (mother_name, child_name, pet_name));
```

However, this has a serious problem. Consider these data:

```
('Daddy', 'Billy', 'Rover')
('George', 'Billy', 'Rover')
('George', 'Billy', 'Fluffy')
```

We do not have a constraint to keep Billy from having two different Mothers, which leads to duplicates of "Rover" in the table. Let's try adding some UNIQUE constraints.

```
CREATE TABLE Families -- wrong but better!
(mother_name VARCHAR(30) NOT NULL
           REFERENCES Mothers (mother_name),
  child_name VARCHAR(30) NOT NULL,
            REFERENCES Children(child_name),
  pet_name VARCHAR(30) NOT NULL UNIQUE
            REFERENCES Pets(pet_name),
  PRIMARY KEY (mother_name, child_name, pet_name));
```

Well, you have solved only part of the problem. I can get around this set of constraints by changing my table to:

```
('Daddy', 'Billy', 'Rover')
('George', 'Billy', 'Fluffy')
```

Billy still has two Mothers. We cannot use a UNIQUE(mother_name, child_name) constraint because this would not allow the child to have more than one pet. Change "George" to "Daddy" to see what I mean. Likewise a UNIQUE (child_name, pet_name) constraint is redundant since the pet_name is unique. We are hitting the limits of Standard SQL uniqueness constraints.

One way around this is with a table level CHECK() constraint or a CREATE ASSERTION statement, thus

```
CREATE ASSERTION Only_One_Mother_per_Kid
CHECK (NOT EXISTS
       (SELECT *
          FROM Family AS F1
```

```
        GROUP BY child_name
        HAVING COUNT (mother_name)) > 1));
```

The logical question at this point is why not use this type of constraint to enforce the "child and pet" rule, thus

```
CREATE ASSERTION Only_One_Kid_per_Pet
CHECK (NOT EXISTS
        (SELECT *
          FROM Family AS F1
          GROUP BY pet_name
        HAVING COUNT (child_name)) > 1));
```

These table level CHECK() constraints obviously generalize up the hierarchy. However, because they have to be tested every time the table changes, they can be quite expensive to execute, they do not improve access to data, and they are not widely implemented yet. You would have to use a TRIGGER in most SQL products.

10.2.2 Disjoint Hierarchies

A simple way to enforce a disjoint hierarchy is with a matrix design. The relationship is stored in a table that connects each parent node to their proper child.

```
CREATE TABLE StudentTypes
(student_id INTEGER NOT NULL PRIMARY KEY
          REFERENCES Students (student_id)
          ON UPDATE CASCADE
          ON DELETE CASCADE,
 in_state_flg INTEGER DEFAULT 0 NOT NULL
        CHECK (in_state IN (0, 1),
 out_of_state_flg INTEGER DEFAULT 0 NOT NULL
          CHECK (out_of_state IN (0, 1),
 foreign_flg INTEGER DEFAULT 0 NOT NULL
        CHECK (foreign IN (0,1),
 CHECK ((in_state_flg + out_of_state_flg + foreign_flg) = 1));
```

To get to the particular attributes that belong to each subclass, you will need a table for that subclass. For example,

```
CREATE TABLE OutOfStateStudents
(student_id INTEGER NOT NULL PRIMARY KEY
           REFERENCES StudentTypes (student_id)
           ON UPDATE CASCADE
           ON DELETE CASCADE,
 state_code CHAR(2) NOT NULL, -- USPS standard codes
 ...);
CREATE TABLE ForeignStudents
(student_id INTEGER NOT NULL PRIMARY KEY
           REFERENCES StudentTypes (student_id)
           ON UPDATE CASCADE
           ON DELETE CASCADE,
 country_code CHAR(3) NOT NULL, -- ISO standard codes
 ...);

CREATE TABLE InStateStudents
(student_id INTEGER NOT NULL PRIMARY KEY
           REFERENCES StudentTypes (student_id)
           ON UPDATE CASCADE
           ON DELETE CASCADE,
 county_code INTEGER NOT NULL, -- ANSI standard codes
 high_school_district INTEGER NOT NULL,
 ...);
```

A more complex set of relationships among the subclass can also be enforced by making the CHECK() constraint more complex. The constant in the StudentTypes table can be changed from 1 to (n), the equality can be replaced with a less than, and so forth.

```
CHECK (subclass_1 + subclass_2 + .. + subclass_n) <= (k))
```

Another trick is to use powers of 2 so that each combination has a unique total; you can also use elaborate CASE expressions with many business rules embedded in them.

Another version of the same approach uses a two-part key in the subclass tables where one column is a constant that tells you what the table contains. Let's use abbreviation codes for "in state", "out of state", and "foreign" students.

```
CREATE TABLE StudentTypes
(student_id INTEGER NOT NULL PRIMARY KEY
            REFERENCES Students (student_id)
            ON UPDATE CASCADE
            ON DELETE CASCADE,
  residence_type CHAR(3) DEFAULT 'ins' NOT NULL
            CHECK (residence:type IN ('ins', 'out', 'for')));
```

Note that if the key had been (student_id, residence:type), then a student could appear in more than one subclass and we could add check constraints to enforce various combinations of those subclasses.

To get to the particular attributes that belong to each subclass, you will need a table for that subclass. For example,

```
CREATE TABLE OutOfStateStudents
(student_id INTEGER NOT NULL PRIMARY KEY
  residence_type CHAR(3) DEFAULT 'out' NOT NULL
            CHECK (residence_type = 'out'),
  FOREIGN KEY (student_id, residence_type)
  REFERENCES StudentTypes (student_id, residence_type)
  ON UPDATE CASCADE
  ON DELETE CASCADE,
  state CHAR(2) NOT NULL, -- USPS standard codes
  ...,
PRIMARY KEY (student_id, residence_type));

CREATE TABLE ForeignStudents
(student_id INTEGER NOT NULL
  residence_type CHAR(3) NOT NULL
            CHECK (residence_type 'for'),
  FOREIGN KEY (student_id, residence_type)
  REFERENCES StudentTypes (student_id, residence_type)
  ON UPDATE CASCADE
  ON DELETE CASCADE,
country_code CHAR(3) NOT NULL, -- ISO standard codes
  ...,
PRIMARY KEY (student_id, residence_type));

CREATE TABLE InStateStudents
(student_id INTEGER NOT NULL
```

```
residence_type CHAR(3) NOT NULL
        CHECK (residence_type 'ins'),
FOREIGN KEY (student_id, residence_type)
REFERENCES StudentTypes (student_id, residence_type)
 ON UPDATE CASCADE
 ON DELETE CASCADE,
county_code INTEGER NOT NULL, -- ANSI standard codes
high_school_district INTEGER NOT NULL,
...,
PRIMARY KEY (student_id, residence_type));
```

The DRI actions will enforce the class membership rules for us, but at the cost of redundant columns.

10.2.3 Representing 1:1, 1:m, and n:m Relationships

One of the basic tricks in SQL is representing a one-to-one or many-to-many relationship with a table that references the two (or more) entity tables involved by their primary keys. This third table has several popular names, such as "junction table" or "join table," but we know that it is a relationship. This type of table needs to have constraints to assure that the relationships work properly.

For example, given two tables,

```
CREATE TABLE Boys
(boy_name VARCHAR(30) NOT NULL PRIMARY KEY
 ...);

CREATE TABLE Girls
(girl_name VARCHAR(30) NOT NULL PRIMARY KEY,
 ...);
```

Yes, I know using names for a key is a bad practice, but it will make my examples easier to read. There are many different relationships that we can make between these two tables. If you do not believe me, just watch an old Jerry Springer show sometime. The simplest relationship table looks like this:

```
CREATE TABLE Pairs
(boy_name VARCHAR(30) NOT NULL
        REFERENCES Boys (boy_name)
```

```
                ON UPDATE CASCADE
                ON DELETE CASCADE,
 girl_name VARCHAR(30) NOT NULL,
                REFERENCES Girls(girl_name)
                ON UPDATE CASCADE
                ON DELETE CASCADE);
```

The Pairs table allows us to insert rows like this:

```
('Joe Celko', 'Lady GaGa')
('Joe Celko', 'Kate Middleton')
('William Windsor', 'Kate Middleton')
('Joe Celko', 'Lady GaGa')
```

Oops! I am shown twice with "Lady GaGa" because the Pairs table does not have its own key. This is an easy mistake to make, but fixing it so that you enforce the proper rules is not obvious to a beginner.

```
CREATE TABLE Orgy
(boy_name VARCHAR(30) NOT NULL
        REFERENCES Boys (boy_name)
        ON DELETE CASCADE
        ON UPDATE CASCADE,
 girl_name VARCHAR(30) NOT NULL,
        REFERENCES Girls(girl_name)
        ON UPDATE CASCADE
        ON DELETE CASCADE,
 PRIMARY KEY (boy_name, girl_name)); -- compound key
```

The Orgy table gets rid of duplicated rows and makes this a proper table. The primary key for the table is made up of two or more columns and is called a compound key because of that fact.

```
('Joe Celko', 'Lady GaGa')
('Joe Celko', 'Kate Middleton')
('William Windsor', 'Kate Middleton')
```

However, the only restriction on the pairs is that they appear only once. Every boy can be paired with every girl, much to the dismay of the Moral

Majority. I think I want to make a rule that guys can have as many gals as they want, but the gals have to stick to one guy.

The way I do this is to use a NOT NULL UNIQUE constraint on the girl_name column, which makes it a key. It is a simple key because it is only one column, but it is also a nested key because it appears as a subset of the compound PRIMARY KEY.

```
CREATE TABLE Polygamy
(boy_name VARCHAR(30) NOT NULL
        REFERENCES Boys (boy_name)
        ON UPDATE CASCADE
        ON DELETE CASCADE,
 girl_name VARCHAR(30) NOT NULL UNIQUE, -- nested key
        REFERENCES Girls (girl_name)
          ON UPDATE CASCADE
          ON DELETE CASCADE,
 PRIMARY KEY (boy_name, girl_name)); -- compound key
```

The Polygamy is a proper table, without duplicated rows, but it also enforces the condition that I get to play around with one or more ladies, thus

```
('Joe Celko', 'Lady GaGa')
('Joe Celko', 'Kate Middleton')
```

The ladies might want to go the other way and keep company with a series of men.

```
CREATE TABLE Polyandry
(boy_name VARCHAR(30) NOT NULL UNIQUE -- nested key
        REFERENCES Boys (boy_name)
        ON UPDATE CASCADE
        ON DELETE CASCADE,
 girl_name VARCHAR(30) NOT NULL,
        REFERENCES Girls (girl_name)
        ON UPDATE CASCADE
        ON DELETE CASCADE,
 PRIMARY KEY (boy_name, girl_name)); -- compound key
```

The Polyandry table would permit these rows from our original set.

```
('Joe Celko', 'Kate Middleton')
('William Windsor', 'Kate Middleton')
```

The Moral Majority is pretty upset about this Hollywood scandal and would love for us to stop running around and settle down in nice stable marriages.

```
CREATE TABLE Marriage
(boy_name VARCHAR(30) NOT NULL UNIQUE -- nested key
        REFERENCES Boys (boy_name)
        ON UPDATE CASCADE
        ON DELETE CASCADE,
  girl_name VARCHAR(30) NOT NULL UNIQUE -- nested key,
        REFERENCES Girls (girl_name)
        ON UPDATE CASCADE
        ON DELETE CASCADE,
  PRIMARY KEY (boy_name, girl_name)); -- compound key
```

The Marriage table allows us to insert these rows from the original set.

```
('Joe Celko', 'Lady GaGa')
('William Windsor', 'Kate Middleton')
```

Think about this table for a minute. The PRIMARY KEY is now redundant. If each boy appears only once in the table and each girl appears only once in the table, then each (boy_name, girl_name) pair can appear only once.

From a theoretical viewpoint, I could drop the compound key and make either boy_name or girl_name the new primary key or I could just leave them as candidate keys. However, SQL products and theory do not always match. Many products make the assumption that the PRIMARY KEY is in some way special in the data model and will be the way that they should access the table most of the time.

In fairness, making special provision for the primary key is not a bad assumption because the REFERENCES clause uses the PRIMARY KEY of the referenced table as a default. In many SQL products, this can also give you a covering index for the query optimizer.

Hierarchical Encoding Schemes

A HIERARCHY IS A useful concept for classifying data as well as retrieving them. The encoding schemes used to represent data are often hierarchical. Tree structures are a natural way to model encoding schemes that have a natural hierarchy. They organize data for searching and reporting along that natural hierarchy and make it very easy for a human being to understand. But what do you use for this natural organizational principle? Physical, temporal, or procedural options often exist, but many hierarchical encoding schemes are more circumstantial, traditional, and just plain arbitrary.

11.1 ZIP Codes

The most common example of a hierarchical encoding scheme is the ZIP code, which partitions the United States geographically. Each digit, as you read from left to right, further isolates the location of the address first by postal region, then by state, then by city, and finally by the post office that has to make the delivery. For example, given the ZIP code 30310, we know that the 30000 to 39999 range means the southeastern United States. Within the southeastern codes, we know that the 30000 to 30399 range is the state of Georgia and that 30300 to 30399 is metropolitan Atlanta. Finally, the whole code, 30310, identifies substation 'A' in the west end section of the city. The ZIP code can be parsed by reading it from left to right, reading first one digit, then two, and then the last two digits.

Many Websites will look up cities in the United States by their ZIP codes, compute the distance between two ZIP codes, and so forth (http://zip.langenberg.com/). Each ZIP code has a preferred city, but a suburb or sister town might fall under the same code if they are small enough or are served by the same post office. Likewise, an address in a town that goes over a state border might have a ZIP code that actually belongs to the other state. In short, it is not a perfect locator for (city, state) combinations, but it is close enough for making contacts by mail or physical location.

In 1983, the postal service began using an expanded ZIP code called ZIP+4, which consists of the original five-digit ZIP code plus a four-digit add-on code. The four-digit add-on number identifies a geographic segment within the five-digit delivery area, such as a city block, office building, individual high-volume receiver of mail, or any other physical unit that would aid sorting and delivery. ZIP+4 codes are not required for first class mail, but must be used with certain classes of bulk mail to aid machine presorting.

11.2 Dewey Decimal Classification

Melville Louis Kossuth Dewey (1851-12-10 to 1931-12-26) had two manias in his life. One was spelling reform and the other was libraries.

As an aside, spelling reform was a hot topic in the United States at that time, and most of the differences between British and American English were established then. Dewey even used "reformed spelling" in several editions of the Dewey Decimal Classification (DDC) system. He changed his name to "Melvil Dui," dropping his middle names, but finally changed the family name back to the original spelling.

He invented the DDC when he was a 21-year-old student assistant in the Amherst college library. What is hard for us to imagine is that before the DDC, every library made up its own classification system without recourse to any standard model. It sounds a lot like IT shops today, doesn't it?

He helped establish the American Library Association in 1876 while he was the librarian of Columbia College (now Columbia University) in New York City; he founded the first library school in 1887 and raised librarianship to a profession.

The Dewey Decimal Classification system had its 23rd revision in 2011. Copies in hardcopy and electronic format can be had from the Online Computer Library Center, Inc. (OCLC) at

OCLC Headquarters

6565 Kilgour Place

Dublin, OH 43017-3395

USA

Website: www.oclc.org

The 500 number series covers "Natural Sciences & Mathematics"; within that, the 510s cover "Mathematics"; finally, 512 deals with "Algebra & Number Theory" in particular. The scheme could be carried further, with decimal fractions for various kinds of algebra.

11.3 Strength and Weaknesses

Hierarchical encoding schemes are great for large data domains that have a natural hierarchy. However, there can be problems in designing these schemes. First of all, because the tree structure does not have to be neatly balanced, some Shop_Categories may need more codes than others and hence more breakdowns. Eastern and ancient religions are shortchanged in the DDC, reflecting a prejudice toward Christian writings. Asian religions were pushed into a very small set of codes. Today, the Library of Congress has more books on Buddhism than on any other religion on Earth.

Second, you might not have made the right choices as to where to place certain values in the tree. For example, in the DDC, books on logic are encoded as 160, in the philosophy section, and not under the 510s, mathematics. In the 19th century, there was no mathematical logic. Today, there is no philosophical logic. Dewey was simply following the conventions of his day. Also, like today's programmers, he found that the system specifications changed while he was working.

Dewey Decimal Table Search for "Logic"

The Hundreds Level (Overview)

000 Computer science, information, and general works

100 Philosophy and psychology

200 Religion

300 Social sciences

400 Language

500 Natural sciences and mathematics

600 Technology (applied sciences)

700 Arts and recreation

800 Literature and rhetoric

900 Geography and history

The Tens Level

160 Logic

The Units Level

161 Induction

162 Deduction

163 Not assigned or no longer used

164 Not assigned or no longer used

165 Fallacies and sources of error

166 Syllogisms

167 Hypotheses

168 Argument and persuasion

169 Analogy

Why this particular breakdown of human knowledge? Well, why not? And it could be much worse. Before the DDC, every library invented its own classifications. Some of the systems were highly personal. Let me give you a quote, which was meant as a joke, but close to the truth. It is from the essay "The Analytical Language of John Wilkins" by Jorge Luis Borges:

> *These ambiguities, redundancies, and deficiencies recall those attributed by Dr. Franz Kuhn to a certain Chinese encyclopedia entitled* Celestial Emporium of Benevolent Knowledge. *On those remote pages it is written that animals are divided into (a) those that belong to the Emperor, (b) embalmed ones, (c) those that are trained, (d) suckling pigs, (e) mermaids, (f) fabulous ones, (g) stray dogs, (h) those that are included in this*

classification, (i) those that tremble as if they were mad, (j) innumerable ones, (k) those drawn with a very fine camel's hair brush, (l) others, (m) those that have just broken a flower vase, (n) those that resemble flies from a distance.

11.4 Shop Categories

In the retail industry, stores will often set up their own shop Shop_Categories to classify their merchandise. For example, if you go to a larger bookstore you will see a separate "Juvenile" section, a section for "Romances," for "Westerns," and so forth. Within these sections, you might find books grouped alphabetically by authors or by further subclassifications.

These shop category tables are hard for beginning SQL programmers to design because they have a hard time conceptually divorcing Shop_Categories from the merchandise. This will be easier to see with an example, which was taken from an actual posting on a Usenet Newsgroup.

First set up a simplified Inventory table that uses the UPC code to identify the merchandise.

```
CREATE TABLE Inventory
(upc CHAR(13) NOT NULL PRIMARY KEY
   CHECK (upc SIMILAR TO '[0-9]{13}'),
 shop_category CHAR(3) NOT NULL
  REFERENCES Shop_Categories (shop_category),
 onhand_qty INTEGER NOT NULL);
```

Each product has a category, but here is what the first attempt at a Shop_Categories table:

```
CREATE TABLE Shop_Categories
(shop_category CHAR(3) NOT NULL PRIMARY KEY
   CHECK (product_cat SIMILAR TO '[0-9][0-9][0-9]'),
 parent_shop_category CHAR(3), -- null means root
 shop_category_name VARCHAR(25) NOT NULL,
 category_count INTEGER DEFAULT 1 NOT NULL
   CHECK (category_count > 0));
```

As you can see, each category has a parent_shop_category, which symbolizes the higher category in a hierarchy. The original poster wanted to know if he could do "some kind of a loop" for each product_cat and tally the quantity on hand into the category_count, with the proper nesting of the Shop_Categories beneath.

There are several design problems in this schema. A better approach is shown later. First, check to see that the product_cat is within the boundaries of the category classification system.

```
CREATE TABLE Inventory
(upc CHAR(13) NOT NULL PRIMARY KEY
   CHECK (upc SIMILAR TO '[0-9]{13}'),
 product_name CHAR(20) DEFAULT 'unknown' NOT NULL ,
 shop_category CHAR(3) NOT NULL
   CHECK (shop_category BETWEEN '000' AND '999'),
 onhand_qty INTEGER NOT NULL);
```

However, the real problem is that the Shop_Categories table is wrong. Using the basic idea of the nested sets model we can set up ranges, such as the Dewey Decimal Classification system, and add more constraints to the table:

```
CREATE TABLE Shop_Categories
(shop_category_name CHAR(20) DEFAULT 'unknown' NOT NULL
            PRIMARY KEY,
 low_shop_category CHAR(3) NOT NULL UNIQUE,
 high_shop_category CHAR(3) NOT NULL UNIQUE,
 CHECK (low_shop_category <= high_shop_category));

INSERT INTO Shop_Categories
VALUES ('Printers (all)', 500, 599),
       ('InkJet Printers', 510, 519),
       ('Laser Printers', 520, 529);
```

Instead of doing a loop and trying to keep the total in a column in the Shop_Categories table, use this VIEW, which will always be right, always up to date, and show all Shop_Categories.

```
CREATE VIEW CategoryReport (shop_category_name, total_qty)
AS SELECT C1.shop_category_name, COALESCE (SUM(onhand_qty), 0)
     FROM Shop_Categories AS C1
          LEFT OUTER JOIN
          Inventory AS P1
```

```
        ON P1.product_cat
            BETWEEN C1.low_shop_category AND C1.high_shop_category
    GROUP BY C1.shop_category_name;
```

If you wanted the Category hierarchy to end with an actual inventory entity, you can enforce this with a declarative referential integrity constraint. In the case of a rare book store with unique items, Shop_Categories would probably not go down to individual titles, but a retail computer store would like to go to the make and model of their equipment, with an entry such as this:

```
INSERT INTO Shop_Categories
VALUES ('Fonebone X-7 Laser Printer', 521, 521);
```

You then use two REFERENCES clauses on the same column to make sure that each inventory item is represented in the Shop_Categories table, thus

```
CREATE TABLE Inventory
(product_name VARCHAR(25) NOT NULL,
 product_cat CHAR(3) NOT NULL UNIQUE
            REFERENCES Shop_Categories(range_start)
            ON UPDATE CASCADE
            ON DELETE CASCADE,
            REFERENCES Shop_Categories(range_end)
            ON UPDATE CASCADE
            ON DELETE CASCADE,
 onhand_qty INTEGER NOT NULL);
```

A good rule of thumb is that you need to use a range of numbers that is larger than what you need now. Data have a way of growing.

11.5 Statistical Tools for Decision Trees

You can buy statistical tools that look at raw data and cluster them by attribute values into a hierarchy based on those data. These are generally used for data mining, so I will only mention them in passing and give a simple example.

Using a sample database from KnowledgeSeeker (Angoss Software), you start with a series of records about the lifestyles of people and their blood pressure—how much they drink, how much they smoke, how much they exercise, what foods they eat, and so forth. The KnowledgeSeeker engine takes these data and produces a tree diagram and a set of rules for predicting blood pressure (the dependent variable) from the other information (independent variables).

At the first level of the tree, we find that age is the most important factor, and we have three subgroups. Within the younger age group (32 to 50 years), you need to stop heavy drinking; within the middle-aged age group (51 to 62 years), you need to stop smoking; and within the oldest age group (63 to 72 years), if you have survived a lifetime of smoking and drinking, you need to watch your diet now. Using this information and a questionnaire, I can predict the likelihood of a new patient having high blood pressure.

However, as my sample size changes or as I add more attributes (say family medical history in the example), my tree might need to be recomputed and decisions reevaluated based on more current and/or complete data available to me.

CHAPTER
12

Graphs in SQL

T HE FOLLOWING SECTION stresses other useful kinds of generalized directed graphs. Generalized directed graphs are classified into nonreconvergent and reconvergent. In a reconvergent graph, multiple paths exist between at least one pair of nodes. Reconvergent graphs are either cyclic or acyclic.

12.1 Adjacency List Model Graphs

The most common way to model a graph in SQL is with an adjacency list model. Each edge of the graph is shown as a pair of nodes in which ordering matters and then any values associated with that edge are shown in another column.

Here is the skeleton of the basic adjacency list model of a graph, with nodes in a separate table. This is the most common method for modeling graphs in SQL. Before we had recursive common table expressions (CTEs), you had to use cursors and procedural code for the interesting algorithms.

```
CREATE TABLE Nodes
(node_id INTEGER NOT NULL PRIMARY KEY,
<< other attributes of the node >>);

CREATE TABLE AdjacencyListGraph
(begin_node_id INTEGER NOT NULL
```

```
REFERENCES Nodes (node_id),

end_node_id INTEGER NOT NULL
REFERENCES Nodes (node_id),

<< other attributes of the edge >>,
PRIMARY KEY (begin_node_id, end_node_id));
```

Technically, the begin_node_id can be the same as the end_node_id, and we can have a node without any edges. They are easy to diagram (see Figure 12.1).

"Other attributes of the edge" are usually called a weight. These attributes model distance or travel time for maps, electrical resistance for circuits, cost of a process in workflow networks, and so forth. They are usually expressed as a numeric value on some scale and we want to do computations with them.

Likewise, "other attributes of the node" are usually a name (say, "5-ohm resistor" in a circuit diagram) or where the weight (travel distance in a road map) is kept in the schema.

12.1.1 SQL and the Adjacency List Model

There are only two approaches with an adjacency list model of a graph. You can use procedural code, which has two more options—a procedure or a cursor—or you can use a recursive CTE, but it is not recommended. Recursion is usually slow, and most SQL products choke at a certain depth, usually some power of two.

Procedural approaches are usually direct translations of known algorithms from your favorite procedural programming languages into SQL/PSM. You replace the arrays with tables that mimic arrays.

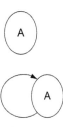

Figure 12.1

While still procedural under the covers, you can use recursive CTEs instead of loops and perhaps gain advantages from the query optimizer and parallelism. The *very* general skeleton of such queries is

```
WITH RECURSIVE
SolutionGraph (source_node, dest_node, <wgt>, ..)
AS
(SELECT source_node, dest_node, <wgt>,
        <other attributes>, <possible counts>
    FROM AdjacencyListGraph
UNION ALL
SELECT G1.source_node, G2.dest_node,
       <computation on wgt>,
       <computation on other attributes>,
       <increment counts>
  FROM SolutionGraph AS G1, Graph AS G2
 WHERE G2.source_node = G1.dest_node
AND G2.dest_node <> G1.source_node
AND NOT EXISTS
    (SELECT *
       FROM Graph AS G3
      WHERE G3.source_node = G1.source_node
        AND G3.dest_node = G2.dest_node
        AND <special conditions>))

SELECT source_node, dest_node,
       <aggregate computation on wgt>,
       <aggregate computation on other attributes>,
       <final counts>
  FROM SolutionGraph
 WHERE <special conditions>
 GROUP BY source_node, dest_node
HAVING <special conditions>;
```

In English, you start with an initial set of nodes and see if they are what you wanted; if not, then add more nodes recursively. This is not the only way to build graph algorithms, but it is a common design pattern. The bad news is that an iterative program can stop at the first right answer; recursive CTEs (and SQL in general) tend to find all valid answers, no matter what the cost.

12.1.2 Paths with CTE

The following queries with CTEs are credited to Frédéric Brouard of France. Sample data and the narrative are so delightful that I am using his material directly.

Perhaps you never go to France. So you may be interested by the fact that in Paris, there are beautiful girls, and in Toulouse a famous dish called Cassoulet, and a small plane constructor call Airbus. So the problem is to go by car from Paris to Toulouse using the speedway network. I will just simplify for you (if you are lost and you do not know the pronunciation to ask people your way to Toulouse, it is simple. Just say "to loose"):

```
CREATE TABLE Journeys
(depart_town VARCHAR(32) NOT NULL,
 arrival_town VARCHAR(32) NOT NULL,
  CHECK (depart_town < > arrival_town),
 PRIMARY KEY (depart_town, arrival_town),
   jny_distance INTEGER NOT NULL
CHECK (jny_distance > 0));

INSERT INTO Journeys
VALUES ('Paris', 'Nantes', 385),
       ('Paris', 'Clermont-Ferrand', 420),
       ('Paris', 'Lyon', 470),
       ('Clermont-Ferrand', 'Montpellier', 335),
       ('Clermont-Ferrand', 'Toulouse', 375),
       ('Lyon', 'Montpellier', 305),
       ('Lyon', 'Marseille', 320),
       ('Montpellier', 'Toulouse', 240),
       ('Marseille', 'Nice', 205);
```

Now we will try a very simple query, giving all the journeys between towns (Figure 12.2):

```
WITH Trips (arrival_town)
AS
(SELECT DISTINCT depart_town
   FROM Journeys
 UNION ALL
```

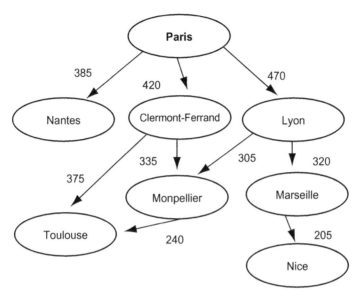

Figure 12.2

```
SELECT arrival_town
   FROM Journeys AS Arrivals,
        Journeys AS Departures
WHERE Departures.arrival_town = Arrivals.depart_town)
SELECT DISTINCT arrival_town FROM Trips;
```

arrival_town

Clermont-Ferrand
Lyon
Marseille
Montpellier
Paris
Nantes
Toulouse
Nice

This query is not very interesting because we do not know from which town we came. We just know the towns where we can go and the fact that we have probably different ways to go to the same place. Let us see if we can have some more information.

First, we want to start from Paris:

```
WITH Trips (arrival_town)
AS
(SELECT DISTINCT depart_town
   FROM Journeys
  WHERE depart_town = 'Paris'
UNION ALL
 SELECT arrival_town
   FROM Journeys AS Arrivals
        INNER Journeys AS Departures
        ON Departures.arrival_town = Arrivals.depart_town)
SELECT arrival_town FROM Journeys;
```

arrival_town

Paris

Nantes

Clermont-Ferrand

Lyon

Montpellier

Marseille

Nice

Toulouse ◀ goal

Montpellier

Toulouse ◀ goal

Toulouse ◀ goal

We have probably three ways to go to Toulouse because we see three occurrences of our goal in this list. Can we filter the destination? Sure!

```
WITH Journeys (arrival_town)
AS
(SELECT DISTINCT depart_town
   FROM Journeys
  WHERE depart_town = 'Paris'
UNION ALL
 SELECT arrival_town
   FROM Journeys AS Arrivals,
        Journeys AS Departures
  WHERE Departures.arrival_town = Arrivals.depart_town)
SELECT arrival_town
```

```
   FROM Journeys
 WHERE arrival_town = 'Toulouse';
```

arrival_town

Toulouse

Toulouse

Toulouse

We can refine this query by calculating the number of steps involved in the different ways:

```
WITH Trips (arrival_town, steps)
AS
(SELECT DISTINCT depart_town, 0
   FROM Journeys
   WHERE depart_town = 'Paris'
UNION ALL
 SELECT arrival_town, Departures.steps + 1
   FROM Journeys AS Arrivals,
        Journeys AS Departures
   WHERE Departures.arrival_town = Arrivals.depart_town)
SELECT arrival_town, steps
   FROM Trips
 WHERE arrival_town = 'Toulouse';
```

arrival_town	steps
Toulouse	3
Toulouse	2
Toulouse	3

The cherry on the cake will be to know the distances of the different ways:

```
WITH Trips (arrival_town, steps, total_distance)
AS
(SELECT DISTINCT depart_town, 0, 0
   FROM Journeys
  WHERE depart_town = 'Paris'
UNION ALL
 SELECT arrival_town, Departures.steps + 1,
        Departures.total_distance + Arrivals.jny_distance
   FROM Journeys AS Arrivals,
        Journeys AS Departures
```

```
  WHERE Departures.arrival_town = Arrivals.depart_town)
SELECT arrival_town, steps, total_distance
  FROM Trips
 WHERE arrival_town = 'Toulouse';
```

arrival_town	steps	total_distance
Toulouse	3	1015
Toulouse	2	795
Toulouse	3	995

The girl in the cake will want to know the different towns we visit by those different ways:

```
WITH Trips (arrival_town, steps, total_distance, way)
AS
(SELECT DISTINCT depart_town, 0, 0,
        CAST('Paris' AS VARCHAR(MAX))
   FROM Journeys
  WHERE depart_town = 'Paris'
UNION ALL
  SELECT arrival_town, Departures.steps + 1,
         Departures.total_distance + Arrivals.jny_distance,
         Departures.way ||', '||Arrivals.arrival_town
    FROM Journeys AS Arrivals,
         Journeys AS Departures
  WHERE Departures.arrival_town = Arrivals.depart_town)
SELECT arrival_town, steps, total_distance, way
  FROM Trips
 WHERE arrival_town = 'Toulouse';
```

arrival_town	steps	total_distance	way
Toulouse	3	1015	Paris, Lyon, Montpellier, Toulouse
Toulouse	2	795	Paris, Clermont-Ferrand, Toulouse
Toulouse	3	995	Paris, Clermont-Ferrand, Montpellier, Toulouse

And now, ladies and gentleman, the recursive query is proud to present to you how to solve a very complex problem, called the traveling salesman problem. This is one of the operational research problems for which Edsger

Wybe Dijkstra found the first efficient algorithm and received the Turing Award in 1972.

```
WITH Trips (arrival_town, steps, total_distance, way)
AS
(SELECT DISTINCT depart_town, 0, 0, CAST('Paris' AS VARCHAR(MAX))
   FROM Journeys
  WHERE depart_town = 'Paris'
UNION ALL
 SELECT arrival_town, Departures.steps + 1,
        Departures.total_distance + Arrivals.jny_distance,
        Departures.way ||', '||Arrivals.arrival_town
   FROM Journeys AS Arrivals,
        Journeys AS Departures
 WHERE Departures.arrival_town = Arrivals.depart_town),

ShortestDistance (total_distance)
AS
(SELECT MIN(total_distance)
   FROM Journeys
  WHERE arrival_town = 'Toulouse')
SELECT arrival_town, steps, total_distance, way
  FROM Trips AS T
       ShortestDistance AS S
 WHERE T.total_distance = S.total_distance
   AND arrival_town = 'Toulouse';
```

12.1.3 Nonacyclic Graphs

In fact, one thing that is limiting the process in our network of speedways is that we have made routes with a single sense. I mean, we can go from Paris to Lyon, but we are not allowed to go from Lyon to Paris. For that, we need to add the reverse ways in the table, such as:

depart_town	arrival_town	jny_distance
Lyon	Paris	470

This can be done by a very simple query:

```
INSERT INTO Journeys
SELECT arrival_town, depart_town, jny_distance
FROM Journeys;
```

The only problem is that previous queries will not work properly:

```
WITH Journeys (arrival_town)
AS
(SELECT DISTINCT depart_town
   FROM Journeys
 WHERE depart_town = 'Paris'
UNION ALL
 SELECT arrival_town
   FROM Journeys AS Arrivals,
        Journeys AS Departures
WHERE Departures.arrival_town = Arrivals.depart_town)
SELECT arrival_town
  FROM Journeys;
```

This query will give you an error message about the maximum depth of recursion being violated. What happened? Simply, you are trying all ways, including cycling ways such as Paris, Lyon, Paris, Lyon, Paris—ad infinitum. Is there a way to avoid cycling routes? Maybe. In one of our previous queries, we have a column that gives the complete list of stepped towns. Why not use it to avoid cycling? The condition will be: do not pass through a town that is already in the way. This can be written as

```
WITH Trips (arrival_town, steps, total_distance, way)
AS
(SELECT DISTINCT depart_town, 0, 0, CAST('Paris' AS VARCHAR(255))
   FROM Journeys
 WHERE depart_town = 'Paris'
UNION ALL
 SELECT arrival_town, Departures.steps + 1,
        Departures.total_distance + Arrivals.jny_distance,
        Departures.way ||', '||Arrivals.arrival_town
   FROM Journeys AS Arrivals,
        Journeys AS Departures
 WHERE Departures.arrival_town = Arrivals.depart_town
   AND Departures.way NOT LIKE '%' || Arrivals.arrival_town || '%')
SELECT arrival_town, steps, total_distance, way
  FROM Trips
 WHERE arrival_town = 'Toulouse';
```

arrival_town	steps	total_distance	way
Toulouse	3	1015	Paris, Lyon, Montpellier, Toulouse
Toulouse	4	1485	Paris, Lyon, Montpellier, Clermont-Ferrand, Toulouse
Toulouse	2	795	Paris, Clermont-Ferrand, Toulouse
Toulouse	3	995	Paris, Clermont-Ferrand, Montpellier, Toulouse

As you see, a new route occurs. The worst in distance, but perhaps the most beautiful!

A CTE can simplify the expression of complex queries. Recursive queries must be employed where recursion is needed. Trust your SQL product to terminate a bad query. There is usually an option to set the depth of recursion either in the SQL engine or as an OPTION clause at the end of the CTE clause.

12.1.4 Adjacency Matrix Model

An adjacency matrix is a square array whose rows are out-node and columns are in-nodes of a graph. A one in a cell means that there is edge between the two nodes. Using the following graph, we would have an array like this:

	A	B	C	D	E	F	G	H
A	1	1	1	0	0	0	0	0
B	0	1	0	1	0	0	0	0
C	0	0	1	1	0	0	1	0
D	0	0	0	1	1	1	0	0
E	0	0	0	0	1	0	0	1
F	0	0	0	0	0	1	0	0
G	0	0	0	0	0	0	1	1
H	0	0	0	0	0	0	0	1

Many graph algorithms are based on the adjacency matrix model and can be translated into SQL. Go to the appropriate chapter for the details of modeling matrices in SQL and, in particular, look at the section on matrix multiplication in SQL. For example, Dijkstra's algorithm for shortest distances between each pair of nodes in a graph looks like this in this array pseudo-code.

```
FOR k = 1 TO n
DO FOR i = 1 TO n
DO FOR j = 1 TO n
IF a[i,k] + a[k,j] < a[i,j]
THEN a[i,j] = a[i,k] + a[k,j]
END IF;
END FOR;
END FOR;
END FOR;
```

You need to be warned that for a graph of (n) nodes, the table will be of size (n^2). The algorithms often run in (n^3) time. The advantage it has is that once you have completed a table, it can be used for lookups rather than recomputing distances over and over.

Running the query against the data set ...

```
INSERT INTO AdjacencyListGraph
VALUES ('a', 'd', 1),
('d', 'e', 1),
('e', 'c', 1),
('c', 'b', 1),
('b', 'd', 1),
('a', 'e', 5);
```

Gives the result SET ...

source_node	dest_node	min_wgt
a	b	4
a	c	3
a	d	1
a	e	2
b	c	3
b	d	1
b	e	2
c	b	1
c	d	2

source_node	dest_node	min_wgt
c	e	3
d	b	3
d	c	2
d	e	1
e	b	2
e	c	1
e	d	3

Doing the Dijkstra algorithm would probably execute significantly faster in a language with arrays than in SQL.

12.2 Split Node Nested Sets Models for Graphs

It is also possible to load an acyclic-directed graph into a nested sets model by splitting the nodes. It is a specialized trick for a certain class of graphs, not a general method such as adjacency list model graphs. Here is a skeleton table with minimal constrains for a nested sets model of a tree.

```
CREATE  TABLE NestedSetsGraph
(node_id INTEGER NOT NULL REFERENCES Nodes (node_id),
 lft INTEGER NOT NULL CHECK (lft >= 1) PRIMARY KEY,
 rgt INTEGER NOT NULL UNIQUE,
  CHECK (rgt > lft),
 UNIQUE (node_id, lft));
```

You split nodes by starting at sink nodes and moving up the tree. When you come to a node of (indegree > 1), replace it with that many copies of the node under each of its superiors. Continue to do this until you get to the root (Figure 12.3). The acyclic graph will become a tree, but with duplicated node values. There are advantages to this model when you want to avoid recursion. You are trading speed for storage space, however.

12.2.1 All Nodes in the Graph

Nodes in the Nodes table might not all be used in the graph, and those that are used can be repeated. It is safer to find nodes in the graph with a simple view instead.

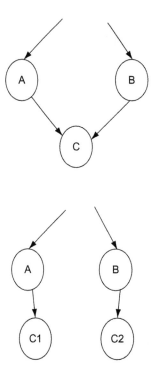

Figure 12.3

```
CREATE VIEW GraphNodes (node_id)
AS
SELECT DISTINCT node_id FROM NestedSetsGraph;
```

This is worth its own subsection because of double counting problems in this model.

12.2.2 Path End Points

A path through a graph is a traversal of consecutive nodes along a sequence of edges. Clearly, the node at the end of one edge in the sequence must also be the node at the beginning of the next edge in the sequence. The length of the path is the number of edges that are traversed along the path.

Path end points are the first and last nodes of each path in the graph. For a path of length zero, path end points are the same node. Yes, it is legal to have an edge that loops back around to the same node. Also, it is legal to have a node without any edges, but you cannot model that with an adjacency list; thank goodness nobody usually cares about those isolated nodes.

If there is more than one path between two nodes, then each path will be distinguished by its own distinct set of number pairs for the nested set representation.

If there is only one path (p) between two nodes but this path is a subpath of more than one distinct path, then the end points of (p) will have number pairs for each of these greater paths. As a canonical form, least numbered pairs are returned for these end points.

```
CREATE VIEW PathEndpoints
(begin_node_id, end_node_id,
begin_lft, begin_rgt,
end_lft, end_rgt)
AS
SELECT G1.node_id, G2.node_id,
G1.lft, G1.rgt, G2.lft, G2.rgt
FROM (SELECT node_id, MIN(lft), MIN(rgt)
FROM NestedSetsGraph
GROUP BY node_id) AS G1 (node_id, lft, rgt)
INNER JOIN
NestedSetsGraph AS G2
ON G2.lft >= G1.lft
AND G2.lft < G1.rgt;
```

12.2.3 Reachable Nodes

If a node is reachable from another node, then a path exists from the one node to the other. It is assumed that every node is reachable from itself.

```
CREATE VIEW ReachableNodes (begin_node_id, end_node_id)
AS
SELECT DISTINCT begin_node_id, end_node_id
FROM PathEndpoints;
```

12.2.4 Edges

Edges are pairs of adjacent connected nodes in a graph. If edge E is represented by the pair of nodes (n0, n1), then (n1) is reachable from (n0) in a single traversal.

```
CREATE VIEW Edges (begin_node_id, end_node_id)
AS
SELECT begin_node_id, end_node_id
FROM PathEndpoints AS PE
WHERE begin_node_id < > end_node_id
AND NOT EXISTS
(SELECT *
FROM NestedSetsGraph AS G
WHERE G.lft > PE.begin_lft
AND G.lft < PE.end_lft
AND G.rgt > PE.end_rgt);
```

12.2.5 Indegree and Outdegree

The indegree of a node (n) is the number of distinct edges ending at (n). Nodes that have zero indegree are not returned. Indegree of all nodes in the graph:

```
CREATE VIEW Indegree (node_id, node_indegree)
AS
SELECT N.node_id, COUNT(E.begin_node_id)
FROM GraphNodes AS N
LEFT OUTER JOIN
Edges AS E
ON N.node_id = E.end_node_id
GROUP BY N.node_id;
```

Outdegree of a node (n) is the number of distinct edges beginning at (n). Nodes that have zero outdegree are not returned. Outdegree of all nodes in the graph:

```
CREATE VIEW Outdegree (node_id, node_outdegree)
AS
SELECT N.node_id, COUNT(E.end_node_id)
FROM GraphNodes AS N
LEFT OUTER JOIN
Edges AS E
ON N.node_id = E.begin_node_id
GROUP BY N.node_id;
```

12.2.6 Source, Sink, Isolated, and Internal Nodes

A source node of a graph has a positive outdegree but zero indegree, that is, it has edges leading from, but not to, the node. This assumes that there are no isolated nodes (nodes belonging to no edges).

```
CREATE VIEW SourceNodes (node_id, lft, rgt)
AS
SELECT node_id, lft, rgt
FROM NestedSetsGraph AS G1
WHERE NOT EXISTS
(SELECT *
FROM NestedSetsGraph AS G
WHERE G1.lft > G2.lft
AND G1.lft < G2.rgt);
```

Likewise, a sink node of a graph has positive indegree but zero outdegree. It has edges leading to, but not from, the node. This assumes that there are no isolated nodes.

```
CREATE VIEW SinkNodes (node_id)
AS
SELECT node_id
FROM NestedSetsGraph AS G1
WHERE lft = rgt - 1
AND NOT EXISTS
(SELECT *
FROM NestedSetsGraph AS G2
WHERE G1.node_id = G2.node_id
AND G2.lft < G1.lft);
```

An isolated node belongs to no edges, that is, it has zero indegree and zero outdegree, but we have agreed to leave them out of the model.

```
CREATE VIEW IsolatedNodes (node_id, lft, rgt)
AS
SELECT node_id, lft, rgt
FROM NestedSetsGraph AS G1
WHERE lft = rgt - 1
AND NOT EXISTS
```

```
(SELECT *
FROM NestedSetsGraph AS G2
WHERE G1.lft > G2.lft
AND G1.lft < G2.rgt);
```

An internal node of a graph has an (indegree > 0) and an (outdegree > 0), that is, it acts as both a source and a sink.

```
CREATE VIEW InternalNodes (node_id)
AS
SELECT node_id
FROM (SELECT node_id, MIN(lft) AS lft, MIN(rgt) AS rgt
FROM NestedSetsGraph
WHERE lft < rgt - 1
GROUP BY node_id) AS G1
WHERE EXISTS
(SELECT *
FROM NestedSetsGraph AS G2
WHERE G1.lft > G2.lft
AND G1.lft < G2.rgt)
```

12.2.7 Converting Acyclic Graphs to Nested Sets

Let's start with a simple graph in an adjacency list model.

```
INSERT INTO Nodes (node_id)
VALUES ('a'), ('b'), ('c'), ('d'),
('e'), ('f'), ('g'), ('h');

INSERT INTO AdjacencyListGraph (begin_node_id, end_node_id)
VALUES ('a', 'b'), ('a', 'c'), ('b', 'd'), ('c', 'd'),
('c', 'g'), ('d', 'e'), ('d', 'f'), ('e', 'h'),
('g', 'h');
```

We can convert this adjacency list model to the nested sets model with a simple stack algorithm. You might want to try to rewrite this with a recursive CTE.

```
-- Stack to keep track of nodes being traversed in depth-first fashion
CREATE TABLE NodeStack
(node_id INTEGER NOT NULL PRIMARY KEY
```

```
REFERENCES Nodes (node_id),
distance INTEGER NOT NULL CHECK (distance >= 0),
lft INTEGER CHECK (lft >= 1),
rgt INTEGER,
CHECK (rgt > lft));

CREATE PROCEDURE AdjacencyListsToNestedSetsGraph ()
LANGUAGE SQL
READS SQL DATA
BEGIN
DECLARE path_length INTEGER;
DECLARE current_number INTEGER;
SET path_length = 0;
SET current_number = 0;
-- Clear the table that will hold the result
DELETE FROM NestedSetsGraph;
-- Initialize stack by inserting all source nodes of graph
INSERT INTO NodeStack (node_id, distance)
SELECT DISTINCT G1.begin_node_id, path_length
FROM AdjacencyListGraph AS G1
WHERE NOT EXISTS
 (SELECT *
FROM AdjacencyListGraph AS G2
WHERE G2.end_node_id = G1.begin_node_id);

WHILE EXISTS (SELECT * FROM NodeStack)
DO
SET current_number = current_number + 1;
IF EXISTS (SELECT * FROM NodeStack WHERE distance = path_length)
THEN UPDATE NodeStack
SET lft = current_number
WHERE distance = path_length
AND NOT EXISTS
 (SELECT *
FROM NodeStack AS S2
WHERE distance = path_length
AND S2.node_id < NodeStack.node_id);
INSERT INTO NodeStack (node_id, distance)
SELECT G.end_node_id, (S.distance + 1)
```

```
FROM NodeStack AS S,
AdjacencyListGraph AS G
WHERE S.distance = path_length
AND S.lft IS NOT NULL
AND G.begin_node_id = S.node_id;
SET path_length = (path_length + 1);
ELSE SET path_length = (path_length - 1);
UPDATE NodeStack
SET rgt = current_number
WHERE lft IS NOT NULL
AND distance = path_length;
INSERT INTO NestedSetsGraph (node_id, lft, rgt)
SELECT node_id, lft, rgt
FROM NodeStack
WHERE lft IS NOT NULL
AND distance = path_length;
DELETE FROM NodeStack
WHERE lft IS NOT NULL
AND distance = path_length;
END IF;
END WHILE;
END;
```

Petri Nets

P ETRI NETS ARE abstract graphic models invented in 1962 by Carl Adam Petri for his
doctoral thesis. Originally, he used them for chemical processes, but they
became popular with computer scientists for modeling concurrency in
computer hardware, such as the CDC 6600.

Petri nets are minimal and very general, but also very rich in
mathematical properties. Do not worry, I will not get into the math—I
write for working programmers. The major use of Petri nets has been
the modeling of systems of events in which it is possible for some events
to occur concurrently, but there are constraints on the concurrence,
precedence, or frequency of these occurrences. They are like a cross
between a state transition diagram (static model) and a board game
(dynamic model). If you want to play with them, get some scratch paper
and a handful of small chips or go to http://www.informatik.uni-hamburg
.de/TGI/PetriNets/introductions/aalst/ where you will find several simple
interactive programs and you can watch the Petri nets for some basic
problems' working.

The diagrams have four parts.

1. Circles called places. Places do not move and they hold tokens.

2. Bars called transitions. Transitions do not move and they fire (I will
   explain that shortly).

3.   Directed arcs that run out of a bar into a place (outputs of the transition) or out of a place and into a bar (inputs of the transition).

4.   Tokens represented as little black dots. These guys do move, like game pieces. They move along the arcs from place to place, as allowed by the transitions.

There are fancy versions of Petri nets with colored tokens, multiple tokens in a place, and rules about how transitions work. This chapter is concerned with the simplest set of rules. A place can hold only one token, tokens are all alike, and a transition can fire only if all of its input places have a token. Petri nets with these rules are called safe nets.

When a transition fires, it looks at all of its input places. If and only if they all have a token, then the input places are emptied and all the output places get a token if they do not already have one. There is an initial marking of tokens in the diagram, which may or may not be important. The order of transition firing may or may not be important. The diagram may or may not arrive at a marking from which it cannot change and it locks. There are ways to test for these properties and do formal proofs.

Figure 13.1 is a simple diagram that locks. Places P1 and P2 start with tokens, which enable transition T1. T1 fires and sends a token to P3. The

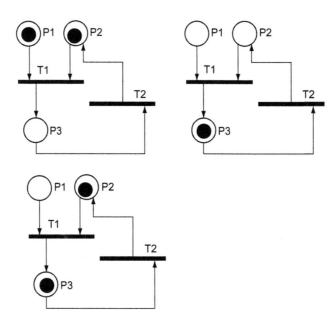

Figure 13.1

token in P2 enables transition T2. T2 fires and P2 gets a token, but P1 stays empty and no more moves are possible in this game.

Figure 13.2 shows two transitions in conflict, which means that the order of transition firings matters. If T1 fires, then P5 gets a token, but not P6. If T2 fires, then P6 gets a token, be changed to but not P5.

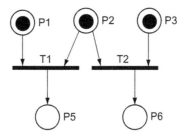

Figure 13.2

Transition rules can be changed to allow parallelism, which would mean that both T1 and T2 fire at the same time so that both P5 and P6 get tokens at the same time. A better approach, however, is to design the Petri net to avoid conflicts so that transitions can be fired in any order and still produce the same final marking

Figure 13.3 is a traffic light that recycles in a fixed pattern. Place P1 is a red light, P2 is green, and P3 is amber.

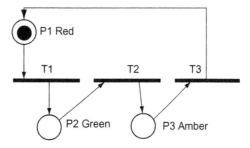

Figure 13.3

Petri nets can be nested inside each other to build complex systems from smaller units. Look at the traffic light example. In the real world, traffic lights come in configurations of several lights at an intersection.

13.1 Data Definition Language for Petri Nets

Tables modeling Petri nets are simple. Because the tokens are entities, they get their own table. The graph is a relationship, so it is in a second table. Here is the initial code.

```
CREATE TABLE Petri_Places
(place_name CHAR(5)NOT NULL PRIMARY KEY,
place_token SMALLINT DEFAULT 0 NOT NULL,

CHECK (place_token IN (0, 1))
CREATE TABLE Petri_Transitions
(transition_name CHAR(3) NOT NULL,
input_place_name CHAR(5) NOT NULL
REFERENCES Petri_Places (place_name),
output_place_name CHAR(5) NOT NULL
REFERENCES Petri_Places (place_name),
PRIMARY KEY (transition_name, input_place_name, output_place_name));
```

Looking at the simple traffic light example, we can load the tables, thus:

```
INSERT INTO Petri_Places (place_name, place_token)
VALUES ('Red', 0), ('Green', 0), ('Amber', 1);

INSERT INTO Petri_Transitions
VALUES ('T1', 'Red', 'Green'),
('T2', 'Green', 'Amber'),
('T3', 'Amber', 'Red');
```

I recommend setting up two very short procedures to clear out the places and one to restore the initial marking. They are very simple. The initialization procedure requires a table with the names of the marked places as shown here. But you could use a row constructor expression in the update statement if you want to make it completely self-contained.

```
CREATE PROCEDURE FireTransition(@in_transition_name CHAR(5))
LANGUAGE SQL
DETERMINISTIC
BEGIN
UPDATE Petri_Places
 SET place_token
   = CASE
     WHEN place_name
       IN (SELECT input_place_name
```

```
        FROM Petri_Transitions
        WHERE transition_name = @in_transition_name)
    THEN 0
    WHEN place_name
      IN (SELECT output_place_name
          FROM Petri_Transitions
          WHERE transition_name = @in_transition_name)
    THEN 1
    ELSE place_token END
WHERE 1 = ALL(SELECT P.place_token)
          FROM Petri_Places AS P
          WHERE P.place_name
            IN (SELECT T.input_place_name
                ROM Petri_Transitions AS T
                WHERE T.transition_name = @in_transition_name))
--display new state of places
--SELECT place_name, place_token FROM Petri_Places;
END.
```

For fun, mark every place and then start firing transitions. In T-SQL, you can get an error message that the procedure has been executed the maximum number of times because of a looping effect in this simple example.

Let's complicate the example a bit. We have a pair of traffic lights hooked together with the rule that they both cannot be green at the same time. Make two copies of the basic traffic light shown in figure 13.3 and put them into a single net, as shown in figure 13.4. The {G1, A1, R1} is one traffic light, and {G1, A2, R2} is the other light. The XX state synchronized them. The SQL for this diagram is

```
INSERT INTO Petri_Places (place_name, place_token)
VALUES ('R1', 1), ('A1', 0), ('G1', 0),
('R2', 1), ('A2', 0), ('G2', 0),
('XX', 1);
INSERT INTO Petri_Transitions (transition_name, input_place_name,
output_place_name)
VALUES
('T1A', 'R1', 'G1'),
('T1A', 'XX', 'G1'),
('T1B', 'G1', 'A1'),
('T1C', 'A1', 'XX'),
('T1C', 'A1', 'R1'),
```

```
('T2A', 'R2', 'G2'),
('T2A', 'XX', 'G2'),
('T2B', 'G2', 'A2'),
('T2C', 'A2', 'XX'),
('T2C', 'A2', 'R2');
```

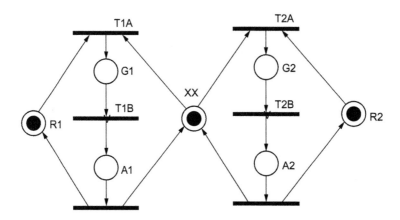

Figure 13.4

References

Celko, J., 1982. Software Practice and Experience 12 (10), 889–895.

Celko, J., 1984. Abacus 2 (1), 40–45.

Peterson, J.L., 1977. Petri nets. ACM Comput. Surv. 9 (3), 223–252. doi:10.1145/356698.356702.

Peterson, J.L., 1981. Petri Net Theory and the Modeling of Systems. Prentice Hall. ISBN 0-13-661983-5.

Petri, C.A., 1962. Kommunikation mit Automaten. Ph.D. Thesis. University of Bonn.

State Transition Graphs

DATA VALIDATION IN a database is much more complex than seeing if a string parameter really is an integer. A commercial world is full of complex rules for sequences of procedures, of fixed or variable life spans, warranties, commercial offers, and bids. All this requires considerable subtlety to prevent bad data getting from in and, if they do, locating and fixing the problem.

Ideally we want to use a declarative data definition language (DDL) to enforce the business rules about this state changes. The tool used by data architects is a state transition diagram. There is an initial state, flow lines that show what are the next legal states, and one or more termination states. Figure 14.1 is a simple state change diagram of possible marital states.

This state transition diagram was deliberately simplified, but it is good enough to explain principles. To keep the discussion as simple as possible, my table is for only one person's marital status over his life. Here is a skeleton DDL with the needed FOREIGN KEY reference to valid state changes and the date that the current state started.

```
CREATE TABLE MyLife
(previous_state VARCHAR(10) NOT NULL,
 current_state VARCHAR(10) NOT NULL,
 CONSTRAINT Improper_State_Change
 FOREIGN KEY (previous_state, current_state)
```

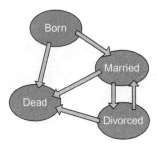

Figure 14.1

```
REFERENCES StateChanges (previous_state, current_state),
start_date DATE NOT NULL PRIMARY KEY, --DateTime for SQL Server 2005
etc.);
```

What is not shown on it are which nodes are initial states (in this case "Born") and which are terminal or final states (in this case "Dead," a very terminal state of being). A terminal node can be the current state of a middle node, but not a prior state. Likewise, an initial node can be the prior state of a middle node, but not the current state. I did not write any CHECK() constraints for those conditions. It is easy enough to write a quick query with an EXISTS() predicate to do this, which I will leave as an exercise for the reader. Let's load the diagram into an auxiliary table with some more constraints.

```
CREATE TABLE StateChanges
(previous_state VARCHAR(10) NOT NULL,
 current_state VARCHAR(10) NOT NULL,
 PRIMARY KEY (previous_state, current_state),
 state_type CHAR(1) DEFAULT 'M' NOT NULL
 CHECK (state_type IN ('I', 'T', 'M')), /*initial, terminal, middle*/
 CONSTRAINT Node_type_violations
CHECK (CASE WHEN state_type IN ('I', 'T')
            AND previous_state = current_state
          THEN 'T'
          WHEN state_type = 'M'
            AND previous_state < > current_state
          THEN 'T' ELSE 'F' END = 'T')
);

INSERT INTO StateChanges
VALUES ('Born', 'Born', 'I'), -- initial state
```

```
('Born', 'Married', 'M'),
('Born', 'Dead', 'M'),
('Married', 'Divorced', 'M'),
('Married', 'Dead', 'M'),
('Divorced', 'Married', 'M'),
('Divorced', 'Dead', 'M'),
('Dead', 'Dead', 'T'); -- terminal state
```

An aspect of this problem that I have not considered is the time dimension. We want to see a temporal path from an initial state to a terminal state. State changes do not happen all at once, but are spread over time. An acorn becomes an oak tree before it becomes lumber and finally my chest of drawers. The acorn does not jump immediately to being a chest of drawers. Some of the changes are controlled by time. I cannot get married immediately after being born, but have to wait to be of legal age. A business offer can expire in a set number of days. You can fill in any number of examples of your own.

For a production system, you would need a more complete set of temporal columns to guarantee that we have no gaps in the history, but this will do for now. We now need a stored procedure to add data to the MyLife table. Here is one solution that is broken deliberately into clear steps for clarity.

```
CREATE PROCEDURE Change_State
(IN in_change_date DATE,
IN in_change_state VARCHAR(10))
LANGUAGE SQL
DETERMINISTIC
BEGIN
DECLARE most_recent_state VARCHAR(10);
SET most_recent_state
    = (SELECT current_state
          FROM MyLife
        WHERE start_date
            = (SELECT MAX(start_date) FROM MyLife));
/* insert initial state if empty */
IF NOT EXISTS (SELECT * FROM MyLife)
   AND in_change_state
       IN (SELECT previous_state
              FROM StateChanges
            WHERE state_type = 'I')
```

```
THEN
INSERT INTO MyLife (previous_state, current_state, start_date)
VALUES (in_change_state, in_change_state, in_change_date);
END IF;
/* must be a real state change & advance forward in time */
IF in_change_state < > most_recent_state
    AND in_change_date
        > (SELECT MAX(start_date) FROM MyLife)
THEN
INSERT INTO MyLife (previous_state, current_state, start_date)
VALUES (most_recent_state, in_change_state, in_change_date);
END IF;
END;
```

The first block of code locates the most recent state of my life, based on the date. The second block of code will insert an initial state if the table is empty. This is a safety feature but there probably should be a separate procedure to create the set of initial states. Because the new state has to be an actual change, there is a block of code to be sure. The changes have to move forward in time. Finally, we build a row using the most recent state as the new previous state, the input change state, and the date. If the state change is illegal, the FOREIGN KEY is violated and we get an error.

If you had other business rules, you could also add them to the code in the same way. You should have noted that if someone makes changes directly to the MyLife Table, he or she can destroy all the data integrity. It is a good idea to have a procedure that checks to see that MyLife is in order. Let's load the table with bad data:

```
INSERT INTO MyLife (previous_state, current_state, start_date)
VALUES ('Born', 'Married', '1990-09-05'),
('Married', 'Divorced', '1999-09-05'),
('Married', 'Dead', '2010-09-05'),
('Dead', 'Dead', '2011-05-10'),
('Dead', 'Dead', '2012-05-10');
```

This poor guy popped into existence without being born properly, committed bigamy, and died twice. And you think your life is tough! Here is a simple validation procedure to catch those errors.

```
WITH Sequenced_State_History
AS
(SELECT previous_state, current_state,
ROW_NUMBER() OVER (ORDER BY start_date)
AS change_seq
FROM MyLife)
/* There is chain of links from the initial state to the current state */
SELECT 'Missing link(s) in History'
FROM Sequenced_State_History AS H1, Sequenced_State_History AS H2
WHERE H1.change_seq + 1 = H2.change_seq
AND H1.current_state <> H2.previous_state
UNION ALL /* has one and only one initial state */
SELECT 'No unique initial state.'
FROM MyLife AS M, StateChanges AS C
WHERE C.state_type = 'I'
AND M.previous_state = C.previous_state
AND M.current_state = C.previous_state
HAVING COUNT(*) <> 1
UNION ALL /* has zero or one terminal state */
SELECT 'Too many terminal states.'
FROM MyLife AS M, StateChanges AS C
WHERE C.state_type = 'T'
AND M.previous_state = C.previous_state
AND M.current_state = C.previous_state
HAVING COUNT(*) > 1;
```

The CTE numbers the steps of the temporal path from an initial node to a middle or terminal node. This chain has to be unbroken, which means going from step (n) to step (n+1) has to be a legal change in the StateChanges table. This chain can have only one initial node, so let's check for that next. Finally, the chain is either still in progress or has reached a single terminal node.

A little note on the programming technique used. The union of separate queries to do one validation at a time can often be made faster by combining some of the queries. However, there are trade-offs; this code is easy to read and maintain and (hopefully) will not be run often. It is also hard to get error messages from a single statement. Look back at the ChangeState() procedure; the two IF and SIGNAL() blocks of code could have been converted into CASE expressions that will generate NULLs, folded into the INSERT INTO statement, and cause the insertion to fail.

```
INSERT INTO MyLife (previous_state, current_state, start_date)
VALUES
 (NULLIF (in_change_state, most_recent_state),
in_change_state,
CASE WHEN in_change_date
<= (SELECT MAX(start_date) FROM MyLife)
THEN NULL ELSE in_change_date END);
```

This is not easy to read or to get error messages that tell you if the in_change_date is invalid in that it violates the time sequence.

14.1 The Temporal Side of Changes

What is still missing is the temporal aspect of state changes. In this example, the ('Born', 'Married') change would have to deal with the minimum age of consent. The ('Married', 'Divorced') change often has a legal waiting period. While technically a business rule, you know that no human being has lived over 150 years, so a gap that size is a data error. The terminal and initial states are instantaneous, however. Let's add more flesh to the skeleton table:

```
CREATE TABLE StateChanges
(previous_state VARCHAR(10) NOT NULL,
current_state VARCHAR(10) NOT NULL,
PRIMARY KEY (previous_state, current_state),
state_type CHAR(1) DEFAULT 'M' NOT NULL
CHECK (state_type IN ('I', 'T', 'M')), /*initial, terminal, middle*/
state_duration INTEGER NOT NULL -- unit of measure is months
CHECK (state_duration >= 0),
CONSTRAINT Node_type_violations
CHECK (CASE WHEN state_type IN ('I', 'T')
AND previous_state = current_state
THEN 'T'
WHEN state_type = 'M'
AND previous_state <> current_state
THEN 'T' ELSE 'F' END = 'T')
);
```

To make up some data, let's assume that the age of consent is 18 (12 months * 18 years = 216), that you have to wait 3 months into your marriage before getting a divorce, and that you have to be divorced 2 months before you can remarry. Of course, you can die instantly.

```
INSERT INTO StateChanges
VALUES ('Born', 'Born', 'I', 0), -- initial state
 ('Born', 'Married', 'M', 216),
 ('Born', 'Dead', 'M', 0),
 ('Married', 'Divorced', 'M', 3),
 ('Married', 'Dead', 'M', 0),
 ('Divorced', 'Married', 'M', 2),
 ('Divorced', 'Dead', 'M', 0),
 ('Dead', 'Dead', 'T', 0); -- terminal state
```

The first question is where to check for temporal violations—during insertion or with validation procedures? My answer is both. Whenever possible, do not knowingly put bad data into a schema; this should be done in the ChangeState() procedure. But someone or something will subvert the schema and you have to be able to find and repair the damage.

Here is a procedure that will tell you what state change in the chain has an improper duration and what the disagreement is.

```
WITH Sequenced_State_History
AS
(SELECT previous_state, current_state, start_date,
        ROW_NUMBER() OVER (ORDER BY start_date) AS change_seq
   FROM MyLife)
/* There is chain of links from the initial state to the current state */
SELECT H2.change_seq, H2.previous_state, H2.current_state,
       CAST ((H2.start_date - H1.start_date) AS INTERVAL YEAR TO SECOND)
AS actual_state_duration,
       C.state_duration AS expected_state_duration
  FROM Sequenced_State_History AS H1,
       Sequenced_State_History AS H2,
       StateChanges AS C
 WHERE H1.change_seq + 1 = H2.change_seq
   AND DATEDIFF (MM, H1.start_date, H2.start_date) <= C.state_duration
   AND C.previous_state = H2.previous_state
   AND C.current_state = H2.current_state;
```

Inserting a new life change is not a simple matter of putting a (previous_state, current_state, start_date) row into the table. To do it right, you can put conditions into the INSERT INTO statement to cause errors when there are bad data.

```
CREATE PROCEDURE Life_Status_Change
(IN in_change_state VARCHAR(10),
 IN in_most_recent_state VARCHAR(10),
 IN in_change_date DATE)
LANGUAGE SQL
DETERMINISTIC
INSERT INTO MyLife (previous_state, current_state, start_date)
VALUES
(NULLIF (in_change_state, in_most_recent_state),
 in_change_state,
 CASE WHEN in_change_date
           <= (SELECT MAX(start_date) FROM MyLife)
      THEN NULL ELSE in_change_date END);
```

A slightly different model will keep a (start_date, expiry_date) pair in the history table. In the case of the MyLife example, durations were minimums for certain changes. You can get married when you are older than 18 years of age and probably should. But a lot of commercial situations have a fixed life span. Warranties, commercial offers, and bids expire in a known number of days. This means adding another column to the StateChanges table that tells the insertion program if the expiration date is optional (shown with a NULL) or mandatory (computed from the duration).

Here is some skeleton DDL for a bid application to explain this better.

```
CREATE TABLE MyBids
(bid_nbr INTEGER NOT NULL,
 previous_state VARCHAR(10) NOT NULL,
 current_state VARCHAR(10) NOT NULL,
 CONSTRAINT Improper_State_Change
 FOREIGN KEY (previous_state, current_state)
 REFERENCES StateChanges (previous_state, current_state),
 start_date DATE NOT NULL PRIMARY KEY,
 expiry_date DATE, -- null means still open.
```

```
CHECK (start_date <= expiry_date),
PRIMARY KEY (bid_nbr, start_date),
etc.
);
```

The DDL has a bid number as the primary key and a new column for the expiration date. Obviously the bid has to exist for a while, so add a constraint to keep the date order right.

```
CREATE TABLE StateChanges
(previous_state VARCHAR(10) NOT NULL,
 current_state VARCHAR(10) NOT NULL,
 PRIMARY KEY (previous_state, current_state),
 state_duration INTEGER NOT NULL,
  duration_type CHAR(1) DEFAULT 'O' NOT NULL
CHECK ('O', 'M')), -- optional, mandatory
etc.
);
```

The DDL for state changes gets a new column to tell us if the duration is optional or mandatory. The insertion procedure is a bit trickier. The VALUES clause has more power than most programmers use. The list can be more than just constants or simple scalar variables, but using CASE expressions lets you avoid if-then-else procedural logic in the procedure body.

All it needs is the bid number and what state you want to use. If you don't give me a previous state, I assume that this is an initial row and repeat the current state you just gave me. If you don't give me a start date, I assume you want the current date. If you don't give me an expiration date, I construct one from the State Changes table with a scalar subquery. Here is the skeleton DDL for an insertion procedure.

```
CREATE PROCEDURE Bid_Status_Change
(IN in_bid_nbr INTEGER,
 IN in_previous_state VARCHAR(10),
 IN in_current_state VARCHAR(10),
 IN in_start_date DATE,
 IN in_expiry_date DATE)
LANGUAGE SQL
DETERMINISTIC
```

```
INSERT INTO MyBids (bid_nbr, previous_state, current_state, start_date,
expiry_date)
VALUES (in_bid_nbr, -- required
        COALESCE (in_previous_state, in_current_state),
        in_current_state, -- required
        COALESCE (in_start_date, CAST (CURRENT_TIMESTAMP AS DATE),
(SELECT COALESCE (in_expiry_date,
        in_start_date + S.state_duration YEAR TO SECOND)
   FROM StateChanges AS S
  WHERE S.previous_state = COALESCE (in_previous_state, in_current_state)
    AND S.current_state = in_current_state
    AND S.duration_type = 'M'))
);
```

Hierarchical Database Systems (IMS)

I AM GOING TO assume that most of the readers of this book have only worked with SQL. If you have heard of a Hierarchical Database System, it was mentioned in a database course in college and then forgotten. In some ways, that is too bad. It helps to know how earlier tools worked so that you can see how new tools evolved from old ones.

The following material is taken from a series on IMS that appeared in www.DBAzine.com. This is not going to make you an IMS programmer, but should help give you an overview.

Why IMS? It is the most important prerelational technology that is still in wide use today. In fact, there is a good chance that IMS databases still hold more data than SQL databases.

15.1 Types of Databases

The classic types of database structures are network, relational, and hierarchical. Network and hierarchical models are called network or "navigational" databases because the mental model of data access is that of a reader moving along paths to pick up data. In fact, when Bachman received the ACM Turing Award that is how he described it.

IMS was not the only navigational database, just the most popular. TOTAL from Cincom was based on a Master record that had pointer chains to one or more sets of slave records. Later, IDMS and other products generalized this navigational model.

CODASYL, the committee that defined COBOL, came up with a standard for the navigational model. Finally, the ANSI X3H2 Database Standards Committee took the CODASYL model, formalized it a bit, and produced the NDL language specification. However, at that point, SQL had become the main work of the ANSI X3H2 Database Standards Committee and nobody really cared about NDL and the standard simply expired.

Because this is a book on hierarchies and relational databases, I am going to ignore the network model on the assumption that it is too old and the products too varied to be of interest. I am also going to ignore object-oriented and other "postrelational" databases on the assumption that they are too young, too varied, and uncommon to be of interest.

IMS from IBM is the one hierarchical database management system still in wide use today. It is stable, well defined, scalable, and very fast for what it does.

The IMS software environment can be divided into five main parts:

1.   Database

2.   Data Language I (DL/I)

3.   DL/I control blocks

4.   Data communications component (IMS TM)

5.   Application programs

Figure 15.1 is a diagram of the relationships of IMS components. We discuss some of these components in more detail, but not in great detail.

15.2 Database History

Before the development of DBMSs, data were stored in individual files. With this system, each file was stored in a separate data set in a sequential or indexed format. To retrieve data from the file, an application had to open the file and read through it to the location of desired data. If data were scattered through a large number of files, data access required a lot of opening and closing of files, creating additional I/O and processing overhead.

To reduce the number of files accessed by an application, programmers often stored the same data in many files. This practice created redundant data and the related problems of ensuring update consistency across multiple files. To ensure data consistency, special cross-file update programs had to be scheduled following the original file update.

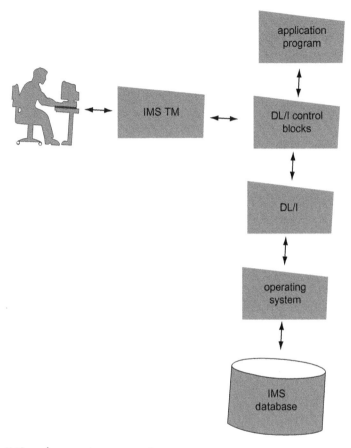

Figure 15.1 IMS environment components.

The concept of a database system resolved many data integrity and data duplication issues encountered in a file system. A properly designed database stores data only once in one place and makes it available to all application programs and users. At the same time, databases provide security by limiting access to data. The user's ability to read, write, update, insert, or delete data can be restricted. Data can also be backed up and recovered more easily in a single database than in a collection of flat files.

Database structures offer multiple strategies for data retrieval. Application programs can retrieve data sequentially or (with certain access methods) go directly to desired data, reducing I/O and speeding data retrieval. Finally, an update performed on part of the database is immediately available to other applications. Because data exist in only one place, data integrity is ensured more easily.

The IMS database management system as it exists today represents the evolution of the hierarchical database over many years of development and improvement. IMS is in use at a large number of business and government installations throughout the world. IMS is recognized for providing excellent performance for a wide variety of applications and for performing well with databases of moderate to very large volumes of data and transactions.

15.2.1 Data Language I

Because they are implemented and accessed through the use of DL/I, IMS databases are sometimes referred to as DL/I databases. DL/I is a command-level language, not a database management system. DL/I is used in batch and online programs to access data stored in databases.

Application programs use DL/I calls to request data. DL/I then uses system access methods, such as the Virtual Storage Access Method, to handle the physical transfer of data to and from the database.

IMS databases are often referred to by the access method they are designed for, such as HDAM (Hierarchical Direct Access Method), HIDAM (Hierarchical Indexed Direct Access Method), PHDAM (Partitioned HDAM), PHIDAM (Partitioned HIDAM), HISAM (Hierarchical Indexed Sequential Access Method), and SHISAM (Simple HISAM).

These are all IBM terms from their mainframe database products and I will not discuss them here.

IMS makes provisions for nine types of access methods, and you can design a database for any one of them. However, SQL programmers are generally isolated from the access methods that their database engine uses. We will not worry about the details of the access methods that are called at this level.

15.2.2 Control Blocks

When you create an IMS database, you must define the database structure and how data can be accessed and used by application programs. These specifications are defined within the parameters provided in two control blocks, also called DL/I control blocks:

1. Database description (DBD)
2. Program specification block (PSB)

In general, the DBD describes the physical structure of the database, and the PSB describes the database as it will be seen by a particular application program. The PSB tells the application which parts of the database it can access and the functions it can perform on data. Information from the DBD and PSB is merged into a third control block, the application control block (ACB). The ACB is required for online processing but is optional for batch processing.

15.2.3 Data Communications

The IMS Transaction Manager (IMS TM) is a separate set of licensed programs that provide access to the database in an online, real-time environment. Without the TM component, you would be able to process data in the IMS database in a batch mode only.

15.2.4 Application Programs

Data in a database is of no practical use to you if it sits in the database untouched. Its value comes in its use by application programs in the performance of business or organizational functions. With IMS databases, application programs use DL/I calls embedded in the host language to access the database. IMS supports batch and online application programs. IMS supports programs written in ADA, assembler, C, C++, COBOL, PL/I, Pascal, REXX, and WebSphere Studio Site Developer version 5.0.

15.2.5 Hierarchical Databases

In a hierarchical database, data are grouped in records, which are subdivided into a series of segments. Consider a department database for a school in which a record consists of the segments Dept, Course, and Enroll. In a hierarchical database, the structure of the database is designed to reflect logical dependencies—certain data are dependent on the existence of certain other data. Enrollment is dependent on the existence of a course and, in this case, a course is dependent on the existence of a department to offer that course.

The terminology changes from the SQL world to the IMS world. IMS uses records and fields and calls each hierarchy a database. In the SQL world, a row and column are similar to record and field, but are much smarter and more general. In SQL, a schema or database is a collection of related tables, which might map into several different IMS hierarchies in the same data model. In other words, an IMS database is more like a table in SQL.

15.2.6 Strengths and Weaknesses

In a hierarchical database, data relationships are defined by the storage structure. The rules for queries are highly structured. It is these fixed relationships that give IMS extremely fast access to data when compared to an SQL database when the queries have not been highly optimized.

Hierarchical and relational systems have their strengths and weaknesses. The relational structure makes it relatively easy to code ad hoc queries. However, an SQL query often makes the engine read through an entire table or series of tables to retrieve data. This makes searches slower and more processing intensive. In addition, because the row and column structure must be maintained throughout the database, an entry must be made under each column for every row in every table, even if the entry is only a place holder (i.e., NULL) entry.

With the hierarchical structure, data requests or segment search arguments may be more complex to construct. Once written, however, they can be very efficient, allowing direct retrieval of data requested. The result is an extremely fast database system that can handle huge volumes of data transactions and large numbers of simultaneous users. Likewise, there is no need to enter place holders where data are not being stored. If a segment occurrence isn't needed, it isn't created or inserted.

There are always trade-offs. SQL gives you portability and flexibility. IMS and other network DB systems give you speed, low overhead (i.e no statistics, no DRI actions or triggers and minimal meta data). Essentially you tune an IMS database for one and only one set of applications and SQL is generic, so it is not surprised by a changing world.

15.3 Sample Hierarchical Database

To illustrate how the hierarchical structure looks, I'll design two very simple databases to store information for the courses and students in a college. One database will store information on each department in the college, and the second will contain information on each college student. In a hierarchical database, an attempt is made to group data in a one-to-many relationship.

An attempt is also made to design the database so that data that are logically dependent on other data are stored in segments that are hierarchically dependent on data. For that reason, we have designated Dept as the key, or root, segment for our record because other data would not exist without the existence of a department. Each department is listed

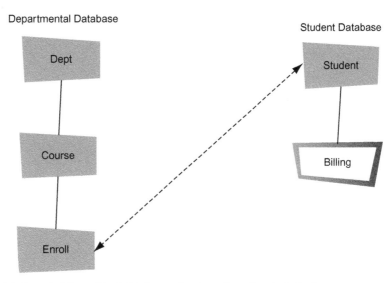

Figure 15.2 Sample hierarchical databases for department and student.

only once. We provide data on each course in each department. We have
a segment type Course, with an occurrence of that type of segment for
each course in the department. Data on the course title, description, and
instructor are stored as fields within the Course segment. Finally, we have
added another segment type, Enroll, which will include student IDs of the
students enrolled in each course.

In Figure 15.2, we also created a second database called Student. This database
contains information on all the students enrolled in the college. This database
duplicates some data stored in the Enroll segment of the Department database.
Later, we will construct a larger database that eliminates duplicated data. The
design we choose for our database depends on a number of factors; in this case,
we will focus on which data we will need to access most frequently,

The two sample databases, Department and Student, are shown in
Figure 15.2. The two databases are shown as they might be structured in
relational form in three tables.

```
CREATE SCHEMA College;

CREATE TABLE Courses
(course_nbr CHAR(9) NOT NULL PRIMARY KEY,
 course_title VARCHAR(20) NOT NULL,
 description VARCHAR(200) NOT NULL,
```

```
dept_id CHAR(7) NOT NULL
        REFERENCES Departments (dept_id)
    ON UPDATE CASCADE);
CREATE TABLE Students
(student_id CHAR(9) NOT NULL PRIMARY KEY,
 student_name CHAR(35) NOT NULL,
 address CHAR(35) NOT NULL,
 major CHAR(10));

CREATE TABLE Departments
(dept_id CHAR(7) NOT NULL PRIMARY KEY,
 dept_name CHAR(15) NOT NULL,
 chairman_name CHAR(35) NOT NULL,
 budget_code CHAR(3) NOT NULL);
```

15.3.1 Department Database

Segments in the Department database are as follow.

Dept: Information on each department. This segment includes fields for the department ID (the key field), department name, chairman_ name's name, number of faculty, and number of students registered in departmental courses.

Course: This segment includes fields for the course number (a unique identifier), course title, course description, and instructor's name.

Enroll: Students enrolled in the course. This segment includes fields for student ID (the key field), student name, and grade.

15.3.2 Student Database

Segments in the Student database are as follow.

Student: Student information. It includes fields for student ID (key field), student name, address, major, and courses completed.

Billing: Billing information for courses taken. It includes fields for semester, tuition due, tuition paid, and scholarship funds applied.

The dotted line between the root (Student) segment of the Student database and the Enroll segment of the Department database represents a logical relationship based on data residing in one segment and needed in the other.

15.3.3 Design Considerations

Before implementing a hierarchical structure for your database, you should analyze the end user's processing requirements because they will determine how you structure the database. In particular, you must consider how the data elements are related and how they will be accessed.

For example, given Parts and Suppliers, the hierarchical structure could subordinate parts under suppliers for the accounts receivable department or subordinate suppliers under parts for the order department.

15.3.4 Example Database Expanded

At this point we have learned enough about database design to expand our original example database. We decide that we can make better use of our college data by combining the Department and Student databases. Our new College database is shown in Figure 15.3.

The following segments are in the expanded College database.

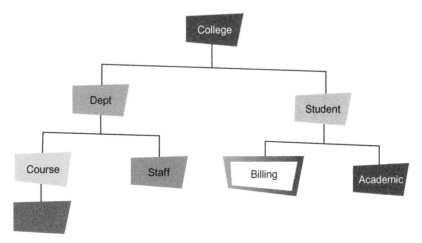

Figure 15.3 College database (combining department and student databases).

College: The root segment. One record will exist for each college in the university. The key field is the College ID, such as ARTS, ENGR, BUSADM, and FINEARTS.

Dept: Information on each department within the college. It includes fields for the department ID (the key field), department name, chairman_name's name, number of faculty, and number of students registered in departmental courses.

Course: Includes fields for the course number (the key field), course title, course description, and instructor's name.

Enroll: A list of students enrolled in the course. There are fields for student ID (key field), student name, current grade, and number of absences.

Staff: A list of staff members, including professors, instructors, teaching assistants, and clerical personnel. The key field is employee number. There are fields for name, address, phone number, office number, and work schedule.

Student: Student information. It includes fields for student ID (key field), student name, address, major, and courses being taken currently.

Billing: Billing and payment information. It includes fields for billing date (key field), semester, amount billed, amount paid, scholarship funds applied, and scholarship funds available.

Academic: The key field is a combination of the year and the semester. Fields include grade point average (GPA) per semester, cumulative GPA, and enough fields to list courses completed and grades per semester.

15.3.5 Data Relationships

The process of data normalization helps you break data into naturally associated groupings that can be stored collectively in segments in a hierarchical database. In designing your database, break the individual data elements into groups based on the processing functions they will serve. At the same time, group data based on inherent relationships between data elements.

For example, the College database (Figure 15.3) contains a segment called Student. Certain data are naturally associated with a student, such as student ID number, student name, address, and courses taken. Other data that we will want in our College database, such as a list of courses taught or administrative information on faculty members, would not work well in the Student segment.

Two important data relationship concepts are one to many and many to many. In the College database, there are many departments for each college (Figure 15.3 shows only one example), but only one college for each department. Likewise, many courses are taught by each department, but a specific course (in this case) can be offered by only one department.

The relationship between courses and students is many to many, as there are many students in any course and each student will take several courses. Let's ignore the many-to-many relationship for now—this is the hardest relationship to model in a hierarchical database.

A one-to-many relationship is structured as a dependent relationship in a hierarchical database: the many are dependent upon the one. Without a department, there would be no courses taught: without a college, there would be no departments.

Parent and child relationships are based solely on the relative positions of the segments in the hierarchy, and a segment can be a parent of other segments while serving as the child of a segment above it. In Figure 15.3, Enroll is a child of Course, and Course, although the parent of Enroll, is also the child of department. Billing and Academic are both children of Student, which is a child of College. (Technically, all of the segments except College are dependents.)

When you have analyzed the data elements, grouped them into segments, selected a key field for each segment, and designed a database structure, you have completed most of your database design. You may find, however, that the design you have chosen does not work well for every application program. Some programs may need to access a segment by a field other than the one you have chosen as the key or another application may need to associate segments that are located in two different databases or hierarchies. IMS has provided two very useful tools that you can use to resolve these data requirements: secondary indexes and logical relationships.

Secondary indexes let you create an index based on a field other than the root segment key field. That field can be used as if it were the key to access segments based on a data element other than the root key.

Logical relationships let you relate segments in separate hierarchies and, in effect, create a hierarchic structure that does not actually exist in storage.

The logical structure can be processed as if it exists physically, allowing you to create logical hierarchies without creating physical ones.

15.3.6 Hierarchical Sequence

Because segments are accessed according to their sequence in the hierarchy, it is important to understand how the hierarchy is arranged. In IMS, segments are stored in a top-down, left-to-right sequence (Figure 15.4). The sequence flows from the top to the bottom of the leftmost path or leg. When the bottom of that path is reached, the sequence continues at the top of the next leg to the right.

Understanding the sequence of segments within a record is important to understanding movement and position within the hierarchy. Movement can be forward or backward and always follows the hierarchical sequence. Forward means from top to bottom, and backward means bottom to top. Position within the database means the current location at a specific segment. You are once more doing depth-first tree traversals, but with a slightly different terminology.

15.3.7 Hierarchical Data Paths

In Figure 15.4, numbers inside the segments show the hierarchy as a search path would follow it. Numbers to the left of each segment show the segment types as they would be numbered by type, not occurrence, that is, there may

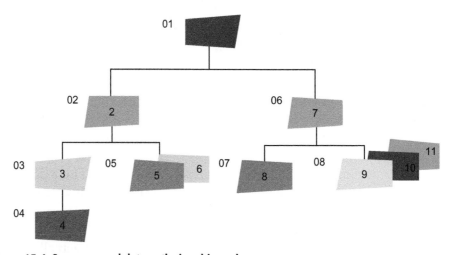

Figure 15.4 Sequence and data paths in a hierarchy.

be any number of occurrences of segment type 04, but there will be only one type of segment 04. The segment type is referred to as the segment code.

To retrieve a segment, count every occurrence of every segment type in the path and proceed through the hierarchy according to the rules of navigation:

1. top to bottom

2. front to back (counting twin segments)

3. left to right

For example, if an application program issues a GET-UNIQUE (GU) call for segment 6 in Figure 15.4, the current position in the hierarchy is immediately following segment 06. If the program then issued a GET-NEXT (GN) call, IMS would return segment 07. There is also the GNP (Get Next within Parent) call, which explains itself.

As shown in Figure 15.4, the College database can be separated into four search paths. The first path includes segment types 01, 02, 03, and 04. The second path includes segment types 01, 02, and 05. The third path includes segment types 01, 06, and 07. The fourth path includes segment types 01, 06, and 08. The search path always starts at 01, the root segment.

15.3.8 Database Records

Whereas a database consists of one or more database records, a database record consists of one or more segments. In the College database, a record consists of the root segment College and its dependent segments. It is possible to define a database record as only a root segment. A database can contain only the record structure defined for it, and a database record can contain only the types of segments defined for it.

The term record can also be used to refer to a data set record (or block), which is not the same thing as a database record. IMS uses standard data system management methods to store its databases in data sets. The smallest entity of a data set is also referred to as a record (or block).

Two distinctions are important. A database record may be stored in several data set blocks. A block may contain several whole records or pieces of several records. In this chapter, we try to distinguish between database record and data set record where the meaning may be ambiguous.

15.3.9 Segment Format

A segment is the smallest structure of the database in the sense that IMS cannot retrieve data in an amount less than a segment. Segments can be broken down into smaller increments called fields, which can be addressed individually by application programs.

A database record can contain a maximum of 255 types of segments. The number of segment occurrences of any type is limited only by the amount of space allocated for the database. Segment types can be of fixed length or variable length. You must define the size of each segment type.

It is important to distinguish the difference between segment types and segment occurrences. Course is a type of segment defined in the DBD for the College database. There can be any number of occurrences for the Course segment type. Each occurrence of the Course segment type will be exactly as defined in the DBD. The only difference in occurrences of segment types is data contained in them (and the length, if the segment is defined as variable length).

Segments have several different possible structures, but from a logical viewpoint, there is a prefix that has structural and control information for the IMS system, and 3 is the prefix for the actual data fields.

In the data portion, you can define the following types of fields: a sequence field and data fields.

> *Sequence (key) field:* The sequence field is often referred to as a key field. It can be used to keep occurrences of a segment type in sequence under a common parent, based on data or value entered in this field. A key field can be defined in the root segment of a HISAM, HDAM, or HIDAM database to give an application program direct access to a specific root segment. A key field can be used in HISAM and HIDAM databases to allow database records to be retrieved sequentially. Key fields are used for logical relationships and secondary indexes.

A key field not only can contain data but also can be used in special ways that help in organizing your database. With a key field, you can keep occurrences of a segment type in some kind of key sequence, which you design. For instance, in our example database you might want to store student records in ascending sequence based on student ID number. To do this, you define the student ID field as a unique key field. IMS will store the records in ascending numerical order. You could also store them in alphabetical order by defining the name field as a unique key field. Three factors of key fields are important to remember:

1.   Data or value in the key field is called the key of the segment.

2.   The key field can be defined as unique or nonunique.

3.   You do not have to define a key field in every segment type

Data field: You define data fields to contain actual data being stored in the database. (Remember that the sequence field is a data field.) Data fields, including sequence fields, can be defined to IMS for use by applications programs.

15.3.10 Segment Definitions

In IMS, segments are defined by the order in which they occur and by their relationship with other segments:

Root segment: The first or highest segment in the record. There can be only one root segment for each record. There can be many records in a database.

Dependent segment: All segments in a database record except the root segment.

Parent segment: A segment that has one or more dependent segments beneath it in the hierarchy.

Child segment: A segment that is a dependent of another segment above it in the hierarchy.

Twin segment: A segment occurrence that exists with one or more segments of the same type under a single parent.

Functions that edit, encrypt, or compress segments are not considered here. The point is that you have a lot of control of data at the physical level in IMS.

15.4 Summary

Those who cannot remember the past are condemned to repeat it.

George Santayana

There were databases before SQL, and they were all based on a graph theory model. What SQL programmers do not like to admit is that less than 20% of all commercial information resides in SQL databases. The majority is still in simple files or older, navigational, nonrelational databases.

Even after the new tools have taken on their own characteristics to become a separate species, the mental models of the old systems still linger. The old patterns are repeated in the new technology.

Even the early SQL products fell into this trap. For example, how many SQL programmers today use IDENTITY or other autoincrement vendor extensions as keys on SQL tables today, unaware that they are imitating the sequence field (a.k.a. the "key field") from IMS?

This is not to say that a hierarchy is not a good way to organize data; it is! But you need to see the abstraction apart from any particular implementation. SQL is a declarative language, while DL/I is a collection of procedure calls inside a host language. The temptation is to continue to write SQL code in the same style as you wrote procedural code in COBOL, PL/I, or whatever host language you had.

The bad news is that you can use cursors to imitate sequential file routines. Roughly, the READ() command becomes an embedded FETCH statement, OPEN and CLOSE file commands map to OPEN and CLOSE CURSOR statements, and every file becomes a simple table without any constraints and a "record number" of some sort. The conversion of legacy code is almost effortless with such a mapping. Also, it is also the worst way to program with a SQL database.

It is hoped that this book will show you a few tricks that will let you write SQL as SQL and not fake a previous language in it.

The www.DBAzine.com Website has a detailed three-part tutorial on IMS from which this material was brutally extracted and summarized.

The best source for IMS materials is at http://www.redbooks.ibm.com/ where you can download manuals directly from IBM.

Reference

Meltz, D., Long, R., Harrington, M., Hain, R., Nicholls, G. 2005. An Introduction to IMS: Your Complete Guide to IBM's Information Management System. IBM Press. ISBN 0132659522.

INDEX

Note: Page numbers followed by *f* indicate figures and *t* indicate tables.

Related Titles from Morgan Kaufmann

SQL Clearly Explained, 3rd Edition
Jan L. Harrington
ISBN: 9780123756978

Joe Celko's SQL for Smarties, 4th Edition
Joe Celko
ISBN: 9780123820228

Relational Database Design Clearly Explained, 3rd Edition
Jan L. Harrington
ISBN: 9780123747303

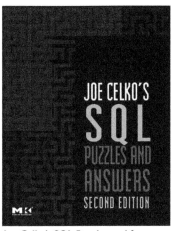

Joe Celko's SQL Puzzles and Answers, 2nd Edition
Joe Celko
ISBN: 9780123735966

Joe Celko's Data Measurements and Standards in SQL
Joe Celko
ISBN: 9780123747228

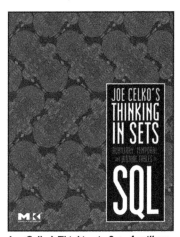

Joe Celko's Thinking in Sets: Auxillary, Temporal and Virtual Tables in SQL
Joe Celko
ISBN: 9780123741370

mkp.com

Printed and bound by CPI Group (UK) Ltd, Croydon, CR0 4YY

03/10/2024

01040315-0001